Deerfield Public Library
920 Waukegan Road
Deerfield, IL 60015

DEERFIELD PUBLIC LIBRARY

3 9094 32064 9377

ALSO BY SIMON CRITCHLEY

What We Think About When We Think About Soccer
Notes on Suicide
ABC of Impossibility
The Problem with Levinas
Bowie
Memory Theater
Stay, Illusion! (with Jamieson Webster)
The Mattering of Matter (with Tom McCarthy)
The Faith of the Faithless
Impossible Objects
How to Stop Living and Start Worrying
The Book of Dead Philosophers
On Heidegger's Being and Time
Infinitely Demanding
Things Merely Are: Philosophy in the Poetry of Wallace Stevens
On Humour
Continental Philosophy: A Very Short Introduction
Ethics—Politics—Subjectivity
Very Little . . . Almost Nothing
The Ethics of Deconstruction

Tragedy, the Greeks, and Us

Tragedy, the Greeks, and Us

Simon Critchley

Pantheon Books, New York

Copyright © 2019 by Simon Critchley

All rights reserved. Published in the United States by Pantheon Books,
a division of Penguin Random House LLC, New York, and
distributed in Canada by Random House of Canada, a division of
Penguin Random House Canada Limited, Toronto.

Pantheon Books and colophon are registered trademarks of
Penguin Random House LLC.

Library of Congress Cataloging-in-Publication Data
Name: Critchley, Simon, [date] author.
Title: Tragedy, the Greeks, and us / Simon Critchley.
Description: First edition. New York : Pantheon Books, 2019. Includes
bibliographical references and index.
Identifiers: LCCN 2018023509. ISBN 9781524747947 (hardcover : alk. paper).
ISBN 9781524747954 (ebook).
Subjects: LCSH: Tragic, The. Tragedy—Greek influences.
Greek drama (Tragedy)—History and criticism. Literature—Philosophy.
Philosophy, Ancient.
Classification: LCC BH301.T7 C75 2019 | DDC 809/.9162—dc23 |
LC record available at lccn.loc.gov/2018023509

www.pantheonbooks.com

Jacket design by Kelly Blair

Printed in the United States of America
First Edition
2 4 6 8 9 7 5 3 1

He was neither profound of thought, nor anything.
Just an ordinary, silly man.
He assumed a Greek name, he dressed like a Greek,
Taught himself to behave—more or less—like a Greek;
And trembled in his soul lest
He mar the tolerable impression
By speaking Greek with dreadful barbarisms,
And have the Alexandrians poke fun at him,
As is their habit—awful people.

And for this reason, he confined himself to a few words,
Fearfully paying attention to the declensions and the
    accent;
And he got bored, no end, having
So many things to say piled up inside him.

—C. P. Cavafy,
The Potentate from Western Libya

CONTENTS

PART I

Introduction

Feeding the Ancients with Our Own Blood

Tragedy shows what is perishable, what is fragile, and what is slow moving about us. In a world defined by relentless speed and the unending acceleration of information flows that cultivate amnesia and an endless thirst for the short-term future allegedly guaranteed through worship of the new prosthetic gods of technology, tragedy is a way of applying the emergency brake.

Tragedy slows things down by confronting us with what we do not know about ourselves: an unknown force that unleashes violent effects on us on a daily, indeed often minute-by-minute basis. Such is the sometimes terrifying presence of the past that we might seek to disavow but that will have its victory in the end, if only in the form of our mortality. We might think we are through with the past, but the past isn't through with us. Through its sudden reversals of fortune and rageful recognition of the truth of our origins, tragedy permits us to come face-to-face with what we do *not* know about ourselves but what makes those selves the things they are. Tragedy provokes what snags in our being, the snares and booby traps of the past that we blindly trip over in our relentless, stumbling, forward movement. This is what the ancients called "fate," and it requires our complicity in order to come down on us.

Yet, the fruit of a consideration of tragedy is not a sense of life's hopelessness or moral resignation, as Schopenhauer thought, but—I think—a deepened sense of the self in its utter dependency on others. It is a question of the self's vulnerable exposure to apparently familiar and familial patterns of kinship (although it sometimes turns out that, like Oedipus, you don't know who your parents are, but if you do know who your parents are, you still don't know *who* they are). One of the most salient but enigmatic features of Greek tragedy is its constant negotiation with the other, especially the enemy other, the foreign other, the "barbaric" other. The oldest extant piece of theater that we possess, Aeschylus's *The Persians,* from 472 BCE, depicts the defeated enemy not with triumph but with sympathy and with an anticipation of the possible humiliation that might face the Athenians should they repeat the *hybris* of the Persians by invading Greece and desecrating the altars of the enemy's gods. Sadly, the Athenians did not heed Aeschylus's lesson, and the brief period of Athenian imperial hegemony in the central decades of the fifth century BCE ended in the humiliating defeat of the Peloponnesian Wars. There is perhaps a moral to be drawn here for our time and place, where the empire knows its heyday is over and we live in a constant state of war. The first rule of war is sympathy with the enemy. This is something that can be seen in the tragedies of Euripides, especially those that deal with the bloody end of the Trojan War, in plays like *The Trojan Women* and *Hecuba.*

As Aristotle put it perspicuously and somewhat blithely nearly a century after the zenith of Greek drama in the second half of the fifth century BCE, tragedy is the imitation of action, *mimesis praxeos.* But what exactly is meant by action? It is far from clear. In play after play of the three great tragedians (Aeschylus, Sophocles, and Euripides), what we see are characters who are utterly disoriented by the situation in which they find themselves. They do not know *how* to act. We find human beings somehow compelled to follow a path of suffering that allows them to raise questions that admit of no easy answer: What will happen to me? How can I choose the right path of action? The overwhelming experience of tragedy is a *disorientation* expressed in one bewildered and frequently repeated question: *What shall I do?*

Tragedy is not about the metaphysical cultivation of the *bios theoretikos,* the contemplative life that is the supposed fruit of philosophy in Aristotle's *Ethics,* or in Epicurus and the other Hellenistic schools. Nor is it about the cultivation of the life of the gods or divine life, *ho bios theois,* which is also the constant promise of philosophy from Plato onward, as we will see. No, tragedy is thinking *in* action, thinking *upon* action, *for the sake of* action, where the action takes place offstage and is often described to us indirectly through the character of a messenger. But this thinking takes the form of a radical questioning: How do I act? What shall I do? If tragedy is *mimesis praxeos,* then it is action that is called into question through tragedy, divided and sliced open. What the experience of tragedy invites is neither the blind impulsiveness of action, nor some retreat into a solitary life of contemplation, but the *difficulty* and *uncertainty* of action in a world defined by ambiguity, where right always seems to be on both sides. Hegel is right to insist that tragedy is the collision between opposed yet mutually justified claims to what is right. But if both sides are right, then what on earth do we do?

Part of the joy of wandering into the ancient world and dealing with seemingly remote phenomena like Attic tragedy (and I will use the adjectives Attic, Athenian, and Greek interchangeably to name the same phenomenon) is how little we know and how little we will ever know. Of the many things we *don't* know about ancient tragedy, the most important and most enigmatic is some sense of what the spectator was expected to take away from these spectacles. The ancient Greek word for "spectator" was *theoros,* from which we get the word *theoria,* theory. *Theoria* is linked to the verb "to see," *theorein,* which takes place in a theater, a *theatron,* to name the act of spectating. If tragedy is the imitation of action, of *praxis,* although the nature of action remains deeply enigmatic, then *praxis* is something seen from a theoretical perspective. Or, better said perhaps, the question of theory and practice, or the *gap* between theory and practice, first opens *in* theater and *as* theater.

Theater is always theoretical, and theory is a theater, where we are spectators on a drama that unfolds: *our* drama. In theater, human action, human *praxis,* is called into question theoretically. Otherwise said, *praxis* is internally divided or questioned by *theoria* in the space of the theater, where the empty space of the theater is a way of calling into question the spaces we inhabit and subverting the divisions that constitute social and political space.

Now, aside from a fragment by the great Sophist Gorgias that we will look at in a little while—and Gorgias is one of the heroes of this book—and Aristophanes' *The Frogs,* where he stages a debate between Euripides and Aeschylus as to who is the best tragedian that I will discuss in Part 5, the only spectator reports on tragedy that we possess come from Plato and Aristotle, who had various axes to grind. In the case of Plato, it is a little like basing your view of the Vikings on the reports of the Christian monks whose monasteries they ransacked. Aristotle appears more benevolent, but appearances can be deceptive. Despite some wonderful and important historical, philological, and archeological work, we have little idea how tragedy was *seen* and what the audience *thought.* We have no online reviews, no blogs, and no tweets. Nor do we even know for sure who attended the plays. For example, we cannot be certain whether any women attended the festivals where the tragedies were performed with such an abundance of female characters.[1] But, in my view, far from being a vice, this epistemic deficit, this lack of knowledge is, I think, a virtue. Tragedy, for me, is the life of skepticism, where the latter is the index for a certain moral orientation in the world, an orientation that seems to emerge from the *disorientation* of not knowing what to do. I hope to make good on this thought as we move through the following chapters.

In a lecture delivered in Oxford in 1908, Wilamowitz— Nietzsche's nemesis, who savaged some of the questionable philological claims of *The Birth of Tragedy*—said,

The tradition yields us only ruins. The more closely we test and examine them, the more clearly we see how ruinous they are; and out of the ruins no whole can be built. The tradition is dead; our task is to revivify life that has passed away. We know that ghosts cannot speak until they have drunk blood; and the spirits which we evoke demand the blood of our hearts. We give it to them gladly.[2]

Of course, the irony here is that Nietzsche says the same thing, namely that it is our blood that makes the ancients speak to us. Without wanting to piggyback on the dizzying recent success of vampire fiction, the latter's portion of truth is that the ancients need a little of our true blood in order to speak to us. When revived, we will notice that when the ancients speak, they do not merely tell us about themselves. They tell us about us. But who is that "us" that might still be claimed and compelled by these ancient texts, by these ruins? And here is both the beauty and strangeness of this thought: This "us" is not necessarily existent. It is us, but in some new way, some alien manner. It is us, but not as we have seen ourselves before, turned inside out and upside down.

Another way of putting this is to say that the "we" that we find in tragedy is *invitational*, an invitation to visit another sense of who we are and who we might become. I borrow this thought from Bernard Williams's *Shame and Necessity*, to which I will return in the following chapter. The idea of invitation has been interestingly developed by Raymond Geuss in the eponymous, final chapter of his *A World without Why* as a kind of procedure, if not a method. For Geuss, one is invited to look at two or more things placed in conjunction without necessarily asking the question why this is the case or seeking for a cause. A pile of dead bodies in a ditch in Iraq is placed alongside the prime minister of the United Kingdom speaking oleaginously in the House of Commons.[3] Here, the idea of invitation can produce an unexpected juxtaposition or disjunction that provokes thinking. In my view, tragedy invites its audience to look at such disjunctions between two or more claims to truth, justice, or whatever without immediately seeking a unifying ground or reconciling the phenomena into a higher unity.

My concern in thinking about tragedy and what I will call "tragedy's philosophy" is to extend an invitation to you to become part of a "we," the "we" that is summoned and called into question by ancient tragedy. More simply stated, every generation has to reinvent the classics. I think it is the responsibility of every generation to engage in this reinvention. And it is the very opposite of any and all kinds of cultural conservatism. If we don't accept this invitation, then we risk becoming even more stupefied by the present and endless onrush of the future. The nice thing is that stupefaction can be really easily avoided by nothing more difficult than reading, and most of the plays are not even that long, which is one reason why I like reading plays. Indeed, although this might sound pompous, I see this as the responsibility of each generation: to pass on something of the deep and unknown past in a way that will speak to the present and arrest us momentarily from the irresistible pull of the future. If the disavowal of the past through the endless production of the new is the very formula for ideology in our societies, then tragedy provides enduring resources for a critique of that ideology that might at least allow for the imagination of a different range of human possibilities. First, however, we need to reach for the emergency brake: STOP!

2

Philosophy's Tragedy and the Dangerous Perhaps

"Tragedy's philosophy" is opposed to "philosophy's tragedy." The thought here is that philosophy as a discursive invention, beginning with the *Republic,* but extending along the millennia into the present, is premised upon the exclusion of tragedy and the exclusion of a range of experiences that we can call tragic, particularly the emotion of grief and the phenomenon of lamentation, which is at the center of so many tragedies, from Aeschylus's *The Persians* onward. I want to suggest that this exclusion of tragedy is, itself, tragic, and this is arguably philosophy's tragedy. I want to defend tragedy against philosophy, or, perhaps better said, to propose that tragedy articulates a philosophical view that challenges the authority of philosophy by giving voice to what is contradictory about us, what is constricted about us, what is precarious about us, and what is limited about us. Philosophy, once again beginning in Plato, appears to be committed to the idea and ideal of a noncontradictory psychic life. Tragedy does not share this commitment. And nor do I. Tragedy is about what Anne Carson calls "that hot bacon smell of pure contradiction."[1] One of the axes I will be grinding in this book is a critique of the very idea of moral psychology and the attempted *moralization* of the psyche that is at work in philosophy and in much else besides, especially Christianity.

Tragedy gives voice to what suffers in us and in others, and how we might become cognizant of that suffering, and work with that suffering, where suffering is that pathos that we undergo, where tragic passion is both something undergone and *partially* overtaken in action (I want to emphasize the word "partially"— agency in tragedy is ever partial). In reading tragedy, we might learn to appreciate both the precariousness of existence and what Judith Butler would call its "grievability."[2] At the source of tragedy is grief and the extreme passions of mourning and lamentation. There are at least thirteen nouns in Attic Greek for words describing grief, lamentation, and mourning. In fact, there are probably many more. Our lack of vocabulary when it comes to the phenomenon of death speaks volumes about who *we* are and what is so impoverished about us.

Now, it is precisely this grief and lamentation that Socrates wants to exclude from the education and life of the philosopher and, most importantly, from the philosophically well-ordered city, regime, or *politeia* described in Plato's *Republic,* which is at once psychic and political or is based on the intended analogy of the psychic and the political: the city and the soul are mirrors of each other. Philosophy is, on this view, a regime that imagines an intense regulation of affect, in particular the affect of grief in the construction of the soul. My larger story, which I will only hint at here but which is developed in detail in Part 4, tracks the exclusion of the tragic poets in Plato in Books II, III, and X of the *Republic* and questions the metaphysical and moral motivation for that exclusion. The mannered ferocity of Plato's denunciation of tragedy seems to conceal a deeper worry about the nature of the philosophical perspective that tragedy seems to embody and its relation to what is, all too simplistically, called "sophistry." There is much to say here: the supposed stability of the distinction between philosophy and sophistry is one of the things I want to press at in order to recover the persuasive force and power of a certain sophistry against the assertions of Socrates and against the reassertion of Platonism that one finds in contemporary philosophers like Alain Badiou. To put it crudely, tragedy's philosophy is sophistry.

My general question could be stated in the following way: What if we took seriously the form of thinking that we find in tragedy, and the experience of partial agency, limited autonomy, deep traumatic affect, agonistic conflict, gender confusion, political complexity, and moral ambiguity that it presents? How might that change the way we think and the way we think about thinking? Might that be tragedy's philosophy as an alternative to philosophy's tragedy? Might that be what Nietzsche meant when he described himself as the first "tragic philosopher" and called for "philosophers of the dangerous perhaps"?[3] To put it a little obtusely, we might say that Nietzsche reads tragedy in order to defend a form of philosophy that is destroyed by philosophy. I want to join Nietzsche in this defense of a tragic philosophy.

3

Knowing and Not Knowing:
How Oedipus Brings Down Fate

As a first step, we might consider the most famous of the Athenian tragedies, the one that has been, since the time of Aristotle's *Poetics,* held up as the highest exemplar of tragedy: *Oedipus the King (Oidipous Tyrannos—Oedipus the Tyrant).* In this infernal, unstoppable, machine of a play, where each line, each word, bristles and bubbles with painful irony and ambiguity, the king is exposed as a tyrant and deposed as a monster and a pollution by the very city that made him king in the first place. But let's back up for a moment and begin at the beginning.

We usually think of tragedy as a misfortune that simply befalls a person (an accident, a fatal disease) or a polity (a natural disaster, like a tsunami, or a terrorist attack like 9/11) and that is outside their control. But if "tragedy" is understood as misfortune, then this is a significant misunderstanding of tragedy. What the thirty-one extant Greek tragedies enact over and over again is not a misfortune that is outside our control. Rather, they show the way in which we collude, seemingly unknowingly, with the calamity that befalls us.

Tragedy requires some degree of complicity on our part in the disaster that destroys us. It is not simply a question of the malevolent activity of fate, a dark prophecy that flows from the inscrutable but often questionable will of the gods. Tragedy requires our collusion with that fate. In other words, it requires no small measure of freedom. It is in this way that we can understand the tragedy of Oedipus. With merciless irony (the first two syllables of the name Oedipus, "swollen-foot," also mean "I know," *oida*), we watch someone move from a position of seeming knowledge—"I, Oedipus, whom all men call great. I solve riddles; now, Citizens, what seems to be the problem?" (I paraphrase)—to a deeper truth that it would appear that Oedipus knew nothing about: he is a parricide and a perpetrator of incest. On this reading, which Aristotle endorses, the tragedy of Oedipus consists in the recognition that allows him to pass from ignorance to knowledge.

But things are more complex than that as there's a backstory that needs to be recalled. Oedipus turned up in Thebes and solved the Sphinx's riddle after refusing to return to what he believed was his native Corinth because he had just been told the prophecy about himself by the oracle at Pytho, namely that he would kill his father and have sex with his mother.

Oedipus *knew* his curse. And, of course, it is on the way back from the oracle that he meets an older man who actually looks a lot like him, as Jocasta inadvertently and almost comically admits later in the play (line 742), who refuses to give way at a crossroads and whom he kills in a fine example of ancient road rage. One might have thought that, given the awful news from the oracle, and given his uncertainty about the identity of his father (Oedipus is called a bastard by a drunk at a banquet in Corinth, which is what first infects his mind with doubt), he might have exercised caution before deciding to kill an older man who seems to have resembled him.

One lesson of tragedy, then, is that we conspire with our fate. That is, fate requires our freedom in order to bring our destiny down upon us. The core contradiction of tragedy is that *we both know and we don't know at one and the same time and are destroyed in the process.* In this book, we will keep circling around this difficult, indeed intolerable, thought: How can we both know and not know?

Such is the complex function of *prophecy* in tragedy. In the tragedy of Oedipus, we watch someone who believes they possess an unencumbered sense of freedom become undone and destroyed by the force of fate. What is so delicate in Oedipus's experience is that his being is not simply causally determined by fate, by necessity. No, fate requires Oedipus's partially conscious complicity in order to bring about its truth. Characters in tragedy are not robots or preprogrammed puppets. In its movement from a delusional self-knowledge and the fantasy of an unencumbered freedom to an experience of an insight into truth that costs us our eyes, tragedy gives voice to an experience of agency that is partial and very often painful. It shows the limits of our attempted self-sufficiency and what we might think of as our autonomy. It shows our heteronomy, our profound dependency. Tragedy gives voice to the complex relations between freedom and necessity that define our being. Our freedom is constantly compromised by that which catches us in the nets of the past, in the determination of our past and future being by fate. Tragedy enacts that which snags at our being and pulls us back to a past that we disavow in our constant thirst for the short-term future. Such is the weight of the past that entangles the tragic protagonist (and us) in its meshes. As Rita Felski says, "The weight of what has gone before bears down ineluctably on what is yet to come."[1] To disavow the past is to be destroyed by it—such is tragedy's instruction.

In tragedy, time is out of joint and the linear conception of time as a teleological flow from the past to the future is thrown into reverse. The past is not past, the future folds back upon itself, and the present is shot through with fluxions of past and future that destabilize it. Time flexes and twists in tragedy. Its script is you and me, as David Bowie said. Tragedy is the art form of between times, usually between an old world that is passing away and a new world that is coming into being. This is true of Greek tragedy, of Elizabethan tragedy, and perhaps the tragedy of our times. In tragedy, time is always out of joint. Its conjunction is disjunction.

Tragedy has a kind of boomerang structure where the action that we throw out into the world returns to us with a potentially fatal velocity. Oedipus, the solver of riddles, becomes the riddle himself. Sophocles' play shows him engaged in a relentless inquiry into the pollution that is destroying the political order, poisoning the wells, and producing infant mortality. But he *is* that pollution.

The deeper truth is that Oedipus knows something of this from the get-go, but he refuses to see and hear what is said to him. Very early in the play, blind Tiresias tells him to his face that *he* is the perpetrator of the pollution that he seeks to eradicate. But Oedipus just doesn't hear Tiresias. This is one way of interpreting the word "tyrant" in Sophocles' original Greek title: *Oidipous Tyrannos*. The tyrant doesn't *hear* what is said to him and doesn't *see* what is in front of his eyes.

But we are tyrants too. We look, but we see nothing. Someone speaks to us, but we hear nothing. And we go on in our endlessly narcissistic self-justification, adding Facebook updates and posting on Instagram. Tragedy is about many things, but it is centrally concerned with the conditions for actually seeing and actually hearing. In making us blind, we might finally achieve insight, unblock our ears, and stop the droning surf of the endless song of ourselves: me, me, me, this is all for me (really?).

There is a wonderful Greek expression recalled by Anne Carson, "Shame lies on the eyelids."[2] The point is that the tyrant (and we could list many recent examples) experiences no shame. But we also have no shame. We are also little, shameless tyrants, especially when it comes to our relations to those we think of as our parents and our children. I think of Walter White from *Breaking Bad,* who insisted until almost the end of the final episode of that long show that he did everything, *everything,* for his family and not for himself. This is tyranny and this is perversion. Finally, his wife gets him to admit that he also became the meth king of New Mexico, the Heisenberg of the southwestern United States, because he enjoyed it. That's a start. At least he is acknowledging a desire, a perverse desire.

Greek tragedy provides lessons in shame. When we learn that lesson and finally achieve some insight, as Oedipus does, then it might cost us our sight and we might pluck out our eyes—for shame. The political world is stuffed overfull with sham shame, ham humility, and carefully staged tearful apologies: I'm so sorry; I'm so, so sorry. But true shame is something else.

4

Rage, Grief, and War

Anne Carson, in *Grief Lessons*—her extraordinarily bold translations of Euripides—writes, "Why does tragedy exist? Because you are full of rage. Why are you full of rage? Because you are full of grief."[1] This is absolutely right. Antigone rages because she is full of grief for her brother Polynices, who is refused burial rites by the leader of the city, Creon. Clytemnestra rages at Agamemnon because of her grief for her daughter Iphigenia, slaughtered like a young foal in order to ensure favorable winds in the sails of the Greek ships on their way to Troy. Hecuba rages at the murder of her daughter Polyxena, only to discover that all her other children have been killed as well. Hecuba's grief seems to know no bounds. In the afterlife, she is told, she will be turned into a dog.[2]

We might add a further question to Carson's list: If tragedy is the rage that follows from grief, then why is one full of grief? Because we are full of war and people have been killed. Tragedy might be defined as a grief-stricken rage that flows from war. We live in a world whose frame is war and where justice seems to be endlessly divided between claim and counterclaim, right and left, conservative and progressive, believer and nonbeliever, freedom fighter and terrorist, or whatever. Each side believes unswervingly in the rightness of its position and the wrongness or, as is usually said, *evil* of the enemy. Such a belief legitimates violence, a destructive violence that unleashes counterviolence in return. We seem trapped in a cycle of bloody revenge and locked into vicious circles of grief and rage caused by war.

Such is what often seems to pass for international politics in our world. This is where, I think, a reflection on Greek tragedy might at the very least illuminate our current predicament and tell us something about our present.

The history of Greek tragedy is the history of war, from the war with the Persians in the early fifth century BCE to the Peloponnesian Wars that rumbled on until that century's end; from the emergence of Athenian imperial hegemony to its dissolution and humiliation at the hands of Sparta. In 472 BCE, Aeschylus's *The Persians* deals with the aftermath of the Battle of Salamis in 480 BCE. It was therefore a good deal closer to the Athenians than 9/11, say, is to us. More than half of our surviving tragedies were composed after the outbreak of the Peloponnesian Wars in 431 BCE. *Oedipus the King* was first performed in 429 BCE, two years after the beginning of the war, during a time of plague that is estimated to have killed one-quarter of the Athenian population. The plague that established the entire environment of Sophocles' play is not some idle musing. It was very real indeed. It killed Pericles, the leader of Athens, in the autumn of that very same year, 429 BCE. The frame of tragedy is war and its devastating effects on human life.

Greek tragedy, particularly with its obsessive focus on the aftermath of the Trojan War, especially in the delightful excessiveness of Euripides, is largely *about* combat veterans. But it was also performed *by* combat veterans. Actors were not flimsy thespians who had majored in performance studies with an abstract interest in social engagement, but soldiers who had seen combat. Tragedy was played before an audience that either participated directly in war or that was indirectly implicated in war. All were traumatized by it and everyone felt its effects. War was the life of the city and its pride, as Pericles argued. But war was also the city's fall and undoing.

Yet, Greek tragedy is a war story without a John Wayne figure, without a swaggering individualist who is the sole source of good in a world gone bad. On the contrary, in Greek tragedy, the hero is not the solution to the problem, but the problem itself. The hero is the source of the plague that is killing the city. This is one reason why Sophocles' tragedy is called *Oidipous Tyrannos*. The king is a tyrant who is polluting the city, and the only resolution to the drama is Oedipus's expulsion and exile. This is the great virtue—the realism—of ancient tragedy, as opposed to the idealized violence, empty empathy, and hollow sentimentality of many contemporary war fictions. If tragedy is a drama performed by war veterans before an audience of veterans, then it pictures a world without heroes and without tyrannical leaders who delude and goad the people into making war.

How might we respond to the contemporary situation of war? It might seem that the easiest and noblest thing to do is to speak of peace. Yet, as Raymond Williams says in his still hugely relevant book from 1966, *Modern Tragedy,* "To say peace when there is no peace" is to say nothing.[3] To which the obvious response is: *say war*. But that would be peremptory. The danger of easy pacifism is that it is inert and self-regarding. It is always too pleased with itself. But the alternative is not a justification of war. It is rather the attempt to understand the complex tragic dialectics of political situations, particularly apparently revolutionary ones.

Williams goes on to claim, "We expect men brutally exploited and intolerably poor to rest and be patient in their misery, because if they act to end their condition it will involve the rest of us, and threatens our convenience or our lives."[4] Often, we simply want violence and war to go away because it is an inconvenience to us and to our lovely lives. As such, we do not only fail to see our implication in such violence and war, we completely disavow it.

The virtue of Greek tragedy is that it makes such disavowal more difficult by confronting us with a situation of grief-stricken rage and disorder. The virtue of seeing the bloody events of the contemporary world in a tragic light is that it exposes us to a disorder that is not just *their* disorder. It is *ours* too. Our war, our rage, our (disavowed) grief. To see political events tragically is always to accept our complicity in the disaster that is unfolding. We are the audience in the theater of war, and we too are responsible. As such, tragedy can enable us to begin to comprehend a situation of war, violence, and grief, without simply condemning it or mouthing empty words of peace. More difficult still is imagining the resolution of such a situation, but a tragic worldview has to be the starting point for any such aspiration.

5

Gorgias: Tragedy Is a Deception That Leaves the Deceived Wiser Than the Nondeceived

This book has a motto from Gorgias, the Sicilian rhetorician who introduced much of the teaching of oratory to Athens in the latter half of the fifth century BCE, and who seems to have been directly influential even on the writing of tragedy, as in Helen's amazing speech in her defense in Euripides' *The Trojan Women* (we will come to that in Part 3 and speak of Gorgias at greater length). We possess an undated fragment preserved in Plutarch that gives us our earliest "theoretical" response to Attic tragedy, that is, some sense of what the *theoros,* the spectator, saw in the spectacle of tragedy. Gorgias writes,

> Tragedy, by means of legends and emotions, creates a deception in which the deceiver is more honest than the nondeceiver, and the deceived is wiser than the non-deceived.[1]

The Greek word that is doing all the work in this passage is *apate,* which Liddell and Scott's *Greek-English Lexicon* tells me means cheating, trickery, fraud, guile, deceit, and cunning.[2] It also connotes a stratagem in war. Altogether, it's a pretty bad thing.

But consider the logic of the fragment: tragedy is a deception or an act of fraud or trickery, in which the deceiver is more honest than the nondeceiver and the deceived is wiser than the nondeceived. What Gorgias seems to describe, perhaps even celebrate, is precisely that which Socrates sees as the great danger of tragedy.

This is the danger of deception, the power of persuasion to induce the affective effects of imitation, of *mimesis,* which Socrates subjects to a corrosive metaphysical and moral critique in the *Republic.* The metaphysical critique concerns the nature of *mimesis* and its threefold removal from the world of forms. The moral critique concerns the allegedly pernicious effects of excessive emotions, like lamentation—in the case of tragedy—and laughter—in the case of comedy. This is how philosophy begins.

By contrast, Gorgias would appear to be suggesting that tragedy (and a fortiori all art) is the acquisition of wisdom through deception, through an emotionally psychotropic experience that generates a powerful emotion. As Stephen Halliwell points out in a fascinating paper on this topic, Gorgias's view would appear to be confirmed by a fragment from Timocles' lost play, *Women Celebrating the Dionysia* (which I would have loved to have seen!). Here tragedy is described as a *parapsyche,* an emotional consolation, cooling or coping with life's troubles, but also as a *psychagogia,* an enthralling persuasion that can also denote a conjuring of souls from the nether world.[3] Interestingly, as we will see in Part 5 Aristotle also describes the effect of tragedy in terms of *psychagogia.*

In other words, the wisdom of tragedy flows not just from deception, but from a kind of necromancy, the conjuring of ghostly illusion. Thinking once again of our oldest extant play, *The Persians,* the drama ends with the conjuring of the ghost of Darius the Great, who admonishes his son, Xerxes, before warning the Greeks not to engage in *hybris.* Tragedy is full of ghosts, ancient and modern, and the line separating the living from the dead is continually blurred. This means that in tragedy *the dead don't stay dead and the living are not fully alive.* What tragedy renders unstable is the line that separates the living from the dead, enlivening the dead and deadening the living.

So, what kind of *parapsyche* does tragedy provide? Where is the cooling consolation in all this hauntology? We might say that tragedy consoles through an imaginative enthrallment with an almost trancelike, otherworldly state that is linked, for Timocles and Aristotle and us, to pleasure, *hedone.* As Horatio calls out to the Ghost early in *Hamlet,* "Stay, Illusion!" This, of course, raises the perplexing question as to the nature of tragic pleasure. What kind of hedonism is the pleasure we take in tragedy, which depicts not just suffering and death, but the ghostly porosity of the frontier separating the living from the dead? Is the greatest aesthetic pleasure the theatrically distanced experience of pain? And what exactly is the pleasure we take in spectacles of pain? I would like to let these questions resonate for us awkwardly, thinking of Artaud's Theatre of Cruelty, Bataille's holy disgust, Hermann Nitsch's blood orgies, the extremity of Sarah Kane's theater, and perhaps the movies of Lars von Trier.

What Plato sees as the great danger of tragedy is celebrated by Gorgias as revealing the power of persuasion and the affective effects of imitation. For Socrates, tragedy and the other mimetic arts can lead us to have sympathy for morally suspect characters. For Socrates, it is an awful danger, the danger of deception and fiction, the danger of a vicious ordering of political life on the basis of a lie (and, as usual, Socrates has a point). We should never forget that the festival of the Great Dionysia was first instituted around 532 BCE under the leadership—indeed the apparently benevolent tyranny—of Pisistratus and his growing political ambition. Also, according to Plutarch, the famous lawgiver Solon left one of the first dramatic representations in disgust because he saw, like Rousseau a couple of millennia later, that theater would lead to the degradation and sickness of the body politic—Socrates makes this point at the end of Book VIII of the *Republic,* as we will see in Chapter 34. There is an implicit connection between democracy and theater as public institutions in the city, conspiring with each other to lead to tyranny. This is why, for Plato, the tragic poets must be excluded. What obsesses Socrates in the *Republic* is the question of tyranny and the link between democracy and theater, where *demokratia* is what Plato calls in the *Laws* a *theatrokratia* (701a), a theatrical regime of power, what we might call a society of the spectacle, that will always leave the door open to tyranny. This is why, for Plato, the only true antidote to *theatrokratia* is *philosophia*.[4]

The vast question that Gorgias's fragment raises is that of the necessity and indeed moral and political productivity of deception, of fiction, of fraud, of illusion. Does, as Nietzsche will suggest, our firstly Platonic and subsequently Christian will to truth blind us to the power of art in general and tragedy in particular? By contrast, can we assert with the young Nietzsche that it is only as an aesthetic phenomenon that existence and the world is truly justified? Might the wisdom of tragedy, a deception where the deceived is wiser than the nondeceived, begin to emancipate us from that Platonic and Christian moralization at the core of truth? Is deception both the undoing of truth and the truth of truth? Such are some of the questions at stake in the relation between philosophy and tragedy, in tragedy's philosophy as a riposte to philosophy's tragedy. As can perhaps be surmised, the stakes here are pretty high.

Justice as Conflict (for Polytheism)

Let's think about Aeschylus's *Oresteia,* our one complete extant tragic trilogy, and a possibly unique example of one story being spread over three plays. What we witness in the bloodbath of the *Agamemnon* and *The Libation Bearers* (*Choephoroi*) is the history of violence upon which the apparently pacific political order rests. We see characters completely caught up in cycles of revenge where there is seemingly no end to the violence and no end to its dogmatic justification by its perpetrators. "Behold, a masterpiece of justice" (*Agamemnon,* lines 1403–05) declares Clytemnestra as she exhibits in a macabre tableau the murdered corpses of her husband, Agamemnon, and his concubine, Cassandra. Orestes claims justice as he slaughters his mother, Clytemnestra, and the chorus comments, "Justice turns the wheel" (*Libation Bearers,* line 315). If justice is on both sides, then what exactly is justice? As Aeschylus says in *Prometheus Bound,* "The wheel turns" (line 515).

What the goddess Athena attempts in the final play in the trilogy, the *Eumenides,* is to use reasoning and persuasion (*peitho*) in order to arrest the cycle of violence and find some way of stopping the bloodshed and finding a settlement. The first thing one notices is that in tragedy *justice is conflict.* It is a fight between opposed parties who are prepared to act violently in its name. The second thing one notices is that, as a counterbalance to violence, there is the activity of what we might call, following Stuart Hampshire, "adversary reasoning" or "adversarial reasoning" in tragedy, where we think from the adversary's position and use reason in order to *audi alteram partem,* to hear the other side.[1] In tragedy, this adversarial reasoning takes place very often either in a law court, as is the case in the *Eumenides,* or it is staged as a legal dispute, as in the debate between Hecuba and Helen in *The Trojan Women.* Very often, at the core of tragedy is the law, and we should not forget that the law court is also a theater and remains such to this day.

If one were optimistically inclined, one might see tragedy as providing an object lesson in resolving conflicts reasonably in a world of overwhelming enmity. I am unsure whether I am that optimistic, because what we also see in tragedy is the weakness of rational argumentation in the presence of violence (in Greek, *Bia,* who is actually a mute dramatic presence onstage in Aeschylus's *Prometheus Bound*) and the persistence of forms of arbitrary decision making. In *The Trojan Women,* Menelaus is the judge between Hecuba and Helen, but although he is persuaded by the strength of Hecuba's arguments, he still refuses to put Helen to death for her betrayal and for causing the Trojan War. The force of the stronger argument is sometimes ignored and due process replaced by an arbitrary decision.

Yet, what is common to the optimistic and pessimistic interpretations of the use of reason (given that the opposition between optimism and pessimism is questionable anyhow) in tragedy is the following: any strong monolithic conception of reason, capital *R,* must be abandoned and we must accept that reasoning is always a two-sided process of fragile negotiation in a world of constitutive and irreducible violence. This also means accepting that reason is essential, but essentially limited in its power, that it requires the use of rhetoric and persuasion, and that it can surely fail. What kind of reasonable settlement can enforce a bond in a conflict where there are passionate but utterly opposed claims to justice on both sides? Such is one of the questions that tragedy seeks to explore and is arguably a description of the world that we inhabit and have always inhabited.

What is preferable about the world of Greek tragedy is that it is a *polytheistic* world with a diversity of conflicting and deeply flawed gods and rival conceptions of the good. It is my conviction, following Hampshire, that the lesson of the adversarial reasoning of tragedy is that it is prudent to abandon *any* notion of monotheism, whether it is either of the three Abrahamic monotheisms, a Platonic monotheism rooted in the metaphysical primacy of the Good, or indeed the secular monotheism of liberal democracy and human rights that still circles around a weak, deistic conception of God. The motto on the back of the dollar bill might be slightly improved if it read *In Gods we trust (and sometimes distrust)*. Admittedly, this is not very catchy.

Tragedy's philosophy begins from the irreducible *facticity* of violence and the fragile necessity of reasoning in a world of conflictual force, a polytheistic world that continues to think of itself as monotheistic. If the acceptance of tragedy's philosophy entails the abandonment of modern theological shibboleths like faith in progress, which is underpinned by a linear conception of time and history that tragedy twists out of joint, then it might also possess the virtue of a modest political realism that has to begin where philosophy should begin, in my view, with disappointment. But although philosophy might begin in disappointment, it does not end there. On the contrary, disappointment is the graveyard of those philosophies and worldviews that insist manically upon affirmation, vitality, wonder, and creation.

7

Tragedy as a Dialectical Mode of Experience

Is tragedy something that is available to us in the contemporary world? Far from claiming, with someone like George Steiner, that tragedy is dead, I would argue, with Raymond Williams, that it offers the most powerful template for diagnosing the seemingly intractable conflicts that define the present and finding reflective resources for thinking beyond them.[1] It is in this spirit, I think, that we could and should approach the struggles of our time. A tragic sensibility obliges us to see our implication within the conflicts of the present and our responsibility for them. If the present is defined by disaster, then tragedy shows us our complicity with it.

The question of tragedy should not be confined to its existence (or nonexistence) as a dramatic genre that might or might not exist in the theater. Rather it is a *mode of experience* that can be found well outside the theater, in film, in TV, in politics, and—most powerfully perhaps—in our domestic lives, our familial relations and kinship structures. Furthermore, tragedy is a *dialectical mode of experience.* Specifically, it is a mode of reversal, inversion, and negation where we are implicated at each step. Tragedy is an object lesson in dialectical thinking. It is a staging of dialectics, which is why Hegel, following on from his friend Hölderlin, had such a profound grasp of tragedy, even if the former sometimes confined it within the horizon of reconciliation on the one hand, and dissolution on the other. Perhaps tragedy is neither and both.

What is perhaps new in my thinking with its focus on tragedy's philosophy is this dialectical turn. In opposition to forms of vapidly hopeful idealism that leads only to despair, I see tragedy's philosophy as offering a bracing, skeptical realism that heavily qualifies what we think of as hope, but perhaps also deepens it into a form of courage.

PART II

Tragedy

8

Tragedy as Invention, or the Invention of Tragedy: Twelve Theses

Let me begin by laying out twelve theses on tragedy, which can serve as signposts for what follows:

1. Tragedy is an invention: at once political, literary, and anthropological, namely taking place at the level of subjectivity. If we are compelled by the moment of Attic tragedy, which combines the three elements of its invention, then the etiological question of its birth or origin is the wrong question to ask.

2. Tragedy is not the expression of a religiously legitimized ritual. It is rather a metaritual or an institution premised upon a temporal disjunction, specifically the disjunction of past and present. The time of tragedy, ancient and modern, is always out of joint.

3. Tragedy is self-consciously *anachronistic;* it disrupts the order of historical time, even as it feeds from a bedrock of what is perceived as historical reality. That bedrock is not sufficient for tragedy, but it is necessary.

4. Tragedy is the self-consciousness of *fictionality,* where the deceiver is more honest than the nondeceiver, and the deceived is wiser than the nondeceived—this is Gorgias's insight. The lie of tragedy is its truth.

5. The subject of tragedy is not the tragic hero—and emotional identification with character is *not* the alpha and

omega of tragedy—but the city-state, or *polis,* specifically the city-state in its novel litigious antagonism, in its breakage with the past in the form of myth and in the discourses of law and reason.

6. Very importantly, tragedy is the experience of moral ambiguity. The right is always on both sides and invariably also wrong. Justice is conflict, as I said in the Chapter 5, which means that justice is divided. Justice is not one, but at least two. This can be found everywhere in tragedy, but it is most obviously evident in the *Oresteia.*

7. Tragedy is gender trouble. It is the travesty of the politics of sexual difference at the core of the political order. Tragedy queers norms. But the effect of that queering is deeply uncertain.

8. The tragic coupling of the human and the divine that is all over tragedy is not some premodern remnant, some supernatural or superstitious residue, and it is not to be explained through an evolutionary narrative that culminates in the achievement of autonomy where we legislate for ourselves.

9. The significance of tragedy cannot be explained away through some either progressivist philosophy of history (Hegel, Marx) or through a regressivist conception (Nietzsche, Heidegger).

10. Tragedy reveals a world only partially intelligible to human agency, where autonomy is necessarily limited by the acknowledgment of dependency. This is one way of understanding Aristotle's theme of *hamartia,* not as a tragic flaw but as a basic experience of human fallibility and ontological limitedness. The belief in autonomy is the moment of *hybris* that precedes tragic ruination, or *ate.*

11. The tragic hero is a problem, not the solution to a problem. The hero is a riddle, not the solution to a riddle. The human being in tragedy is both an agent and the one

acted upon, both innocent and guilty—something baffling, incomprehensible, and monstrous.

12. As Euripides—for Aristotle, "the most tragic" (*tragikotatos*) of the tragic poets—arguably shows most powerfully, the mood of ancient tragedy is *skeptical,* it is about the dissolution of all the markers of certitude that finds expression in the repeated question "What shall I do?" Such questions are not the beginning of an experience of rational argumentation, but reason's terminus. This skeptical mood is also common in modern tragedy, most obviously in Shakespeare, which implies that the distinction between ancient and modern tragedy, and, consequently, antiquity and modernity, is not as secure and stable as one might imagine or wish. Tragedy means giving up any theology or metaphysics of history based on the distinction of ancients and moderns.

9

A Critique of the Exotic Greeks

Are the Attic Greeks really such exotic people? Are they really so unlike us? The more I read and think about these questions, the less I am drawn to exoticist explanations. We are, of course, not in the same situation as the ancient Greeks, historically, socially, politically, or even environmentally. As the great poet and self-described "impresario of the Ancient Greeks," Louis MacNeice, wrote, "It was all so unimaginably different / And all so long ago."[1] But the temptation to situate the Greeks in a position of utter otherness must be resisted, I think, or at the very least questioned.

There is a widespread view, let's call it "early Nietzschean," that one can find in a book such as Erika Simon's *The Ancient Theater* (1972) and that I bought hook, line, and sinker as an undergraduate in the early 1980s (as I did the arguments of Bruno Snell's 1946 book, *The Discovery of the Mind,* which claims that the Homeric and tragic Greeks lacked a fully developed theory of the mind, intention, and agency).[2] On this view, tragedy arises out of ritual, religious ritual, specifically in honor of the God Dionysos. Now, both Aristotle and Nietzsche agree on this point, although they employ it for very different ontological ends. In the *Poetics,* as we will see in Part 5, Aristotle says that the beginning of tragedy lies with the dithyramb and the members of the chorus are followers of Dionysos, to whom Thespis added the first actor (1449a). Aristotle adds that tragedy arose out of satyric drama, although it acquired grandeur, *megethos, only* when it separated itself from satyr plays. Aristotle's concern is with defining the being of tragedy as it found full expression in the plays of the fifth century BCE. As is well known, Nietzsche accords much more ontological importance to the genesis of tragedy in Dionysian religious worship. Erika Simon's view picks up from Nietzsche's thought, claiming that tragedy begins in religious ritual and worship, where judgment in the tragic contest, or *agon,* was given by priests. On this view, we are given an explanation of tragic costume, because the actors had to be heavily disguised for religious reasons in order to achieve the loss of individuality and allow for *ekstasis,* or "standing outside oneself." There is thus an implicit connection between *mimesis* and *ekstasis,* between tragic imitation and the loss of self, a loss that has a religious significance, which Nietzsche describes as the overcoming of the *principium individuationis,* a dissolution of self that occurs through the intoxicating power of music.[3]

Given my agnostic claims in the last chapter, I am hardly in a position of epistemic authority to declare that Simon's view is wrong, and the threat of *ekstasis* is clearly part—and a big part—of Socrates' worries about including tragedy in the education of the guardians in the *Republic.* But I am skeptical of this view, the fantasy of the ecstatic Greeks, the exotic, othered, god-languishing early Greeks, the Greeks imagined by thinkers like Heidegger and, even more so, by Heideggerians. Some recent classical scholarship is also highly skeptical of the claim that tragedy emerges out of religious ritual, specifically Dionysian worship. Ian Storey and Arlene Allan suggest that the location of the Theater of Dionysos might well have been accidental and that the southeast slope of the Acropolis was simply the best place to locate a theater in a rapidly expanding city.[4] In addition, of the thirty-one tragedies that we possess from the fifth century, only one has anything to do with Dionysos, obviously Euripides' late play *The Bacchae,* and it is—to say the very least—a complex case. Indeed, Dionysos also appears in comedy, as in Aristophanes' *The Frogs.* The most common topics in ancient tragedies are connected with the events preceding or succeeding the Trojan War and the affairs of the House of Atreus and the Palace of Thebes. For example, we have sixty titles of tragedies by Aeschylus—supposedly the most "ritualistic" of the tragedians—and two-thirds of them involved episodes from the Trojan War. Are Ajax or Agamemnon or Oedipus masks for Dionysos, the dying, suffering god, as Nietzsche suggests? It is a tempting, seductive theory, but there is absolutely no reason to accept it, and the fact that it is tempting perhaps says more about our intellectual weakness for generalized etiological explanations than the theory's strength.

The temptation to explain tragedy on the basis of ritual is very powerful. Simon Goldhill discusses the Cambridge Ritualists of the early twentieth century who—under the influence of Nietzsche and Frazer—approached the performance of tragedy as ritual. Gilbert Murray (although he taught at Oxford) was associated with the group and saw Greek tragedy as arising out of a dancing ritual around the "year spirit" (*eniautos daimon*) of Dionysos.[5] Murray's views are continued in the work of his successor at Oxford, E. R. Dodds, whose *The Greeks and the Irrational* (1951) was deeply influential, and who also translated *The Bacchae*. One can find related views in René Girard, for whom "Tragedy is the child of sacrificial crisis."[6] This is an obviously compelling way of understanding dramas like *The Bacchae* or indeed *Oedipus the King,* where Oedipus can be seen as the scapegoat that has to be sacrificed so that the city can continue life. To be clear, I am not saying that the interpretation of tragedy as ritual is completely misguided. Rather, tragedy might be better approached as metaritual: namely, it is the rational *reenactment* or *reappropriation* of mythic ritual within the context of a new aesthetic, institutional, and political regime. It comments on ritual as it is enacted before our eyes, which is what happens in so many of the tragedies.

Of course, a subtle anthropologist might object at this point and say that I am misunderstanding the nature of ritual and that all ritual is metaritual, namely that it is a self-conscious reenactment of a given practice and that it is not irrational, but that it has a rationality inherent to that practice. If that is the case, then I have no objection to calling tragedy ritual. But that is *not* what is usually meant by those who identify tragedy with ritual. They long for some fantasy of a precognitive, preconscious, trancelike sacral automatism that can be ideologically identified with the desire for authenticity. If we can speak of tragedy as an *inauthentic* ritual, then I have no problem with it.

Tragedy *might* have had a religious origin, but one is entitled to ask So what? Many things have a religious origin, like major European universities (Paris, Oxford), the legal profession, and the institutionalized pedophilia of the Catholic Church, but that doesn't entail that their activity must be defined in relation to its origin and confined within it. As Scott Scullion notes in a fascinating paper, "The primeval Dionysiac tragedy in the ancient sources belongs to the neverland of aetiological conjecture."[7] In my view, there is a lamentable tendency to *exoticize* Attic tragedy, doubtless as part and parcel of some more or less reactionary critique of whatever people mean by "modernity," to invoke that benighted noun. The early Nietzschean *doxa* appears to want to imagine that the spectators of ancient tragedy were in some sort of prerational, ritualistic stupor, some intoxicated, drunken dumbfounded state. Lurking behind this *doxa,* I suspect there is an authoritarian, antimodern fantasy: Wouldn't it be wonderful if a religiously and ritualistically saturated art form legislated for society without the ceaseless disputation and dissent that are a consequence of modern rationality? Which raises the question: perhaps, contra Heidegger, origins are the wrong things to look for when it comes to artworks. As Patricia Easterling rightly writes, "There is no reason why a complex and continuously developing institution should be best explained in terms of an account of its origins."[8] When it comes to tragedy, I would suggest that we suspend the habit of etiological conjecture and focus on the thing itself. Perhaps this obsession with origins is part and parcel of a

Protestant, intellectual tic that wants to destroy the inheritance of tradition in the name of a reactivated primal and pure source.

The problem perhaps lies in the very title of Nietzsche's 1872 *The Birth of Tragedy,* which is less an account of tragedy than a defense of a Schopenhauerian artists' metaphysics with an affirmative rather than resigned twist. The authoritarian fantasy driving the idea of the Dionysian in the early Nietzsche is clear. He writes,

> Transform Beethoven's "Hymn to Joy" into a painting; let your imagination conceive the multitudes bowing to the dust, awestruck—then you will approach the Dionysian.[9]

As the later Nietzsche would himself have said: no, no, and thrice no. It is to Nietzsche's great credit that he matured, abandoned his Schopenhauerianism and his Wagnerism, and adapted his views on the Dionysian. One of the problems with etiological speculation on the birth of tragedy is that it invites prognostications on either the death of tragedy or its possible rebirth. It is my conviction that questions of the birth, death, and rebirth of tragedy are less important than the *life* of tragedy, and seeking to understand the vital moment that it occupies. It is the moment of Greek tragedy that concerns Jean-Pierre Vernant and Pierre Vidal-Naquet, and to which I will now turn.

Discussion of Vernant and Vidal-Naquet's
Myth and Tragedy in Ancient Greece

The influential essays that make up Vernant and Vidal-Naquet's *Myth and Tragedy in Ancient Greece* were published in two volumes in 1972 and 1986.[1] The first question to ask is why is the title of the book on myth *and* tragedy? What is the meaning of the conjunctive? The thought here is that tragedy emerges only toward the end of the sixth century at the moment when the language of myth ceases to have a hold on the political realities of the city. Tragedy is not a form of mythical narrative, "myth was both *in* tragedy and at the same time rejected by it."[2] Tragedy is not simply mythic, as many people assume; it is the *problematization* of myth. Tragedy is born at the moment when myth starts to be seen from the viewpoint of the citizen and in relation to law and the city.

Vernant and Vidal-Naquet's studies seek to understand the *moment* of Greek tragedy. Laying aside the idealistic, generalizing rhetoric of the philosophical discourse on the tragic, Greek tragedy appears at a historical turning point that is limited and dated: "It is born, flourishes and degenerates in Athens, and all almost within the space of a hundred years."[3] Tragedy is thus a *moment*—is this still relevant to our moment? Arguably. We will come back to that.

The decisive fact in approaching the moment of tragedy is that tragedy was an invention. Therefore, the question of the origin of tragedy, or its birth, should be prudently used only to gauge the innovative aspects of tragedy, that is, tragedy's *discontinuity* with regard to both prior religious practices, like the cult of Dionysos, and ancient poetic forms, like the epic poetry of Homer and Hesiod. Vernant and Vidal-Naquet argue, against Nietzsche and against many others, that the truth of tragedy is not to be found in an obscure, more or less "primitive" or "mystical" past secretly haunting the theater stage. Rather, tragedy decisively shifts the Greek cultural horizon on three levels:

1. At the level of social institutions, tragedy or tragic competitions were introduced and administered by the chief magistrate, the *archon,* down to the smallest details, using the same rules as applied to democratic assemblies and the law courts. From this point of view, tragedy could be said to be a manifestation of the city turning itself into theater, presenting itself onstage before its assembled citizens. As we noted earlier, this is what the aged Plato calls, with a clear critical intent, *"theatrokratia,"* where *demokratia* is identified with theater and theater with democracy, and both are identified with tyranny. Tragedy is democracy turning itself into a spectacle, which, of course, is also Rousseau's worry in his 1758 *Letter to D'Alembert*. Opposition to theater is opposition to democracy.

2. At the level of literary form, tragedy is fundamentally different from preceding genres, like epic and lyric, Homer or Pindar: it was written to be seen and heard, and carefully planned as a vast public spectacle. Remember that Aristotle will say at the end of the *Poetics* that the fact that tragedy is accessible to the "many" does not make it inferior to epic; indeed, the opposite is the case for Aristotle.

3. Most important, at the level of human experience, there is the development (we can't say "invention," I think) of

what Vernant and Vidal-Naquet call "tragic consciousness." Human beings and their actions were not presented as stable realities but as problems, unanswerable questions, riddles whose double meanings remain enigmatic however often decoded. For example, epic poetry exalted heroic values, virtues, and high deeds. But in tragedy, through the interplay of dialogue, the hero becomes a subject of debate. The hero becomes a problem:

When the hero is thus publicly brought into question in fifth-century Athens, it is the individual Greek in the audience who discovers himself to be a problem, in and through the presentation of the tragic drama.[4]

This is why the question of the origin of tragedy is the wrong path to follow, as it fails to account for the nature of tragedy's invention, i.e., its relative *modernity*. The importance of the relation of tragedy to religion has thus been overstated. For example, for Vernant and Vidal-Naquet, the function of the mask is aesthetic, not ritualistic. This claim becomes clearer in the first essay in the second volume of the book from 1986, "The God of Tragic Fiction." On this point, modern scholarship in the wake of Nietzsche seems to answer the question of the fifth-century audience as reported by Plutarch, "What has it to do with Dionysos?," by trying to reconnect ancient tragedy with its religious origins in the cult of Dionysos.[5] Vernant and Vidal-Naquet are highly skeptical of such claims and I agree with them. If anything, it is satyric drama rather than tragedy that represents the Dionysian roots of theater, but interestingly, satyr plays are instituted as part of the City Dionysia by Athens after and not before tragedy.

Philologically, attempts have been made to link tragedy to goat song by a speculative etymology linking tragedy to *tragos,* the he-goat. But no goats were sacrificed at the City Dionysia. Goats don't seem to be so important to an understanding of tragedy. To quote the title of the 2009 George Clooney movie, the spectators of Attic tragedy were not men who stare at goats. So, we should forget about goats and visions of animal (or human) sacrifice. It says more about our fantasies and our weariness with the modern world than it does about tragedy. Of course, to say that tragedy is an invention is also to say that tragedy is not traditional. It is not the expression of a stable society governed by *Sittlichkeit,* a stable set of mores that make up social life, which is a Hegelian fantasy that Hegel himself perhaps didn't quite believe. Tragedy, like democracy, is a break with tradition. It is an ancient version of modernity, a deliberate aesthetic innovation or self-conscious modernization.

Tragedy is the disjunctive art of discontinuity rather than the continuity of tradition or a form of life (inter alia, I have little idea what philosophers mean when they appeal to "forms of life," which always seems like a crypto-conservative gesture). Tragedy is concerned with the contradiction between the past and the present. For example, at one moment in *Seven Against Thebes,* Eteocles, son and brother of Oedipus, acts like a good democratic ruler; at another moment his *daimon* recalls him to bloodthirsty blood conflict and the consequences of dark family prophecy, and the play might have been called *Eteokles Tyrannos.* Tragedy is not about the past or the present, but about their inextricable and fatal entanglement, which leads to disaster. It leads us to disaster too.

For Vernant and Vidal-Naquet, the Dionysian element is present in tragedy not in terms of birth or origins, which simply elude us, but in terms of the self-consciousness of fiction that tragedy enacts.[6] The spectator in the theater was aware of both the real existence of the characters onstage and the completely illusory nature of what those characters characterized. The figures onstage were not what they seemed. Tragedy, like cinema for us, is both real and unreal at once. Two in one, as François Truffaut says in *La Nuit américaine.* For Vernant and Vidal-Naquet, the new cultural space opened up by ancient tragedy in Greek culture is that of *mimesis,* the space of the imaginary, pure artifice. In other words, tragedy induces a self-consciousness of fictionality, of the productivity of illusion and imitation. This is precisely what Socrates cannot abide and what Gorgias describes as *apate,* deception. Against any ideology of naturalism, a consciousness of fiction is obviously essential to drama. It is its enabling condition and cognitive consequence.

The true protagonist in so much tragedy—as in Aeschylus's *Seven Against Thebes* or the *Eumenides*—is not the tragic hero, but the city itself.[7] Similarly, to use Nietzsche's term, what commits suicide in tragedy, as Hegel realized better than anyone else in the *Phenomenology of Spirit,* is the Athenian city-state, through war. It is this long suicide that is critically observed in tragedy, especially in Euripides, but equally in Aristophanic comedy. For example, it is a central theme of *The Frogs,* as we will see in Part 5.

Otherwise said, the true material of tragedy is the political thought of the democratic city-state. For example, the earliest allusion to the voting habits of the assembly is in Aeschylus's *The Suppliant Maidens* from 463 BCE (but there are other later examples, such as Euripides' *Orestes).* But what is particularly striking, and which Vernant and Vidal-Naquet bring out so powerfully, is the proximity between tragedy and legal thinking (of course, this is also true of Shakespeare; think of the trial scene in *The Merchant of Venice* or again in *King Lear*—the law court is also a theater). Obviously, the affinity between the theater and the law court is most obvious in the *Eumenides,* which is the only drama that takes place in the heart of Athens itself, on the Areopagus. But tragedy is full of legal vocabulary.

The Greeks did not have an idea of absolute law or even constitutional law founded on principles and organized into a coherent system: "For them there are, as it were, differing degrees of law."[8] This is more like common law in England. Also, although classical Athens was a very litigious society, mercifully they did not have lawyers. Citizens represented themselves. For Vernant and Vidal-Naquet, the meaning of law or right *oscillates* in Greek tragedy, like the use of *kratos,* or power, in *The Suppliant Maidens* (both democratic power and violent power) or *nomos* in the *Antigone* (both divine law and human law).

> What tragedy depicts is one *dike* in conflict with another, a law that is not fixed, shifting and changing into its opposite. To be sure, tragedy is something quite different from a legal debate. It takes as its subject the man actually living out this debate, forced to make a decisive choice, to orient his activity in a universe of ambiguous values where nothing is ever stable or unequivocal.[9]

Tragedy places a distance between itself and the myths of the heroes at the center of the drama. Tragedy arises at the point when a gap opens up between the new legal and political thought of the democratic city on the one hand, and mythic and heroic traditions of the archaic past on the other. But this gap must still be narrow enough for the conflict to be a painful one. We may no longer believe in our myths, but we have to pay a price for not believing in them. The tragic hero is not a reality in which we are somehow meant to believe. The hero has become a problem and heroism has become a problem, a vast question mark.

This gap between the past and the present is the *anachronism* of tragedy, a kind of disjunction in the order of time, the out-of-jointness of time. What is so odd in Attic tragedy is the way in which characters from the mythic past are presented dealing with contemporary crises of legitimacy, between the claims of family and city, say. Or again, what is so peculiar is the anachronism involved in characters, indeed divinities, from the ancient, heroic past of the city, like Athena, employing the very latest rhetorical techniques of sophistical and legal disputation, as is the case in the *Eumenides.*

The world of Attic tragedy is a world of *ambiguity,* a world without certainty, a world where questions always seem to remain open, but where the wounds of the past still bleed unhealed into the present, producing a disjunction and an experience of disorientation, often leading the chorus to exclaim What will happen to me? What shall I do? The question I have asked myself for many years is very simple: In what does the power of ancient tragedy consist? Why does it continue to speak to us so powerfully?

Moral Ambiguity in Aeschylus's Seven Against Thebes *and* The Suppliant Maidens

My hypothesis in this book is that tragedy is the experience of moral ambiguity. Justice is always on both sides and one is swayed one way and the other by argument and counterargument. Justice is slowly twisted into its opposite and vice versa. The truth of tragedy—the truth of what Gorgias would see as its lie—consists in bearing ambiguity, living with ambiguity. Justice (or power or law or whatever the key term that is in play in the play) is not one, but is at least two, possibly more.

This ambiguity is staged, for example, in Aeschylus's *Seven Against Thebes,* from 467 BCE. The peculiarly undramatic action of this quietly amazing play closes with a disputatious disagreement about justice. There is the talk of a curse on the race, the *genos,* of the Palace of Thebes and the house of Oedipus (line 650). This is the transgenerational curse that appears in so many tragedies and whose vehicle is the family. Then, a number of things happen: first, there is the fatal combat between the two brothers, Eteocles and Polynices. Second, a beautiful symmetry is shown by the lamentation of Antigone and Ismene, where the former shows none of the animosity toward the latter that can be found in Sophocles' *Antigone.* Third, Antigone declares "I will bury him," and "I am not ashamed of this anarchical [*anarchion*] act of disobedience to the city." Fourth, she adds, powerfully, "strange thing is the common blood [*deinon to koinon*]" (lines 1029–32). Incidentally, *deinon* is the word at the heart of Heidegger's reading of the *Antigone,* which he renders as *das Unheimliche,* "the uncanny."[1] At this point, with the uncanniness of the common, in the final lines of the drama the chorus of Theban women, who have been understandably nervous throughout the play, as they fear being raped and enslaved by the invading forces, exclaim, "What shall happen to me? What shall I do? What shall I plan?" (lines 1055–56). Not only is the chorus uncertain and divided around the question of justice, of what is the right thing to do, they literally divide into two groups, A and B, stating the justice of either side:

First Half-Chorus
Let the state do or not
What it will to the mourners of Polynices.
We will go and bury him;
We will go as his escort.
The grief is common to the race
But now one way and now another
The city approves the path of justice.

Second Half-Chorus
But we will go with the other, as the city
And justice jointly approve.
For after the Blessed Ones and the strength of Zeus
He is the one who saved the city
From utter destruction, from being overwhelmed
By the wave of foreign invaders. (lines 1067–79)

With those words, the drama ends. What's more, *Seven Against Thebes* is very probably the last play in a trilogy, of which the other two plays are lost. So, the denouement is not reconciliation, which we are told by a certain *doxa* is what ancient tragedy is about, especially the *Oresteia,* but precisely a dispute, what the French call a *différend,* where the city identifies itself around a fundamental difference on the question of justice. In truth, the core experience of *Seven Against Thebes* is *doubling.* There is the double death of Eteocles and Polynices, which simultaneously saves the city and dooms it. There is the doubling of Antigone and Ismene, which mirrors that of their brothers and their own future strife. And there is the doubling of dirge for the two brothers, which divides the chorus into two halves. Everything and everyone is doubled and doubled over in the play.

Is the ambiguous doubling of Greek tragedy somehow linked to democracy? Are these two inventions linked? Yes, if we can think about democracy as learning to bear ambiguity and the acceptance of a certain skepticism and a *différend* about justice. It is this ambiguity that philosophy, in the person of Socrates and all the way to Husserl and Heidegger, cannot bear. For philosophy, ambiguity is a sign of crisis that has to be arrested and avoided through an appeal to some higher, ideal transcendental source of meaning or intelligibility that can be a basis for political authority. For tragedy, that crisis is life and has to be lived as such.

Examples are important, so let's consider the question of democracy in Aeschylus's *The Suppliant Maidens* (*Hiketides*), which was traditionally thought to be his oldest play, although now it is dated to 470 BCE, two years after *The Persians.* Paul Cartledge claims that this is the first known reference to democratic assembly voting.[2] The action is very simple: the Danaids are the suppliants, who, although apparently Egyptian, are from an Argive lineage and ask for refuge in Argos from King Pelasgus. There is a reality/appearance problem in this play: the Danaids appear to be Egyptian, of a sunburnt or dark race (lines 154–55), King Pelasgus chauvinistically notes,

> So outlandishly
> Arrayed in the barbaric luxury

Of robes and crowns, and not in Argive fashion
Nor in Greek. (lines 237–40)

But the Danaids claim refuge on the basis of their Greek ancestry. The claiming of refuge and the welcoming of the foreigner
are important themes in Attic tragedy; for example King Theseus
of Athens grants refuge to Oedipus in *Oedipus at Colonus*. As the
chorus of Danaids says, "Everyone is quick to blame the alien"
(line 974). A line that is echoed by Danaus, their father,

Time becomes the touchstone of the alien,
Who bears the brunt of every evil tongue,
The easy target of calumny. (lines 992–94)

To risk considerable understatement, these are words that resonate strongly with the experience of immigration and the claiming of refuge and asylum in recent times. But the essential conflict
in the drama in *The Suppliant Maidens* is between the claims of
blood legitimacy and democratic legitimacy. That is, the Danaids
claim refuge based on blood, but King Pelasgus claims that he can
accept them into the city—and at risk of war—only if his people
agree to it in a vote: "I would make no promises until / I share
with all the citizens." After a nasty conflict with a rather vulgar
Egyptian herald, King Pelasgus declares the outcome of the vote,
which is unanimous.

Thus unanimous the vote
Decreed, never to surrender them [i.e., the Danaids] to
    force.
Joined, doweled and bolted stays this law,
That neither scratched on tablets, nor book sealed,
You hear announced by the tongue of freedom's voice. (lines
    941–45)

Here is a very precise example of the anachronism of tragedy, where King Pelasgus from the mythical and misty past of Argos is presented making arguments for a democratic voting procedure. It is also probably not accidental that the reference to freedom's voice, or free-spoken (*eleutherostomou*), is announced in the festival of Dionysos Eleuthereus, the God of liberation.

12

Tragedy, Travesty, and Queerness

In talking of tragedy, Terry Eagleton cites Yeats's splendid lines "For nothing can be sole or whole / That has not been rent."[1] In other words, tragedy does not so much reflect a social reality, it calls it into question, by depicting it rent, twisted, doubled over, and divided against itself. As Vernant and Vidal-Naquet write,

> The tragic message gets across to [the spectator] only provided he makes the discovery that words, values, men themselves, are ambiguous, that the universe is one of conflict, only if he relinquishes his earlier convictions, accepts a problematic vision of the world and, through the dramatic spectacle, himself acquires a tragic consciousness.[2]

Tragic consciousness is about accepting ambiguity, that there are "zones of opacity and incommunicability in the words that men exchange" . . . and not just men. Nowhere is this ambiguity greater than in the relation between the sexes in Greek tragedy. If the frame of tragedy is war, then it is a sex war.

A really helpful guide on the question of sex and gender in Greek tragedy is Nicole Loraux, a student of Vernant and Vidal-Naquet, and author of a very important series of books, for example, *The Experiences of Tiresias, The Invention of Athens,* and *Mothers in Mourning.*[3] In her wonderfully entitled 1987 short book, *Tragic Ways of Killing a Woman,* it is a question of the deaths of wives and virgins: Clytemnestra and Iphigenia, Hecuba and Polyxena, Jocasta and Antigone. For Loraux, it is a question of what glory is available to women, given the glory that surrounds the heroic male death, like the suicide of Ajax or the transfiguration of Oedipus in *Oedipus at Colonus*. The paradox is that for a woman's death to be glorious it must be manly. Both Clytemnestra and Antigone are described as manly women because of their assertiveness and rebelliousness. As Loraux writes, "The woman in tragedy is more entitled to play the man in her death than the man is to assume any aspect of woman's conduct, even in his manner of death."[4] This leads to the paradox that if women are free in tragedy, then this freedom is realized only in death, in succumbing to necessity: "For women there is liberty in tragedy— liberty in death."[5]

Far from seeing figures like Antigone as one-faceted feminist heroes, say for example in Brecht's 1948 retelling of the story where she is an antifascist freedom fighter, for Loraux there is thus a deep and abiding ambiguity in the tragic representation of gender. She writes,

> This is what is meant by ambiguity, and there must have been an ambiguous thrill to the *catharsis* when, during a tragic performance, male citizens watched with emotion the suffering of these heroic women, represented onstage by other male citizens dressed in women's clothes. Women's glory in tragedy was an ambiguous glory.[6]

Tragedy is dress-up, and men—especially Englishmen, it must be said—always love to dress up as women, which is a phenomenon that is completely consistent with misogyny. As Loraux writes, "In the matter of femininity, tragedy is two-faced. . . ." She continues,

> We should accept that tragedy constantly disturbs the norm in the interest of the deviant, but at the same time we must

be aware that under the deviant the norm is often silently present.[7]

What we arguably need is a bifurcated or Janus-faced reading of tragedy, where what appears to be at stake in the drama is both the norm of patriarchy and its subversion.

This leads Loraux to the overwhelming question: What is tragedy for? In other words, "What do spectators in the theatre gain from thinking, in the mode of fiction, things that in everyday life cannot and must not be thought?"[8] What kind of benefit accrues to the city through imagining itself, through theater, in representations that are so at odds with the customs and ways of that city? Loraux asks, Does some sort of "purification," which is another way of thinking about *catharsis,* follow from the extremity of tragic representation?[9]

The answer is that we will never know, as we will never be in the position of spectators in the theater in classical Athens. But, I would contend, it is this not-knowing that is so compelling about Greek tragedy. If the ancients are like vampires that need us and feed on our blood, and if antiquity can become invitational, where we reinvent the classics for our world and invent the "we" that regards the plays, then we can look at the question of gender only through our eyes and try and see through our multiple blindnesses.

I think that an example of such a reading is Judith Butler's *Antigone's Claim.*[10] For Butler, far from representing some pure idea of "the feminine" or the laws of kinship, as Antigone does for both Hegel and Lacan in different yet related ways, she represents the instability, porosity, and fragility of gender identity and the utterly contingent character of social relations and kinship structures. Far from being one pole in an essentialized concept of sexual difference, Antigone is a kind of antigeneration figure for the emergence of new forms of gender identification and family structure. But—and this is important to point out—such a read-

ing of tragedy is not carried out in the name of some new performative heroism of drag or whatever. Norms can be queered,
hetero-normativity can be criticized, but that doesn't mean that
we are somehow free of the Oedipal structures that characterize
tragedy. We are still prisoners of the family, even a queer family.

13

Polyphony

Who was in the audience for the Attic dramas? Simon Goldhill, who has written compellingly on this theme, claims, "The theatre was a space in which all the citizens were actors—as the city itself and its leading citizens were put on display."[1] Paul Cartledge quotes Clifford Geertz on Bali as "the theatre state."[2] But this also serves as an apt description of classical Athens. The play festivals were devices for defining Athenian civic identity, Cartledge writes, "which meant exploring and confirming but also questioning what it was to be a citizen of a democracy, this brand-new form of popular self-government."[3] This much is clear in the plays of Aeschylus, such as *The Suppliant Maidens* and the *Eumenides*: it is always a question of the city.

The Great Dionysia was the largest gathering of Athenian citizens in the calendar and was perceived to be a stage for political celebration. For Goldhill—and we will return to this in Part 5—it is therefore striking that Aristotle barely mentions the *polis* in the *Poetics* and the civic frame of tragedy is silenced. This silencing can be linked with Aristotle's focus on individual character, such as Oedipus, rather than the chorus as the embodiment of the community or the collective. Goldhill writes, "The most significant critical turn in the last thirty years of criticism of ancient tragedy has been precisely the relocation of tragedies within a local and national socio-political context."[4] Such is the influence of Vernant and Vidal-Naquet. It is very important to grasp the civic scale and political import of tragedy and the dramatic festivals of Athens if one is to understand firstly why it is that Plato identifies *demokratia* with *theatrokratia* in the *Laws*. By *theatrokratia*, Plato means literally the sovereign rule of the theater audience. In Cartledge's words, *theatrokratia* refers to "the dictatorship of the mass (or mob) or poor Athenian citizens who formed the majority of the spectatorship, as they formed the ruling majority of the Athenian democratic state as a whole."[5] Secondly, Goldhill claims, with some justification in my view, that it was in part because of the sheer scale and impact of the drama festival on the imagination of the city that Plato is so intent on banning tragedians from the *Republic*. It is only in the light of an understanding of theater as the glue of democracy that one can appreciate the novelty and urgency of Plato's exclusion of the tragic poets and other members of those he calls the "mimetic tribe" (595b). It is not a question of "aesthetics" in the modern sense as the experience of a work of art or our judgment upon it, as much as it is a question of the *aesthetic regime of the political*. Theater is the spectacle of politics looking at itself.

It is difficult to imagine that there was not a strong audience response, particularly in such a competitive context as the festival and with such a large crowd, possibly somewhere between 14,000 and 17,000 souls. Would there have been yelping, cheering, and booing? Might the opinion of the judges of the dramatic contests have been swayed by some ancient version of a clapometer, where prizes were given to the most popular plays? It is unclear, but it is also hard to imagine that such an audience had little consequence for the overall effect of the dramas. Thinking ahead to the kind of audience that Brecht desired for what he called his "epic theater," to be discussed at the end of Chapter 18, I imagine the audience as being *relaxed*, being knowledgeable about what was going on and at ease. Such an audience would be closer to a contemporary sports crowd than the small, anxious huddles of alienated souls (like me) who still go to the theater. And it can't have been too comfortable during the City Dionysia to sit all day on wooden benches in cramped conditions. Did the audience bring cushions? Did they eat and drink during the performances? If so, what? Were there olives, cheese, honey, bread, lamb, wine, and water? On some reports, a hot meal was provided to the audience, which must have been quite a feat of catering.

So, the audience for the Attic dramas was overwhelmingly composed of male Athenian citizens. But what about noncitizens? According to Goldhill, these were divided into four groups: (1) foreigners (*xenoi*—it is not clear how many, but there were certainly representatives of other Greek and possibly non-Greek cities in the audience); (2) resident aliens, or metics; (3) slaves (it is said that some did attend, but there is no evidence one way or the other, although slaves sometimes held great power in antiquity, particularly over the affairs of a household); and (4) women. On the question of whether women attended the plays, Goldhill asserts that "no single piece of evidence can offer a clear and direct answer to the problem."[6] No women participated in the writing, production, performance, or judging of the plays. Women could not claim support from the Theoric Fund, which paid for citizens to attend the plays and replaced their wages as a kind of subsidy. Women could also not attend the Assembly or participate in the law courts either as witnesses or jurors. By contrast, the "Athenian Stranger" from *The Laws* specifies tragedy as the pleasure of "educated women, young men and perhaps almost all the general public."[7] But this is hardly compelling evidence. Other evidence for the participation of women at the dramatic festivals is inferred only by analogy from the presence of women at the Great Panathenaia, which was a festival for the whole city. The problem here is that if it is the city itself that is on display in tragedy and theater in general, then it is a matter of the utmost importance as to whether women were present or absent. But we simply don't know for sure either way.

Which raises the question, picking up on Loraux's work: What was taking place in the performance of femaleness in the characters of Medea, Cassandra, Antigone, Alcestis, Andromache, and the rest? The question haunts this book. What is going on in the *mimesis* of femaleness in tragedy? We know nothing about vocal techniques or whether "femaleness" was indicated by tone of voice, or gesture, or just by the mask. Female roles were probably played by young men, as they were in Shakespearean theater. But whatever was the case—and we will very probably never know—we are dealing with travesty here, with cross-dressing, with a certain regime of queerness, which is most obviously the case with a rather queer man like Tiresias, "throbbing between two lives, / Old Man with wrinkled female breasts."[8]

As Edith Hall makes clear in a fascinating discussion, classical Athens was a xenophobic, patriarchal, imperialist society based on slaveholding and imperial tribute.[9] Yet the figures who are silenced in the public realm are represented in the fictions of theater, as if the democracy that was denied to those figures publicly is somehow extended to them theatrically. Hall examines the tragic representation of Athenians interacting with outsiders, women, and slaves. Firstly, there is the theme of exile, which marks so many of the plays, whether it is Philoctetes, who becomes literally *apolis,* or the women seeking asylum in Aeschylus's *The Suppliant Women,* or Euripides' *Heracleidae,* or the displaced, enslaved, or humiliated women who appear in the *Agamemnon, Hecuba, The Trojan Women,* and elsewhere. Almost every cast of an Athenian tragedy features characters of mixed ethnicity or multiple provenance aside from the *Antigone,* where everyone is Theban, and in *The Persians,* where everyone is Persian. But in both plays we watch people who were foreigners to the Athenians. As Hall points out, only one tragedy, *Philoctetes,* has no women, "and female tragic choruses in the surviving plays outnumber males by twenty-one to ten."[10] This appears to be a paradox.

Women are multiple in tragedy—young daughters, older daughters, wives, aging widows, murderesses, and exemplars of virtue, but the basic contrast is between virgins and wives. There is a clear tendency in the tragedies toward plots with disruptive women who are temporarily or permanently husbandless. Women unsupervised by men are trouble. There is, of course, the extraordinary example of Medea, the murderous barbarian sorceress, who flies off unpunished at the end of the play in the chariot of the sun to Athens. In the meantime, she gives the most extraordinary speech decrying women's position in society: giving birth to a child is worse than standing three times in front of the line of battle. This speech used to be recited in Edwardian London at meetings of the suffragettes.[11] Hall offers a fascinating discussion of the understanding of women in ancient Greek medicine, where sexual intercourse was seen as a cure for female diseases and wives were meant to be sexually active and preferably pregnant.[12] If Phaedra had gone to see a doctor, then he would have prescribed intercourse, as long as it was with her husband and not her stepson. Virgins were also trouble, like Electra and Antigone, because of what was seen as a wild, untamed sexuality. As Hall points out, there are no historical examples of Athenian women acting like Antigone, but nonetheless it must have been somehow imaginable.[13] But in what precise manner, we do not know. Tragedy is often concerned with how highborn women become slaves, like Tecmessa in Sophocles' *Ajax,* Cassandra in the *Agamemnon,* and Hecuba in *The Trojan Women.* This is a form of reversal, or *peripeteia,* that is not acknowledged by Aristotle. And we should not forget the role that slaves play in drama, whether the slave who becomes a shepherd and is briefly tortured by Oedipus (because slaves were known to lie) or the oddly comic Phrygian slave in Euripides' *Orestes.*

We will return to what Aristotle pejoratively calls the "anomaly" of slaves and women in Part 5, but what does the apparent theatrical inversion of the social role of foreigners, slaves, and women in Attic tragedy mean? Hall concludes, hopefully, "Greek tragedy does its thinking in a form which is vastly more politically advanced than the society which produced Greek tragedy."[14] In other words, there is in tragedy the imagining of a political egalitarianism that did not exist in reality. Hall makes the compelling suggestion that tragedy is *polyphonic*.[15] It both legitimizes the chauvinism of Athenian power and glory at the same time as giving voice to that which undermines it. Indeed, Hall links this polyphony directly to developments in rhetoric, where students were taught to think antithetically, as in Gorgias's defense of Helen that we will turn to in Chapter 24. We might say that tragedy is polyphony and antiphony, and this is why we need a *bifurcated* reading of tragedy, sensitive to both the ideological import of tragedy and its subversions.

14

The Gods! Tragedy and the Limitation of the Claims to Autonomy and Self-Sufficiency

There is an important line of thought in Vernant and Vidal-Naquet that in tragedy human action is not strong enough to do without the power of the gods and not autonomous enough to be fully conceived without them. Human action must be aligned with the power of fate, which is more than human.[1] There is a doubling of the point of view in tragedy, both human and divine, that invokes reflection on the part of the hero, on the one hand weighing up the pros and cons of a line of action, and on the other hand risking oneself in a terrain that is strictly unknown and incomprehensible because it is ordained by the gods. Tragedy operates simultaneously at two levels.

In order to illustrate the double-level operation of tragedy, Vernant and Vidal-Naquet give a wonderful analysis of the carpet scene in Aeschylus's *Agamemnon*. On the one hand, Agamemnon steps on a purple carpet or purple-dyed cloth that has been laid down for him by Clytemnestra (no doubt in order to conceal the bloodstains when she murders him). But on the other hand, in taking this simple human step, Agamemnon enters a divine order of time and action, from which the rest of the *Oresteia* unfolds toward Clytemnestra's own murder at the hands of Orestes and its divine denouement on the Areopagus in Athens in the conflict between Athena and the Furies. At this moment of stepping on the carpet, past, present, and future come together and we realize that the sacrifice of Iphigenia was not dutiful obedience to Artemis but the guilty weakness of an ambitious man, and the capture of Troy was not a just war against a foreign aggressor but a brutal act of destruction, violence, and rape. "At this culminating point of the tragedy," Vernant and Vidal-Naquet write, "where all the threads are tied together, the time of the gods invades the stage and becomes manifest in the time of men."[2]

This doubling of the divine and the human is what the spectator sees, the *theoros* in the theater theorizes. But it is also linked to another line of thought in Vernant and Vidal-Naquet, which I would like to press at more critically, namely that what is taking place in tragedy is the *emergence* of something like autonomy. Vernant and Vidal-Naquet write that what is happening in tragedy is that "man himself [*sic*] is beginning to experiment as an agent who is more or less autonomous in relation to the religious forces that govern the universe."[3] Such experimentation will be completed only when man possesses "the category of the will." They go on to claim, "as is well-known, in ancient Greece, there was no true vocabulary to cover willing."[4] We should perhaps always be wary of what is apparently so "well-known." But here's the long, key passage I'd like to ponder, and mark the words "still not acquired":

For there to be tragic action it is necessary that a concept of human nature with its own characteristics should have already emerged and that the human and divine spheres should have become sufficiently distinct from each other for them to stand in opposition; yet at the same time they must continue to appear as inseparable. The tragic sense of responsibility makes its appearance at the point when, in human action, a place is given to internal debate on the part of the subject, to intention and premeditation, *but when this human action has still not acquired enough consistency and autonomy to be entirely self-sufficient.* The true domain of tragedy lies in that border zone where human actions are hinged together with the divine powers, where—unknown to the agent—they derive their true meaning by becoming an integral part of an order that is beyond man and that eludes him.[5]

On this view, tragic responsibility makes its appearance when human beings begin to debate internally about what to do but cannot resolve that debate without reference to an external, divine authority. Before he slaughters his mother, Orestes asks, "What should I do, Pylades?" (line 899). He is reassured that her death is sanctioned by order of Apollo and he does the deed. Or again, the repeated questioning that we find in Attic tragedy, for example the line "What shall I do?" from Sophocles' *Philoctetes,* which circulates from character to character throughout the play, is a question that only a god can answer, which occurs with the deus ex machina of Heracles at the end of the play. Vernant and Vidal-Naquet claim that tragic responsibility takes this form because human beings have not yet acquired enough autonomy and consistency to be entirely self-sufficient. Tragic action lies in that border zone between inner subjective reflection and something external to the subject, in this case the divine.

What we have here is a historicist—or, better, evolutionist or progressivist—thesis, that the Attic Greeks are on their way to the discovery of the will or the mind in the modern sense, but still not quite there. Many readers of my generation will be familiar with this thesis as it arises in the work of Bruno Snell, namely that Greek civilization is about the discovery of the mind, but that those poor ancient Greeks didn't have a concept of the will and for that we have to wait until the emergence of Christianity in St. Paul or St. Augustine. Hannah Arendt tells a similar story in *The Life of the Mind.* But is this right? Are the Greeks, as even Marx recognized in the Introduction to the *Grundrisse,* relevant to us because they are our past? It is a past that we have left behind.[6] Although the Greeks incarnate the norm and standard for art, Marx continues, they are like exotic children, what Marx calls "normal children," with the clear proviso that we are abnormal children of alienated, capitalist modernity. But is our moral or subjective situation really so different from that of the Attic Greeks? Are they such an exotic and distant people? I am not so sure.

The long passage I quoted from Vernant and Vidal-Naquet is cited by Bernard Williams early on in his 1993 book, *Shame and Necessity*.[7] Williams claims, rightly I think, that Vernant and Vidal-Naquet's account is driven by "an evolutionary story" or what he also calls a "progressivist" account of our relation to the ancient Greeks. Namely, that the tragic outlook is "a step in the development of the notion of action." Williams goes on, very clearly, "I do not accept this evolutionary account, and this presents a difficulty."[8] What exactly is the difficulty? Williams writes,

> I want to say all of the following: our ideas of action and responsibility and other of our ethical concepts are closer to those of the ancient Greeks than we usually suppose; the significance of those Greek ideas is expressed in ancient tragedy and indeed is central to its effect; tragedy must be understood as a particular historical development, coming at a particular time; and this historical development involved beliefs about the supernatural, the human, and the daimonic, which we could not possibly accept, which are no part of our world. Can all these things be true together?[9]

Maybe they can, maybe they can't. But I agree with the thrust of Williams's claims here. His view gets more traction, I think, when he contrasts it with other accounts of ethical experience, for example Kantian or Hegelian accounts that would structure morality around distinctions between terms like the religious and the secular, the heteronomous and autonomous, or the ancient and the modern, and which look for the emergence of an autarchic human reason as opposed to impersonal forces that lie beyond humanity, like the gods of antiquity or the Christian God. In the final pages of *Shame and Necessity*, after much detailed and fascinating textual analysis, Williams relaxes his hand on the grip of his argument and dilates the focus of his critique of philosophy. He writes,

> Plato, Aristotle, Kant, Hegel are all on the same side, all believing in one way or another that the universe or history or the structure of human reason can, when properly understood, yield a pattern that makes sense of human life and human aspirations.[10]

Tragedy leaves us with no such sense. It represents something slower moving and flawed about us. In Sophocles, we see

> Human beings as dealing sensibly, foolishly, sometimes catastrophically, sometimes nobly, with a world that is only partially intelligible to human agency and in itself is not necessarily well adjusted to ethical aspirations.[11]

Greek tragedy does not present human beings who are ideally in harmony with themselves, their world, and their gods. There is a gap between what the tragic character is and the ways in which the world acts upon him.

Tragedy's philosophy presents us with a divided and dependent self that lacks self-sufficiency and the capacity for self-legislation and self-determination, *autarchia*. Tragic consciousness is staged in relation to demands that exceed autonomy, that flow from the past, disrupt the present, and disable the future. Further, although this is a separate topic that I have taken up elsewhere, I do not think that the experience of the Greek tragic heroes is so significantly different from their Senecan or Shakespearean successors.[12] Is Hamlet really more autonomous than Hecuba? If so, how much? Can we somehow measure and quantify autonomy? Or are both Hamlet and Hecuba suffering from similar symptoms of radical self-alienation?

The presence of the gods, fate, or supernatural forces in Attic tragedy, like ghosts, need not scare us. The meaning of the gods is a way of naming those aspects of possible experience—forces, structures, circumstances, or just the weight of the past—that lie outside of individual control and that can destroy those individuals. Napoleon allegedly said to Goethe that what fate was in the ancient world, politics is in the modern. There is also the bon mot of Benjamin Constant that the network of institutions and conventions that envelop us from birth to death is equal to the fate of the ancients.[13]

The main point here is that the role of the gods in Attic tragedy is the placeholder for a force or forces that exceed yet determine and can indeed destroy human agency. The gods are names for powers not under our control. It seems to me that Ibsen understood this perfectly, where the function of divine fate is transformed into the transgenerational effects of venereal disease in *Ghosts* or into the latent power of capital itself in *John Gabriel Borkman*. It might also be understood in terms of the fatal force of a genetic inheritance or the quiet, latent presence of cancer cells in the body. Or consider a disturbing conversation I had with the late, great Philip Seymour Hoffman about happiness and truth, namely that you might think that you are happy at a moment, a certain specific moment, but a truth about you might creep up to you from the past and destroy you.[14] It destroyed him.

So, Williams basically defends Vernant and Vidal-Naquet's idea of tragic consciousness, but removes from it any evolutionist or progressivist thesis. His next move is truly radical and far-reaching, but one does not necessarily feel its force because Williams cuts through arguments with an elegant British sterling-silver butter knife rather than a Germanic Nietzschean hammer. In the penultimate paragraph of *Shame and Necessity*, he identifies and brilliantly contests what is arguably the central presupposition of the major tradition in the history of philosophy and its various morality games. Williams writes, and we should note again the *invitational* character of his first-person-plural pronoun, his "we,"

> We are in an ethical condition that lies not only beyond Christianity, but beyond its Kantian and its Hegelian legacies. We have an ambivalent sense of what human beings have achieved, and have hopes for how they might live (in particular in the form of a still powerful ideal that they should live without lies). We know that the world was not made for us, or we for the world, that our history tells no purposive story, and that there is no position outside the world or outside history from which we might hope to authenticate our activities. We have to acknowledge the hideous costs of many human achievements that we value, including this reflective sense itself, and recognize that there is no redemptive Hegelian history or universal Leibnizian cost-benefit analysis to show that it will come out well enough in the end. *In important ways, we are, in our ethical situation, more like human beings in antiquity than any Western people have been in the meantime.* More particularly, we are like those who, from the fifth century and earlier, have left us traces of a consciousness that had not yet been touched by Plato's and Aristotle's attempts to make our ethical relations to the world fully intelligible.[15]

This is a stunning passage with significant implications, but let's be clear about what is at stake: There is no question either of a return to the ancient world or the fantasy of its rebirth of the kind that possessed the youthful Nietzsche. Nor—picking up on where we began this part—is there any question of an idealized exoticism of the Greeks as a way of criticizing the nihilism of modernity (i.e., Heidegger), in line with a conservative *Kulturkritik* that always carries with it a crypto-authoritarian fantasy of order and blind submission. The admission in Williams's words is much more sober: "we" find ourselves in a situation where the belief that human reason (Kant) or reason plus God (Aquinas) or reason plus affect (Spinoza) or reason plus history (Hegel) or whatever might be able to yield a pattern or a system that would make sense of human life, human actions, and human aspirations *has to be given up*. As Williams writes, "Sophocles and Thucydides, by contrast, are alike in leaving us with no such sense."[16]

History tells us no purposive story, whether progressivist (Hegel and Hegelians like Marx) or regressivist (Nietzsche, Heidegger, and neo-Spenglerians like Wittgenstein). If only a God can save us, as Heidegger said, then we know—deep down—there is no such thing. Salvation is the wrong concept when it comes to thinking through and assessing the value of human life. The world was not made for us; nor we for the world, as Ptolemaic systems believed and some of their successors continue to insist. Human beings' relation to the world is a marriage of convenience or adaptation made neither in heaven nor in nature, but on the slaughter bench of history. We are consequences of an awkward process of cultural adaptation and mutation. No totalizing theory or complete theory of everything is going to satisfy our urge to make sense of the whole, certainly not the currently cynical minestrone of cosmology, neuroscience, and American Buddhism. Perhaps this desire for a comprehension of the whole is perversion itself. It is what tragedy describes falling apart, which is what the great poet Hölderlin understood and which is arguably the reason why he was unable to finish his modern tragedy, his mourning play, *The Death of Empedocles*.

In this sense—and this is my wager in this book—we are arguably the extreme contemporaries of those other skeptics, those other realists, the Attic tragedians, and perhaps we might learn something by spending more time in their company. The world is a confusing, noisy place, defined by endless war, rage, grief, ever-growing inequality. We undergo a gnawing moral and political uncertainty in a world of ambiguity. To think in this spirit is to breathe a little of the air of Attic tragedy. This book is not exactly an oxygen cylinder, but more of a small, handwritten map with a set of largely borrowed instructions as to where one might possibly be found.

To be entirely fair to them, Vernant and Vidal-Naquet seem to anticipate some of the force of Williams's critique. Tragedy lays bare the network of contradictory forces that assail all human beings, not just in the ancient Greek world but in all societies and cultures. They write, "Tragedy prompts the spectator to submit the human condition, limited and necessarily finite as it is, to a general interrogation."[17] But this general interrogation cannot aspire, as most philosophy aspires, to the formation of a pattern of concepts that would give us a true picture of reality accessible to rational intelligibility. On the contrary,

> From the point of view of tragedy, human beings and human action are seen, not as realities to be pinned down in their essential qualities, in the manner of the philosophers of the succeeding century [i.e., the fourth century BCE, namely Aristotle], but as problems that defy resolution, riddles with double meanings that are never fully decoded.[18]

More generally stated, tragedy's philosophy enables us to become theoretical spectators in the theater of human complexity, an ambiguous and indeed contradictory reality that is never reducible to what we called above a monotheistic point of view or to some metaphysics. This is why drama and dramatic presentation are essential. They give us a sense of the polytheistic agonism and opacity of human affairs, both their value and vanity.

15

A Critique of Moral Psychology
and the Project of Psychical Integration

Let me open a brief parenthesis here. The problem that Williams is trying to face is linked to what we usually call "moral psychology," namely that there is or must be an analogy or even an identity between the structure of the psyche and some conception of virtue, the good life, morality, or whatever. Furthermore, the very idea of moral psychology is based on the premise that the psyche is moral or should be moral, and the union of morality and psychology is expressed in some idea of what some thinkers call "psychical integration," whether that is a solitary ego, a relational self, or a communal subject.

Think for a moment about the tripartite division of the soul in Plato, into *logistikos, thymos,* and *epithymia*—reason, spiritedness, and appetite. Although Plato recognizes a division within the soul, indeed a conflict between reason and appetite, most famously expressed in the charioteer image in the *Phaedrus*, the goal of the philosophical life is an integration of the three faculties under the rule of reason. Such is the life of the philosopher and the philosophically well-educated guardian, as we will see in Part 4. One could make an analogous case in Aristotle, with the idea of the unity of virtue and happiness in the contemplative life of the philosopher, the divine life or the life of the gods at the end of the *Nicomachean Ethics*. Or, again in Kant, the conviction that there must be an identity, a felt identity moreover, which leads to his odd idea of the "fact of reason," between rationality and freedom, that means that all pathological desire must be subordinated to and organized by pure practical reason expressed in the moral law. Or, finally, the idea in Hegel that Kantian rationality is well intentioned but produces a hopelessly abstract and one-sided view of the self that is divorced from its historical constitution in social norms, *Sittlichkeit,* or in a set of legitimate institutions, such as those of the state.

Other versions of this view could be expressed, and there are clearly exceptions to this rule (one thinks, obviously, of Hume). But we could say that the project of philosophy at its core has the idea and ideal of psychical integration, whether expressed in terms of the relation of justice to the good, the moral law, or a socially articulated freedom. The point I am seeking to make, admittedly rather sketchily, as it is not my main concern in this book, is that one cannot find this idea of psychical integration in tragedy. Indeed, the opposite seems to be the case. We see characters in various states of war with themselves, with fate, with each other, even with the gods. Tragedy is the enactment of the varieties of psychical *disintegration*. This at least has the virtue of a certain realism, of the conflict we experience between the life of the passions, the force of the past and our social, political, and familial formation, and the necessity of reasoning, but also of reason's frailty in the face of such forces.

Much philosophy would appear to be committed to an idea and ideal of the integration of the soul in itself (or "self," "subject," or "mind" if that is preferable) or of my soul with the soul of others under the primacy of reason, whether conceived metaphysically, transcendentally, or as something more socially articulated. It is not that tragedy seeks to refute such a view. Such a view doesn't need to be refuted. We are divided against ourselves in much of our living activity. The burden of proof lies with those theories that aspire to the unity of the psyche and morality. Tragedy describes another state of affairs. It shows us human beings at odds with themselves, often in a state of profound contradiction. This is arguably what tragedy shares with certain traditions of psychoanalysis, but by no means all of them. Perhaps philosophy labors under the delusive ideal of the unity of rationality and freedom, that one's true interests as a rational self correspond to one's other, perhaps baser, interests and can redeem such baseness. Whatever we can say of tragedy, it does not toil under the burden of such an ideal.

16

The Problem with Generalizing about the Tragic

The term *tragikos,* or "tragic," was used as sloppily in Attic Greek as it is in modern journalism. When Socrates refers to *tragikos legein,* "tragic talk," he is referring to words that pretend to grandeur but that only achieve pomposity. Such talk also says nothing about suffering.[1] The identification of tragedy with suffering is characteristically modern. Therefore, when Aristotle calls Euripides *tragikotatos,* "the most tragic" (and I will push hard at this description in Part 5), it is difficult to know how to interpret the term. In the *Rhetoric,* Aristotle dismisses some metaphors as being "too grand and tragic."[2] The tragic is not a closely defined or theoretically rigorous category in antiquity. Stephen Halliwell argues that we should not be moving toward anything like "an essence of the tragic" on the basis of Aristotle.[3] Goldhill writes, "Aristotle's *Poetics,* in short, is a theory of tragedies, not a theory of the tragic."[4] I think this is right.

The concept of the tragic undergoes a spectacular inflation in the Germanophone world at the end of the eighteenth century with the invention of *das Tragische,* the tragic. The latter comes to assume the burden for the possible unification of the domains of pure and practical reason, necessity and freedom, or epistemology and ethics, that Kant had so carefully demarcated but which he had himself tried to bridge in his late work on aesthetics, *Critique of Judgment* (1790). The tragic becomes the name for that domain of experience in which an intellectual intuition of the whole is still possible. As Hölderlin writes, the tragic "is the metaphor of an intellectual intuition."[5] That is, the very experience that Kant had shown was not possible epistemically—we can have no knowledge of God, the soul, or the whole—can still be experienced aesthetically, through an exemplary work of art. The thought developed after Kant is that drama offers such an aesthetic experience and that tragedy is the loftiest genre of drama.

The concern of the philosophy of the tragic is not so much actual theater as the *idea* of tragedy, and this is arguably the problem. From this rather stratospheric, idealized perspective, Aristotle is seen as remaining too vulgar, pragmatic, and empirical. This philosophical idea of the tragic is coined by Schelling in the last of his *Philosophical Letters on Dogmatism and Criticism* from 1795, written when he was just twenty years old.[6] In this vibrant, youthful text, Schelling follows Fichte, the most influential German philosopher after Kant, in saying that there are only two completely consistent philosophical systems, those of Kant and Spinoza. Sadly, those systems completely contradict each other, leaving us with a conflict between Kantian critique and Spinozist dogmatism. As Fichte puts it, Kant begins philosophizing from the basis of an "absolute I," a free self, whereas Spinoza begins from an "absolute object or non-I," namely substance understood as nature or God, as he puts it at the beginning of the *Ethics*. On the one hand, critique wants unconditional freedom, unbounded spontaneity. On the other hand, dogmatism submits to the power of necessity and finds freedom in this submission.

We seem to be stuck in an impasse between two irreconcilable philosophical positions. This is where Schelling introduces a third option, which is what he calls "the tragic." Revealingly, Schelling's understanding of tragedy is based exclusively on a rather particular reading of Sophocles' *Oedipus the King*. Indeed, Schelling presents us with a very philosophical Oedipus, who is torn between the objective power of necessity and the determination to fight freely against the fate that threatens to consume him. What takes place in tragedy is the life-and-death struggle between the free hero and the power of necessity that determines his being through the power of prophecy. For Schelling, the experience of the tragic culminates in what he calls a great or sublime thought: to suffer punishment willingly, freely, for an inevitable crime and so to prove one's freedom in the very loss of freedom, and "to go down with a declaration of free will." On this view, Oedipus proves his freedom through the very loss of his freedom. As Schelling concludes the letter, "there is nothing left but to fight and fall."[7] This is why, for Schelling, the Greeks are sublime and terrible; they can endure and transcend the conflict between freedom and necessity. The question that is left unanswered, and that is very possibly unanswerable, is whether there can be a modern experience of the tragic that would do for us what Sophocles allegedly did for the Greeks.

Schelling develops and indeed radicalizes this line of thinking some years later in his 1802–3 lecture series *The Philosophy of Art*.[8] Indeed, he makes the most extraordinary claims for tragedy, saying that art is the *organon* of philosophy, the instrument through which its highest aim is achieved, and that the tragic is the most sublime fulfillment of this aim. Namely, that if the goal of philosophy is what Schelling now calls the *identity* of freedom and necessity, then this is possible only through the tragic.[9] Tragedy is the keystone in the arch that unites freedom and necessity, practical reason and pure reason. The tragic is the completion of philosophy after Kant.

What we see in Schelling is the beginning of a philosophical tradition that turns on an abstract and general definition of the tragic. This tradition blends together two questionable tendencies: a universalism in aesthetics that has its source in Kant and an idealized Philhellenism whose motivation is political. The philosophical discourse on the tragic is the fateful merging of these two tendencies. *The Philosophy of Art* ends with an all-consuming whimper of nostalgia for the Greeks. Schelling asserts "modernity lacks fate," namely that there is no substantial, public experience of art that would be the modern equivalent of Greek tragedy.[10] Having idealized the sublime Greeks, one is left with the sorry realization that there is and will never be a modern German Sophocles. One can find something very similar in the early Nietzsche's hopeful call for a German rebirth of Greek tragedy out of Wagnerian opera. Happily, Nietzsche abandoned his hope for Wagner and in his later work turned violently against the Germanism of both Wagner and his younger self.

I think we should be cautious about the philosophical habit of generalizing about the tragic, and in particular the lamentable custom of constructing what Goldhill calls "a canon within the canon."[11] Namely, that one or two tragedies might be discussed by a philosopher (usually Sophocles' *Oedipus the King* and the *Antigone*) and not in any particular textual detail, and on that basis a whole number of ontological, moral, and historical assumptions are proffered. It is worth recalling that there are thirty-one extant tragedies, it is not that difficult or time-consuming to read them all, and my experience is that the more one reads, the less easy it becomes to generalize about the tragic, especially when one absorbs all the plays by Euripides. One ambition of this book is to deploy the experience of reading tragedies in order to subvert the philosophical discourse on the tragic that extends back from us through German idealism and romanticism and casts a long shadow across our understanding of Aristotle's *Poetics*. Following Walter Benjamin, I want to argue that such talk of the tragic as presenting something universally human is "vain."[12] This is particularly the case when thinkers like Heidegger wax lyrical about "the essence of Greek *Dasein*" on the basis of a highly partial and selective reading of the *Antigone*.[13]

17

Good Hegel, Bad Hegel

Without a doubt the most influential account of the concept of the tragic is Peter Szondi's *An Essay on the Tragic* from 1978.[1] This small and highly pedagogical text describes the history of the concept of the tragic from Schelling to Benjamin's *The Origin of German Tragic Drama* (1928). What is central to Szondi's account is the identification of the tragic with dialectic. The hero here is obviously Hegel. The tragic process is the "self-division and self-reconciliation" of *Sittlichkeit*, by which Hegel means communal ethical life. Crucially, for Szondi, it is in this interpretation of tragedy that Hegel makes dialectic apparent for the first time. Dialectic has its source in a thinking of tragedy, in the experience of a rhythm of union and separation that we can find in Hölderlin's writings on tragedy and his failed attempt to write a modern Greek tragedy, *The Death of Empedocles.*

For Szondi, the tragic and the dialectical coincide in Hegel. And this is what is wrong with Schelling, namely that he talks of the tragic too abstractly, without taking account of its dialectical, that is, historical, character. Yet, for Szondi, there is a bad and a good Hegel. If you will, there is a Hegel of totality and another of infinity, one who is closed and encloses everything under deadening concepts, and one who is open and rich in living possibilities.[2] Good Hegel is found in the 1802–3 essay on natural right or natural law.[3] Hegel argues against what he sees as the rigid opposition between the universal (conceived as the domain of law) and the particular (conceived as living individuality) in Kant's practical philosophy. Hegel wants to replace the abstract conception of ethics in terms of law and the *Sollen,* or the Kantian moral "ought," with a real one that presents the universal and the particular in their identity. But this identity is not the frozen concept that one finds in Schelling. It is rather identity as "possessing an inner movement which is the very process that will achieve its final form as the dialectic of spirit in the *Phenomenology of Spirit.*"[4] It is this dynamic opposition at the heart of identity that Hegel finds at work in Attic tragedy. In his interpretation of the *Eumenides,* the conflict between Athena and the Furies, the struggle around the nature of justice, takes place "in front of the ethical organization, the Athenian people," and concludes with a reconciliation.[5]

So, tragedy is the objective, dramatic performance of the double-natured character of the substance of what Hegel calls *Geist,* or Spirit, in ethical life. In the *Eumenides,* what is displayed are the twin forces that constitute ethical life in their division, legal contestation and reconciliation. For Hegel, if tragedy is the self-awareness of ethical life that is objectified and placed outside itself in the form of fate, then *comedy* is the dissolution of fate. Hegel writes in the essay on natural law,

> The comedy so separates the two zones of the ethical that it allows each to proceed entirely on its own, so that in the one the conflicts and the finite are shadows without substance, while on the other the Absolute is an illusion. But the true and absolute relation is that the one really does illumine the other; each has a living bearing on the other, and each is the other's serious fate. The absolute relation, then, is set forth in tragedy.[6]

For Hegel, tragedy is always a drama of substance, of the opposed forces that fatefully constitute ethical life. Comedy, by contrast, is the dissolution of substance into subjectivity, where fate dissolves into contingency and necessity empties into licentiousness. One of the axes I am trying to grind in this book is the implausibility of this distinction of the tragic from the comic. By contrast, as I will try and show in Part 5, Euripides—the most tragic, *tragikotatos*—is the supremely tragicomic poet. This is why he is often so delightfully unpleasant.

What about bad Hegel? For Szondi—and I find this argument a little forced, to be honest—bad Hegel can be identified through the later formulation of the tragic in the vast sweep of the *Aesthetics,* his monumental lectures from the 1820s, where the essence of the tragic is defined as the collision between opposed sides, each of which has justification. Each side is true and yet each side is equally involved in guilt. What Szondi rightly objects to in the later Hegel's definition of the tragic is that it is too general and corresponds "to its position in an aesthetic theory."[7] The meaning of this claim becomes clearer in relation to the earlier *Phenomenology of Spirit* from 1807. Contrary to the *Aesthetics,* the *Phenomenology* places the tragic at the center of Hegelian philosophy, and interprets it as the dialectic governing ethical life. Szondi criticizes the ever-enlarging scope of the dialectic in Hegel, from the defining trait of ethical life that finds its reconciliation in love, to "the law of the world and the method of knowledge."[8] The problem is that dialectic has no limits in the later Hegel and becomes a theory of everything.

What is at stake in this debate becomes clearer in a key transitional discussion of Benjamin later in *An Essay on the Tragic.* In a frankly rather willful interpretation of *The Origin of German Tragic Drama,* Szondi claims that Benjamin, like the good Hegel and not the bad, "posits the genesis of the tragic as identical with the genesis of the dialectic, even if he does not characterize it as such."[9] This has the upshot that the dialectical structure of the tragic is not intended to be an anchor or guarantee for some global, general philosophy understood as a theory of everything. Rather, Szondi importantly writes, "it is familiar to the dramaturgical viewpoint."[10] Namely, in order to engage with the concept of the tragic, it is necessary to try and *think theatrically* and not just philosophically, which is what Szondi attempts to do in a series of analyses of plays that form the second half of *An Essay on the Tragic* that culminates in an electrifying reading of Georg Büchner's exhilaratingly bleak *Danton's Death*.

The key quote in Szondi's book is the following, which was anticipated by our discussion above:

> There is no such thing as *the* tragic, at least not as an essence. Rather, the tragic is a *mode*, a particular manner of destruction that is threatening or already completed: the dialectical manner. There is only *one* tragic downfall: the one that results from the unity of opposites, from the sudden change into one's opposite, from self-division. *But it is also the case that only the demise of something that should not meet its demise, whose removal does not allow the wound to heal, is tragic.* The tragic contradiction may not be sublated [*aufgehoben*] in a superordinate sphere, whether immanent or transcendent. If this is the case, then either the object of destruction was something trivial, which as such eludes the tragic and offers itself up to the comic, or the tragic is already vanquished in humor, covered up in irony, or surmounted in faith. Kierkegaard, more than any other, had considered this.[11]

The tragic is not an essence instantiated or not in certain tragedies, based on the judgment (which is always a critic's or a philosopher's judgment) of their exemplarity. Such is the Aristotelian legacy seen through the generalizing looking glass of the tragic. Rather, for Szondi, the tragic is a dialectical modality, a mode of experience, which is specifically the experience of the self-constitution and self-division of ethical life. Even more specifically, for me, the tragic is a dialectical modality of negation, where things fall apart, are rent and sundered. Against Hegel, the tragic does not necessarily allow for "sublation" or higher reconciliation of the opposed forces that make up ethical life. Inverting Hegel's thought in the *Phenomenology,* tragedy reveals the wounds of spirit that will not heal, but that fester and become infected. At that point, genre distinctions between the tragic and the comic or humor begin to blur and fade. What interests me, and I am thinking specifically of some plays by Euripides, especially the *Orestes,* Shakespeare's *Troilus and Cressida,* Ibsen's *Ghosts,* or Sarah Kane's *Phaedra's Love,* is drama as a tragicomedy of infection. Drama is here a disease that is bequeathed to the spectator. As the pimp protagonist Pandarus says in the final words of *Troilus and Cressida,* "Till then I'll sweat and seek about for eases, / And at that time bequeath you my diseases."[12]

18

From Philosophy Back to Theater

We need to go back to the theater. Rather than philosophizing about the tragic on the basis of some universalistic model of aesthetic exemplarity or freezing the essence of the tragic in a philosophical system like a lark's tongue in aspic, we need to see tragedy itself as a dialectical mode of experience that can teach us something important and importantly nontranslatable into philosophy as it is commonly understood. It is not that tragedy is nonphilosophical or antiphilosophical—far from it—but that it is a specific mode of presenting the human situation and inviting us to ponder it, a dramatic, dialectical mode that does not claim to eliminate ambiguity, but might enable us to see the contours of that ambiguity a little more sharply and clearly.

We can relate this thought to other philosophers who have pondered the question of tragedy. Let me mention two who are important to me: Philippe Lacoue-Labarthe and Jacques Taminiaux. In a series of interventions spanning many years that culminate in a pair of short texts from 1998, *Métaphrasis* and *Le théâtre de Hölderlin,* Lacoue-Labarthe sought to liberate Hölderlin not just from the conceptual grid and grip of Heidegger's reading, but also to liberate the theatrical experience of tragedy from what we might call the "antitheatricalism" of a certain idealist reception of tragedy in Schelling, Hegel, Nietzsche, and many others.[1] This liberation tends in the direction of theatrical praxis, not as an end in itself, but as the index for a possible political praxis. One of the many vagaries of Heidegger's reading of Hölderlin is its radically depoliticized character, specifically the way it silences the clear republican sympathies that Hölderlin was seeking to work through in the multiple, ever-incomplete drafts of his modern tragedy, *The Death of Empedocles.* For Lacoue-Labarthe, there is a return to Aristotle in Hölderlin, in the sense of a return to theater, and a kind of rejection of what Lacoue-Labarthe calls "the speculative interpretation" of tragedy and its idealization of the tragic. For Lacoue-Labarthe, Hölderlin's question, and I think this is right, is *"comment faire une tragédie?"* ("how to make a tragedy?").[2] Thus, the speculative, metaphysical interpretation of tragedy has to be purged. Tragedy is the theatrical presentation of the tragic flaw, or *hamartia,* and its *catharsis* in the name of a rethinking of praxis, or action.

One finds a related set of concerns in Jacques Taminiaux's *Le Théâtre des philosophes* from 1995, which is his most satisfying and complete book, in my view.[3] Taminiaux sees the entire philosophical reception of tragedy in terms of a Platonic gesture of the reduction of *praxis* to *poiesis,* that is, the reduction of the human intrigue of drama to the production of an ontology, to philosophical determinations of being. For Taminiaux, there is, in both Hegel and Heidegger, an overly philosophical understanding of tragedy with the very idea of positing the being or essence of the tragic. Such an abstract, philosophical understanding—and here Taminiaux draws as he very often does on the thought of Hannah Arendt—misses the dimension of plurality, the difficulty of situated practical judgment, Aristotle's *phronesis,* and the irreducibility of opinion, or *doxa,* that is at work in tragedy. The two historical exceptions to this thesis are Aristotle, who respects what we might call the practical dimension of tragedy and theater, and Hölderlin, who secretly and prudently returns to Aristotle. I see Taminiaux's book as a theatrical critique of the primacy of philosophical approaches to tragedy, and the entire discourse on the essence of the tragic. For Taminiaux, it is a question of Arendt against Heidegger staged as theater against philosophy.

More examples could be given, and Taminiaux's argument could be contested on many points, but I think the overall point is clear: *we need to go back to theater*. This thought is what drives my interest in theatrical performance and in different accounts of theatrical praxis. We might consider Artaud's theater of cruelty, Grotowski's poor theater, Peter Brook's immediate theater, and the practice of theater groups like the Wooster Group from New York. But perhaps the most obvious analogue to what I have been saying is with Brecht's idea of epic theater, a theater that is highly specific, punctual, and political, but that is also deeply cognitive and philosophical.[4] This is a Euripidean theater that shakes up the audience's expectations and tries to wake them up from the hypnosis or more often slumber they slip into in the theater (why do we fall asleep in the theater?). This is a theater of intelligence and reason rather than feeling and ritual, a reflexive drama that turns the spectator into an observer onstage. It is a theater that presents arguments that might awaken a capacity for action on the part of the audience. This is a theater where smooth narrative flows are constantly interrupted, where music and sound are used to jar the arc of the plot. It is a theater of fits and starts, like jumping images on a strip of film. The audience is composed of experts and relaxed like a sports crowd rather than the cramped, anxious, tiny groups who still go to theater. Epic theater requires profound intelligence on the part of the actors and awakens the intelligence of the audience by producing astonishment. It is a theater that refuses *catharsis* through any identification with the sufferings of the tragic hero and dime store psychology. Epic theater is deeply untragic. In short, as Benjamin writes and as Nietzsche feared in his talk of "aesthetic Socratism" in *The Birth of Tragedy*, epic theater "revives a Socratic praxis."[5] Epic theater is tragedy's philosophy.

This opens a possibly abyssal question: If we need to go back to the theater, then where exactly *is* the theater? What I mean is that if we might understand tragedy as a dialectical mode of experience, a modality of negation, in the way I have proposed, then must this experience be had in what Peter Brook would call the empty space of a theater building? Or might it be had in other spaces and other media, for example film, television, even social media? Can theater in this sense happen as political action, as teaching, as sitting around a table and eating together, in listening to someone speak in a room or on the street? Can theater even happen in philosophy itself, understood not as system or a determination of being, but as dramatic action, as an experience of thoughtful conflict? I see no reason why not.

PART III

Sophistry

19

Against a Certain Style of Philosophy

It is not against philosophy as such that I want to speak in this book as much as against a certain *style* of philosophy that, I believe, originates with Plato. To use an admittedly limited shorthand, we could define this style as dominated by a will to truth that is premised upon a belief that reason and the activity of human rationality can identify and render intelligible that which is. Such a style of philosophy is committed to what we can call "the intelligibility of being." This dominant style of philosophy is ontological in the sense that, however claims about being are determined, whatever shape and content they might have, there is the belief that such claims *can* be made and are truthful. In a word, such a style of philosophy is premised on the idea that human beings can gain true insight into that which is. Of course, such claims are rarely just ontological. They are also moral. The history of philosophy displays a persistent linking of ontological claims to moral claims, in Plato, Aristotle, Aquinas, Spinoza, Kant, and Hegel. The list could be continued. An insight into that which is, is always linked to the claim that such an insight is what is good for the human being.

What I wish to defend in this book is another style of philosophy that is ultimately closer to the patterns of thinking, speaking, and reasoning that can be seen in Attic tragedy, especially the plays of Euripides. Tragedy's philosophy is a style of thinking that can be understood as dramatic performance and is marked by a profound moral ambiguity. Philosophy as drama, then. What we see in Greek tragedy, to lean once again on Bernard Williams, "is a world that is only partially intelligible to human agency and in itself not necessarily well adjusted to ethical aspirations." To this extent, I join Barbara Cassin in her critique of ontology in the name of *logology*, which finds its voice in the Sophists and the tragic poets and which, for me, is premised upon a profound ontological skepticism: the world is only ever partially intelligible to human agency. Any philosophical dream of full intelligibility has to be given up.

As such, the orientation that lies behind or beneath this book is Nietzschean in the sense that can be found in his mature works, such as *Beyond Good and Evil* (1886). Here Nietzsche speaks with a devastatingly witty violence about "The Prejudices of Philosophers," notably the driving or governing prejudice of the will to truth, and pleads for a tragic philosophy that recognizes untruth as a condition of *life*. Nietzsche writes—and I alluded to this in Part 1—"We have to await the arrival of a new species of philosopher . . . philosophers of the dangerous perhaps."[1] It is this "dangerous perhaps" that I see enacted in the language of tragedy, both in its Attic variants but equally in the tragedies of Shakespeare.[2]

20

An Introduction to the Sophists

The discursive invention that we call philosophy and that begins with Plato is premised upon two exclusions that are linked: the expulsion of the tragic poets, which we will track in detail in Chapter 37, and the opposition between philosophy and sophistry. This opposition continues to this day, both in very general terms, i.e., sophistry is deemed a bad, unworthy thing and philosophy is a good, worthy thing; and in more specific terms, as with, say, Alain Badiou's reassertion of Platonism against the alleged relativism of the Sophists or alleged contemporary neo-Sophists.[1] The standard narrative is that the Sophists were itinerant, rather flashy, usually foreign teachers, who taught the arts of rhetoric, oratory, and persuasion to people who could pay their large, indeed sometimes exorbitant, fees. But, so the story goes, they weren't concerned about the truth. Socrates, by contrast, is meant to be our hero because he was interested in the truth and he didn't get paid. So, in a way, anyone (such as myself) who gets paid to teach philosophy is really a Sophist, and if someone wants a salary for teaching philosophy (such as some possible readers of this book), then they want to be Sophists too.

We had a look at an example of the antithetical nature of sophistical thought in the fragment from Gorgias discussed in Part I. Sophistry exploits the concept of *antilogia,* or contradiction, as an argumentative procedure. Gorgias's contradictory thought is that tragedy is a deception or an act of fraud or trickery, in which the deceiver is more honest than the nondeceiver and the deceived is wiser than the nondeceived. What Gorgias seems to describe, then, perhaps even celebrate, is precisely that which Socrates/Plato sees as the great danger of tragedy, the danger of deception, the power of persuasion to induce the affective effects of imitation, of *mimesis*.

I'd like to give a more complex and sympathetic picture of the Sophists than one gets from philosophers. After a general consideration of sophistry and a close textual analysis of the fascinating extant fragments of Gorgias, I will consider the relation between sophistry and tragedy, particularly on the question of the language of tragedy and more particularly still on the ambiguity of tragic language. This will lead to a brief discussion of the nature of rationality in tragedy and its relation to force. In the closing sections of Part 3, I will then consider the image of the Sophist in Plato by looking at the contrasting ways in which sophistry is presented in two dialogues: the *Phaedrus* and the *Gorgias*.

The Greek word *sophistes* originally meant "skilled craftsman" or "wise man," but was used to describe traveling teachers who visited Athens from the mid-fifth century BCE and acquired a negative connotation in the comedies of Aristophanes, like *The Clouds,* and then in the writings of Plato and, later, Aristotle. The word *sophistes* means something like an expert or pundit, one who is wise, *sophos*. Ever since and for us still, the name Sophist is a term of abuse, meaning someone who uses bad argument deliberately to deceive the audience. A Sophist, then, is a fraud. In the *Sophist,* Plato argues that the Sophist is a "mercenary hunter after the young and rich . . . a wholesaler of learning . . . (and) a salesman of his own products of learning" (231d). Aristotle says the same thing in *On Sophistical Refutations,* describing the Sophist as "a money-maker" (165a). Xenophon in the *Memorabilia* calls those who sell wisdom for money "Sophists, just like prostitutes" (I, 1, 11). This brings to mind Cassin's suggestive proposal of looking at the history of philosophy from the standpoint of the prostitute rather than the client, as is usually the case.[2] Of course, it is rather intriguing that Aristophanes, who was a good deal closer to the context than we are, simply lumped Socrates together with the Sophists in his "thinkery" in *The Clouds.* Aristophanes didn't see Socrates through the rose-colored spectacles provided by Plato. Aristides, a Greek orator who lived during Roman times in the second century CE, polemically suggested that the reason for Plato's revulsion at the Sophists "is both his contempt for the masses and for his contemporaries."[3] This doubtless goes too far, but we have to take seriously the question of the relation between Socrates' contestation of sophistry and his critique of Athenian democracy.

Thanks to the reforms of Pericles from around the 460s BCE, Athenian democracy, limited as it was, was still remarkable and placed a high value on oratory, the ability to speak persuasively in public. It might be noted that Thucydides, in the most famous speech that has come down to us from antiquity, Pericles' Funeral Oration, which some claim was inspired by new learning provided by the Sophists, claims that the virtue of the Athenians in part consists in the capacity of being instructed through speeches (*logoi*). At the same time as the democratic reforms, there was a spectacular rise in lawsuits generated through the popular courts, which, it should be remembered, consisted of large panels of up to 501 citizens. Athens was also a society without lawyers, where citizens had to defend themselves if they were accused, as Socrates does in the *Apology.*

Following the defeat of the Persians and the formation of the Delian League, Athens had become very powerful and very wealthy in a relatively short space of time, and—*plus ça change*—the city attracted foreigners, "professors" of a kind, like Protagoras from Abdera on the Thracian coast, Prodicus from the Aegean island of Ceos, and Gorgias from Leontini in Sicily. They converged on Athens to give dazzling set-piece public orations and apparently very expensive private tutoring to those who could pay.

If a suitably wealthy young man wanted to get on in public life, then he hired a Sophist to train him to speak persuasively. The Sophists made apparently an awful lot of money instructing the wealthy young men of Athens and elsewhere (and, like contemporary star academics, they were constantly traveling).

Almost nothing survives of the voluminous writings of the original or older Sophists, particularly with the first and most famous of them, Protagoras. Three doctrines are associated with Protagoras, although evidence here is scanty and skewed by Plato.

1. Man is the measure of all things. Protagoras's fragment, which displays his use of *antilogia,* reads, "Of all things the measure is man, of the things that are, that they are, and of the things that are not, that they are not."[4] In Plato's hands, this leads to what we would now call subjectivism in relation to knowledge and relativism in relation to virtue. Each man judges what is true for him but this is not true for all. It is a question of virtue as that which is advantageous. This view is attacked in the *Theaetetus* and the *Protagoras* where the image of the philosopher is constantly presented as not being concerned with the human measure, but with the divine measure and the possibility of *ho bios theois,* the life of the gods. Obviously, the key question is whether virtue can be taught. For the Sophists, apparently it can. For Plato, it cannot. But there is no evidence that Sophists like Gorgias claimed to teach virtue. I want to defend the sophistical emphasis on the human measure as opposed to the philosophical preoccupation with the divine measure. Linked to this, I see the entire problematic of relativism as a by-product of philosophy's obsession with universalism. Once that universalist obsession is pushed to one side, then the problem of relativism also disappears in a puff of smoke and we might finally be able to engage in a more realistic and plausible account of the life of virtue and its relation to place and, indeed, other places.

2. Skepticism about the gods: "Concerning the Gods, I am not in a position to know either that they exist, or that they do not exist, for there are many obstacles in the way of such knowledge, notably the intrinsic obscurity of the subject and the shortness of human life."[5] This seems an eminently reasonable approach to the question, as opposed to Socrates, who, in the *Phaedo, Republic,* and *Gorgias,* is consistently arguing for the immortality of the soul and the afterlife as the reward for the philosophical life of virtue. Given the evident limitedness of human intelligence and the brevity of life, perhaps we should just put the question of God or the gods to one side.

3. The view that everything can be contradicted, the technique of *antilogia,* which was taught as a rhetorical skill. This linked to the use of double arguments *dissoi logoi,* which meant looking at both sides of a case, in order to make the weaker argument stronger and vice versa.[6] A fragment of Protagoras reads, "To make the weaker cause the stronger."[7] This is taken to an absurd conclusion by Aristophanes in *The Clouds,* who has two characters, one called "Stronger Argument" and the other called "Weaker Argument."

21

Gorgiasm

The greatest of the Sophists, in my view, for whom we have a lot more precious textual evidence, is Gorgias, and I would like to focus on him. There is an amusing book called *Lives of the Sophists* from the third century CE by Philostratus, which is short of absolutely any intellectual merit but full of nice anecdotes.[1] When Protagoras introduced a fee for his lectures, Philostratus quips that we prize those things we spend money on more than those we don't. Gorgias apparently charged incredibly high fees and was the wealthiest of the Sophists. Philostratus adds that there was even a verb in Greek, "to Gorgianize," *gorgiazein,* meaning to engage in oratory of a grand and florid style, or to speak in an excessive manner, to speak like Gorgias. Philostratus reports that Gorgias was praised for his great eloquence, his daring and unusual expressions, and the sudden transitions in his discourse.[2]

Gorgias probably lived circa 483–375 BCE, which means that he lived to be 108 years old. Philostratus confirms this, although there is no way of knowing if it is true (Diogenes Laertius often claims that pre-Socratic thinkers enjoyed extraordinary longevity). He arrived in Athens in 427 BCE, when he was already in his mid-fifties, as an ambassador for his native city, Leontini, after the outbreak of the Peloponnesian Wars. Gorgias delivered a number of show speeches to the Athenian assembly with great success, displaying what was seen as the new Sicilian form of rhythmic prose. He was acquainted with and on some reports (the *Suda*) the student of Empedocles, and knew of Parmenides, as he ridiculed the latter's type of being-talk in his own spoof, "On Not-Being," to which we will turn presently (if it is indeed a spoof, which is unclear). We are fortunate to have two versions of reports of "On Not-Being" and two short, brilliant examples of the set-piece speech, or *epideixis,* the stunningly beautiful text "The Encomium of Helen" and the rather less beautiful "The Defense of Palamedes."

There are many odd, ancient anecdotes connected with Gorgias. According to the satirist Lucian, he died by abstaining from food with all his faculties intact. According to the wonderfully dull Diogenes Laertius, Gorgias was the father of the sophistic arts, as Aeschylus was the father of tragedy. Diodorus of Sicily reports that Gorgias's eloquence astonished the Athenians, winning them over to support an alliance against Syracuse, which had attacked his hometown of Leontini. This would all end badly for Athens, with the military disaster of the Sicilian Expedition, reported in detail by Thucydides. Gorgias's speeches are repeatedly described in testimonies as highly poetic. Pausanias describes a statue of Gorgias at Olympia as "undistinguished." There was also a gilded statue of Gorgias (in some reports it was made of solid gold) in the temple to Apollo at Delphi that he dedicated himself. He was very wealthy and clearly a little vain. Amazingly, in 1876, the inscribed base of the statue was found during excavation. It finishes with the words "His statue stands too in the vale of Apollo / Not as a show of his wealth, but of the piety of his ways."

No doubt in order to parade his piety, there are also reports that Gorgias went about in purple clothes, the royal or imperial color (the same is said of Empedocles). This is a good example of sophistical bling. The Sophists are widely reported as dressing well, as opposed to Socrates, who usually went barefoot, wore an old cloak, and—as Nietzsche enthusiastically reports—was ugly. In Plato's *Meno,* it is said that Gorgias allowed any Greek to question him on any topic and he would improvise a response.[3]

On the topic of his teaching and methods, Gorgias did not teach any set of doctrines, but a method, a *hodos,* which was, in his view, value-free. He gave the highest status to the power of rhetoric, and I'd now like to summarize and interpret in turn the three main extant texts by Gorgias. The first is called *To me on*— "the not-being," "the nonexistent," "what is not"—and it is a set-piece example of sophistic *antilogia,* or contradiction, characterized by the technique of *elenkos*, refutation. I will then go on to examine "The Encomium of Helen" and "The Defense of Palamedes" and try and analyze in detail the use of antithetical language in order to show how the weaker can always become the stronger and how the seemingly indefensible, namely Helen, the cause and object of the Trojan War, can be rationally defended and exonerated of any guilt.

What particularly interests me, in relation to the wider argument of this book, are the evident links between the antithetical language of Gorgias and the language of Greek tragedy, specifically the plays of Euripides, more specifically still *The Trojan Women,* where both Cassandra and Helen herself deploy techniques of Gorgiastic reasoning to show that the weaker is the stronger and how in apparent defeat lies victory. What we see in Euripides is a quite different picture of the nature of rationality and morality than we find in the Platonic dialogues, a rationality that describes the effects of force and violence, but doesn't imagine that these effects can be ameliorated through reason alone. What emerges in tragedy is a notion of justice as an inherently conflictual activity in a world of war and constitutive violence, a world that is characterized by profound moral ambiguity. In brief, what tragedy presents us with is a world of disappointed or decayed democracy. Such a world does not require an idealistic Platonic response, but a *historical* response, of the kind found in Thucydides. The decay of democracy does not require a move into a form of universalist idealism, but contextual realism.

22

The Not-Being

Some have read "On the not-being" as a spoof or parody of the ontological pretensions of Eleatic philosophers like Parmenides (which has significant implications for German philosophers like Heidegger), to speak about being as either one or many or indeed anything at all. In Fragment 3, Parmenides says that it is the same thing to think and to be, and goes on, in Fragments 6 and 7, to say that we should choose the path of being, which is identified with possibility, whereas non-being or nothingness is not possible. Being is described as *eukuklou,* well-rounded like a sphere.[1] It is this sphere that Gorgias sets about smashing to pieces through a series of bewilderingly complex proofs. Gorgias undermines and appears to ridicule anyone who claims to speak about being. For Gorgias, arguably in distant anticipation of Nietzsche, the concept of being is a fiction and all philosophical theories that aim to uncover an underlying ontological reality are arrogantly implausible, indeed delusional. Gorgias is certainly an anti-Platonist skeptic *avant la lettre,* and maybe the first example of a genuine nihilist, a term that I use nonabusively. It is also important to emphasize that the text is what Gorgias elsewhere calls in "The Encomium of Helen" a *paignion,* an amusement, a plaything, a toy. If this fragment is a refusal of any and all philosophy of being, then it is also a *comic* undermining of any and all philosophical talk about being. Perhaps comedy itself, from Aristophanes onward, is the dramatic undermining of ontology. There are two reports of the fragment, one from Sextus Empiricus (second century CE), the other from a text called *On Melissus, Xenophanes, and Gorgias* that somehow wound up in the Aristotelian corpus. One can and should respect the difference between these two texts, in particular on their relative proximity to skepticism. I will follow Sextus's version, as it is clearer.[2]

Gorgias argues three theses:

1. Nothing exists.
2. If anything exists, it is unknowable or inapprehensible by humans.
3. If anything is apprehensible by humans, it is incommunicable to one's neighbor.

Let's take the theses in turn:

1. Nothing exists. If anything exists, it is either being or not-being, or both being and not-being.

(a) It cannot be not-being, for not-being does not exist. If it did exist, it would at the same time both be and not be, which is impossible.

(b) It cannot be being, for being does not exist, as shall now be demonstrated, Gorgias nicely adds. If being exists, then it must either be uncreated or created.

(i) If it is uncreated or eternal, it has no beginning, and having no beginning, it is infinite. But if it is infinite, it has no position, i.e., no body or location. If it has no position, it is nowhere, ergo it does not exist.

(ii) If it is created, it is either created out of either being or not-being. If it is created out of being, then it has not been created, as being would already exist. If it is created out of not-being, then that is absurd because not-being cannot create anything. Nothing comes of nothing.

(iii) Neither can being be a mixture of eternal and created, since they are opposed.

(iv) Being is not one, as some claim, like Parmenides, because if it exists as one, it has size, and if it has size, it is infinitely divisible and therefore potentially many.

(v) Neither is being many, as Empedocles might have claimed, because the many is made up of many ones, and since the one doesn't exist, nor does the many.

(c) A mixture of being and not-being is in itself impossible as it makes no sense for the same thing to both be and not be.

2. If anything exists, it is unknowable and inconceivable. This will now be shown, says Gorgias. If things thought about (what we can call "percepts") are not existent, i.e., they are thoughts and not things, then the existent is not thought. All that is thought are things that do not exist, the percepts that flash through our minds. Consider the opposite view: one might say that all the things that are thought exist (like Berkeley, *esse est percipi*). But this is stupid, because I can think that chariots run across the sea or that men fly like birds or think of a unicorn. Furthermore, if things thought are existent, then the nonexistent things will not be thought. But this is absurd, for many nonexistent things are thought, like Scylla and Charybdis. Therefore, things that are thought do not exist, and if anything exists, then we know nothing of it and cannot even conceive it.

3. If anything is capable of being apprehended, it cannot be communicated. This will now be shown. The means by which we indicate the existence of things is *logos,* speech. But speech is not identical with things. Not at all. All that we communicate to another is speech, which is not that which exists. I do not communicate a color or a sound. I communicate in a word, but a word is not by definition a thing. Therefore, if anything exists and is comprehended, it is incommunicable.

Nothing exists. QED. Gorgias proves his claim in the first thesis and appears to add the second and third theses as wonderfully excessive argumentative flourishes to show that even if it could be proved that something existed, it would be unknowable and incommunicable. The argument is exquisite and, as I said, very funny, with great satirical force. According to Jean-François Lyotard, in his "Gorgias Notice" from *Le Différend,* the effect of the argument of "On the not-being" is a radical, exuberant, and comic nihilism. It is a little like Freud on the logic of the borrowed kettle:

1. That he had returned the kettle undamaged.
2. That it was already damaged when he borrowed it.
3. That he had never borrowed it in the first place.[3]

Or it is like the logical structure of some of the best jokes: Groucho Marx with his hand on Chico's pulse, "Either this man is dead or my watch has stopped." Or again, when Chico is being pursued by some unwelcome people who suddenly appear, and he asks Groucho what to do. Groucho says, "Tell them you're not here." Chico responds, "They won't believe me." To which Groucho replies, "They will when you start speaking." Some jokes possess the power of *antilogia* and the ways in which we can learn to live with contradiction. Eric Kaplan recalls the joke at the end of *Annie Hall,* when the Woody Allen character tells a joke about a man whose brother thinks he is a chicken. When pressed on why the man won't turn in his brother to the doctors, he says, "Because I need the eggs." The legendary Columbia philosopher Sidney Morgenbesser was once asked whether he accepted the view that something could be p and not-p at the same time. He answered, "I do and I don't."[4] According to Gorgias, he wasn't kidding.

23

I Have Nothing to Say and I Am Saying It

The first thing to note is that the kind of sophistical procedure enacted by Gorgias in "On the not-being" constitutes the challenge to which Socrates repeatedly responds and leads to the invention of that discursive practice called *philosophia*. At the very least, sophistry needs to be read and understood before being condemned and cannot simply be arrogantly swept aside in the name of truth, certainty, or some sort of reassertion of Platonism, as is the case with figures like Badiou and his acolytes. Such a Platonizing gesture reduces philosophy to some kind of policing function where the criminal is always the Sophist and the Sophist is always the criminal. The way in which to condemn someone as a nonphilosopher is to brand him or her a Sophist.

I am close to Barbara Cassin on this point and agree with her view that it is simply not satisfactory to construct the model of philosophy over against the "bad other" of sophistry. This reduces philosophy to the act of violence, what she calls "using the stick."[1] Rather, what is being offered by Gorgias in his undermining of any and all ontologies is a *logology*. Indeed, I am very intrigued by Cassin's claim that "the first women I came across in philosophy were the Sophists. They constitute for the Platonic-Aristotelian orthodoxy an unassimilable heterodoxy."[2] Obviously, we could let that insight resonate with the question of gender in relation to philosophy on the one hand, and drama on the other, which is a prominent subplot in this book.

But is it justified to claim that Gorgias's fragment is just a parody or spoof on the Parmenidean style of reasoning, where philosophy is identified with the determination of being and where the history of metaphysics is understood, with Heidegger, as a series of such determinations that descend into ever-deeper oblivion or forgetfulness (*Vergessenheit*)? Might one not also say that this strange little fragment is closer to self-parody? Might it not be read as a completely knowing, self-conscious, and self-aware statement of the self-undermining character of all language, Gorgias's included? Rather than seeing "On the not-being" as just a contradiction of ontology, might we not see it as a performative *self*-contradiction that is completely self-conscious and perhaps intrinsic to any and all linguistic acts? Gorgias asserts in "The Encomium of Helen" that speech is a mighty lord, and this is indeed true. But does not Gorgias demonstrate, at and as the very inception of philosophy, the self-undermining character of all language, his own included? Rather than being just an *anti-logia* to ontological discourse, "On the not-being" might also be an *auto-antilogia* where Gorgias freely and willingly undermines himself, works against himself, undoes himself. As John Cage said in his famous "Lecture on Nothing": "I have nothing to say, and I am saying it."[3]

I think here, obviously, perhaps, of Samuel Beckett. There is Malone's famous line "Nothing is more real than nothing," but also the ceaseless patterns of negation that characterize Beckett's texts, which are indeed *Textes pour rien,* where emphasis should be placed on the preposition: these are texts *for* nothing, even for *the* nothing, for the being *not*. This is not the place to begin a taxonomy of the words "nothing" and "non-being" in Beckett, which would take us from very early texts, like his essay on Proust, to the three late prose texts contained in *Nohow On,* a title that I willfully want to hear as an echo of Gorgias's *"to me on."* But the link between Gorgias and Beckett that I would like to suggest concerns what Beckett calls "the syntax of weakness," and which arguably characterizes his language throughout his work. Consider some examples from *The Unnameable:*

> But my good-will at certain moments is such, and my longing to have floundered however briefly, however feebly in the great life torrent streaming from the earliest protozoa to the very latest humans, that I, no, parenthesis unfinished. I'll begin again. My family.[4]

And this:

> And would it not suffice, without any change in the structure of the thing as it now stands as it always stood, without a mouth being opened at the place which even pain could never line, would it not suffice to, to what, the thread is lost, no matter.[5]

And finally:

> I resume, so long as, so long as, let me see, so long as one, so long as he, ah fuck all that, so long as this, then that, agreed, that's good enough, I nearly got stuck.[6]

And so it goes on. And on. A nohow on where we do not know how to go on, but we do nonetheless, until we don't anymore. Beckett's sentences are a series of weak intensities, a series of antithetical inabilities, unable to go on and unable not to go on, a double inability, a double not that ties us in a double knot, like the negations of Mr. Knott in Beckett's *Watt,* which is overfull with whatnots. Such a syntax of weakness is based on the insight that speech is indeed, as Gorgias says, a mighty lord, but what language does is to constantly move in patterns of negation that undermine that power. The mighty lord is also a bonded servant. Logology is not some new superontology, but ultimately the undoing of language itself. This undoing is not done in the name of some knowing, secretly masterful cynicism, but in the namelessness and unnameability of a more modest skepticism. If Gorgias robs us of our ability to ontologize or to offer new determinations of being, then such an orientation is perhaps not ultimately divorced from a minimal moral orientation that tries to separate itself from being, where not-being and the beyond being perhaps touch together. And perhaps this is human, which of course is nothing much, nothing to write home about, but "a lobster couldn't do it," as Beckett quips. But who knows, maybe we should ask some lobsters.

24

Helen Is Innocent

Let's turn to the second and most famous text by Gorgias, "The Encomium of Helen," which was very probably written as an *epideixis,* or display speech, in order to show the all-conquering power of persuasive speech. It would appear that the so-called linguistic turn did not begin in the twentieth century with the work of Heidegger or the later Wittgenstein; it starts before "philosophy" proper, with Gorgias. "Philosophy" is a response to and an attempted refutation of the sophistical linguistic turn. The "Encomium" is not so much a genuine defense of Helen as much as evidence that speech is a powerful lord who can defend the seemingly indefensible, namely that the material cause of the multiple murders and miseries of the Trojan War—Helen, whom Euripides describes as coming from Hell—cannot be found guilty. The text is something between prose and poetry in the Attic Greek and a work of genuine beauty, in particular in its use of rhythm, rhyme, and alliteration.

Why did Helen do what she did? Gorgias lists six possible reasons:

For either it was by the will of Fate
and the wishes of the Gods
and the votes of Necessity
that she did what she did
or by force reduced

or by words seduced
or by love possessed.[1]

If it was any of the first three reasons—fate, or the will of the gods, or necessity—then obviously Helen cannot be held accountable because such things are outside her control. If she was abducted by force, ravished, and raped, then this also obviously was not her fault. As we should all know, rape is not the victim's crime but that of the rapist, in this case Paris.

And love? Is Helen to blame if she falls in love? Gorgias reasons, "Love has the divine power of the gods, / how could a lesser being reject and refuse it?"[2] If the body of Alexander "presented to her soul eager desire and contest of love, / what is wonderful in that?"[3] As Woody Allen once said, "The heart wants what the heart wants." Interestingly, even Socrates would be obliged to agree with this view, as he insists in the *Phaedrus* that love is a god.

But we've left out one last possible reason: What if it were speech that persuaded her and deceived her soul? Here we come to Gorgias's main point: "Speech is a powerful lord." "It can stop fear and banish grief / and create joy and nurture pity."[4] Gorgias continues, with great eloquence,

There come upon its hearers
fearful shuddering
and tearful pity
and grievous longing
and at the good fortunes and evil actions
of others' affairs and bodies
through the agency of words
the soul experiences suffering of its own.[5]

Of course, Gorgias's thought here is close to that of Aristotle in the *Poetics,* where tragedy as a privileged form of poetic language can induce the affects of pity and fear in the soul of the spectator.

Gorgias goes a little further and sees speech as a kind of incantation, witchcraft, or magic.

> Inspired incantations conveyed through words
> become bearers of pleasure [*epagogoi hedones*]
> and banishers of pain [*apagogoi lypes*].[6]

It is reported in Plato that Gorgias's brother Herodicus was a doctor, and words are compared with drugs (*Gorgias*, 448b): "The effect of speech upon the structure of the soul / Is as the structure of drugs over the nature of bodies."[7]

Thus, if Helen came under the influence of the lordly power of speech, then it is as if she was "ravished by the force of pirates." Therefore, she cannot be held responsible. Gorgias infers from this, "She did not do wrong [*edikesen*], but was unfortunate [*etykhesen*]."[8] If we were in a court of law and this was a trial—and remember that the Sophists' teaching was explicitly aimed toward use in Athenian law courts—then Helen would have to be found not guilty. The case against her would have been dismissed. It is a great example of sophistical *elenkos,* or refutation.

The beauty of "The Encomium of Helen" is its rhapsodic power, but also its utter self-awareness. Gorgias knows exactly what he is doing and what effect he is creating with his words. It is an utterly persuasive speech on the power of persuasive speech. But the last lines of the speech pull the rug from under our feet. Gorgias concludes, with a wry smile, "My purpose was to compose a speech as an encomium of Helen / and an amusement for myself."[9]

Obviously, this is what motivates the charge of nihilism. Gorgias doesn't necessarily believe anything that is said in the speech. He is simply showing that such a case for Helen can rationally and persuasively be made. The competent deployment of reason does not require belief on the part of the reasoner, although it might well induce such belief in the listener. The question we will turn to next is the relation between sophistical language and the language of tragedy. We will see that tragedians like Euripides seem to know Gorgias rather well and to have learned his arguments by heart.

The third text by Gorgias is "The Defense of Palamedes," which can be dealt with more briefly but which has been massively influential in the history of legal reasoning.[10] More properly, the text is a self-defense. Palamedes had been "framed" by Odysseus as retribution for exposing the latter's trickery in trying to get out of fighting in the Trojan War. A letter was forged from Priam, the enemy king, and a quantity of gold was found in Palamedes' tent in the camp of the Argives outside Troy. Palamedes is charged with treason. The speech is a closely reasoned, forensic dismantling of the prosecution case that exposes the fallaciousness of the claims made against Palamedes. It skillfully makes Palamedes look like the patriot and turns Odysseus into a traitor. He also elegantly flatters his audience of Greek warrior aristocrats (knowledge and flattery of one's audience are essential to the activity of persuasion). Of course, Palamedes' defense was unsuccessful, and he was executed. Gorgias's point is that if he had been trained in oratory by him, he would have been found innocent. Sadly, Gorgias wasn't around during the Trojan War. Too bad for Palamedes.

Permit me one last example from Gorgias, which is a particularly beautiful excerpt from a funeral oration written to be spoken over the Athenian dead during the Peloponnesian Wars. It is perhaps the strongest example of the antithetical construction that was introduced by the Sophists and was of course a staple of many traditions of rhetoric (examples of such oxymoronic language are legion in Shakespeare, Donne, and many others):

> Wherefore though they have died
> desire for them has not died,
> but lives on,
> though they live not,

immortal in bodies not immortal
[*all' athanatos ouk en athanatois somasi zei ou zonton*].[11]

Of course, these words bring to mind Pericles' funeral oration over the war dead as it is recorded in Thucydides. It is more than likely that Pericles was influenced by the new learning that was brought into Athens by the Sophists, and in the funeral oration he claims that the virtue of the Athenians consists in being instructed by speeches, whereas for others, like the Spartans, "ignorance makes them brave and thinking makes them cowards."[12] The Spartans might have been terrific warriors, but they were not, in the Athenian view, particularly clever. This, of course, suggests anew the relation between sophistry and democracy and the opposition to both by philosophy.

25

Tragedy and Sophistry—The Case of Euripides' The Trojan Women

Let's go back to tragedy and try and think about its relation to sophistry. There are direct connections between the language of sophistry and tragedy, particularly in the plays of Euripides. Here we witness the weaker argument becoming the stronger and vice versa in the practice of *antilogia*. This occurs both in terms of action and plot, where Euripides inherits the plays of Aeschylus, say, but then subjects them to a kind of twisting or 180-degree rotation. But *antilogia* also appears in the very language of the plays, with their fascination with ambiguous, doubling, or ironic utterance, and particularly in the use of antithetical language, as when Sophocles' Antigone refers to herself as "No wife, no bride" (Sophocles, *Antigone* 917) or when Electra defines herself through a series of negations, "I cannot not grieve" (Sophocles, *Electra* 181) and "I must not violate Electra" (line 495—we will return to Sophocles' *Electra* in Part 5). Or again, Euripides' Hecuba, looking at the murdered body of her daughter, Polyxena, cries out, "Maiden nonmaiden, bride nonbride."[1]

In his essay "The Language of Tragedy," Simon Goldhill engages in a brief but compelling discussion of Gorgias. What is particularly striking is the adoption of the sophistical interest in arguments of paradoxical reversal, "manipulated with extraordinary *élan* by Euripides."[2] In play after play, we see the weaker argument become the stronger. Think of the case of Cassandra in Euripides' *The Trojan Women*, who demonstrates that her city is more blessed than the Greeks' and shows how the besieged and defeated Trojans are better off and more noble than the victorious Greeks. This strategy of inversion or reversal is typical of Gorgias. Cassandra says, "The Trojans have that glory which is loveliest: / They died for their own country" (Euripides, *The Trojan Women* 386–87). Thus, the apparent defeat of the Trojans is actually their victory, for they acted honorably in losing, whereas the Greeks behaved like beasts in winning the war. Furthermore, given that Cassandra can see the future (although she is never believed), she knows that Clytemnestra will murder Agamemnon (and her too), which will lead to the ruination of the house of Atreus that we know from the *Oresteia*. She says to her mother, the endlessly weeping Hecuba,

> O Mother, weep no more for me.
> You beneath the ground, my brothers, Priam, faith of us all,
> I will be with you soon and come triumphant to the dead
>   below,
> Leaving behind me, wrecked, the house of Atreus, which
>   destroyed our house. (lines 457–60)

In apparent defeat lies true victory. The weaker will destroy the stronger. Atreus will fall (which it does). Victory is defeat.

This technique of rhetorical training and its transposition into tragic language must not be viewed, Goldhill insists, "a regrettable fall from the purity and passion of a putative Aeschylean *Gesamtkunstwerk*."[3] After all, the first great trial scene is in Aeschylus's *Eumenides*. Goldhill quips, "Indeed, the judgement 'mere rhetoric' is always a critical laziness." Rather, there is an intimate link between the language of tragedy and sophistry.

> That some sophists wrote tragedies and that tragedians manipulate sophistic rhetoric is not a casual overlap of interest. It testifies to the active, public debate about man, lan-

guage and the polis in democratic Athens. Tragedy's use . . .
of rhetoric in action is an integral part of its engagement with
the public life of the contemporary city."[4]

As we will presently see, philosophy in the person of Socrates
rejects sophistical rhetoric in the same way as it disengages from
the public life of the city, governed by "the many." Philosophy's
antirhetorical prejudice is *antipolitical.*

Language takes on a polyvalence and opacity in tragedy. Following Vernant and Vidal-Naquet, the dramatic conflict will often
circle around opposed meanings in the same word, like *dike* in the
Oresteia (are the Furies right, or is Orestes?), *nomos* (should we be
guided by the law of the gods or human law in the *Antigone*?), or
kratos (does power lie with the king or with the people in Aeschylus's *The Suppliant Women*?). Language is also as much about the
failure to communicate as its success; think of Cassandra's speech
in the *Agamemnon,* where she sees the truth clearly and accurately
but cannot persuade anyone to believe her. There seems to be a
persistent, performative gap between truth and persuasion.

The huge importance of persuasion in tragic language should
be noted, which stands opposed to violence or force, in Greek *bia.*
Tragedy is persuasion in action and, more importantly, persuasion
as action. Goldhill discusses Sophocles' *Philoctetes,* where the latter gradually persuades Neoptolemus, who has been sent to force
him back to Troy, until Heracles appears in a *deus ex machina* and
the matter is settled by a kind of divine violence or force. Obviously, honey-tongued Odysseus is the figure who best embodies
persuasion. Neoptolemus says to Odysseus, "Do you really not
think it is disgraceful to tell lies?" "No," says Odysseus, "if safety is
what the lie brings."[5] Can we defend lying? Truly, it seems.

Let's return to *The Trojan Women,* which contains one of the
most extraordinary examples of persuasion in tragedy and shows
the depth of the influence of Sophists like Gorgias on the language
of tragedy. In my view, it was not Socrates who helped Euripides

write his plays, as Nietzsche either slyly or suspiciously suggests in *The Birth of Tragedy*. It was probably Gorgias. For her instrumental role in causing the Trojan War and being such a woman of questionable virtue, Hecuba wants Helen killed. Her abandoned husband, Menelaus, initially agrees: "I did not come to talk with you. I came to kill" (line 905). But when Helen objects that the demands of justice should grant her the right to defend herself, an informal law court is set up, with Hecuba pleading the case for the prosecution and Menelaus acting as judge. What is amazing about Helen's speech is that—anachronistically—she has clearly been reading Gorgias's "Encomium of Helen." Helen responds to the claim that she be put to death with a carefully structured sophistical argument: first point, second point, consider the logical consequences, etc., etc. She speaks like a lawyer and uses the technique of paradoxical reversal: her adultery benefitted the Greeks as it enabled them to defeat the barbarians:

> Yet Hellas' fortune was my own misfortune. I,
> Sold once for my body's beauty stand accused, who should
> For what has been done wear garlands on my head. (lines
> 935–37)

Indeed, Helen seems to follow the precise line of defense that was prepared for her by Gorgias. How can she be guilty? She claims that she was "a bride of force" (*bia*) (line 962) and not choice. Furthermore, if she was seduced by love to couple with Paris, then love is a mighty force, which no mortal can withstand. Who is stronger than Aphrodite? Helen asks. No one, of course (which is also Gorgias's point). So, if she is just a little bit to blame for leaving her husband, sleeping with the enemy, and causing a long and bloody war, then, she adds, "Should I not be forgiven?" (line 950). In a lovely final flourish, Helen adds that if anyone should be to blame, it is clearly Hecuba, as she was Paris's mother, therefore the cause of all the trouble in the first place.

Hecuba replies to Helen in lucidly rational terms, replying point by point and refuting her arguments decisively. She should win the argument on purely rational grounds. But here's the twist: although Menelaus is persuaded by Hecuba's superior argument, Hecuba is undercut and loses. Helen is not killed on the spot, and although Menelaus pushes her away, she is let on board his ship and returns to Sparta. There is an ancient story that when Menelaus approached Helen on board ship with a sword, she dropped her top, and at the sight of her breasts he was so taken with her beauty that all thought of punishment instantly vanished. Indeed, in the trial scene, Hecuba seems (anachronistically, again) to know this tale. She pleads, "Let her not be put in the same ship as you" (line 1049). To which Menelaus replies with a joke, "What can you mean? That she is heavier than she was" (line 1050). Hecuba, perhaps knowing the case is futile, adds, "A man in love once never is out of love again," or "once a lover, always a lover" (line 1051). In brief, Helen seduces Menelaus.

In the language of tragedy, particularly in Euripides but it is also present in Aeschylus and Sophocles, there is a willful manipulation of the founding, legitimating myths that the city has inherited. Tragedy "charts the way in which the self-aware modernity of the democratic polis is formulated in relation to Homeric and other narratives of the past."[6] The complex and multiform relations between past and present in tragedy and especially its bold anachronism, where gods from the archaic past engage in sophistical, legal debate, show that the old stories are no longer sufficient for life in the city. Ancient tragedy is not ancient. It is quintessentially modern.

26

Rationality and Force

Tragedy is a symptom of the fifth-century linguistic turn that placed enormous value on rationality, argumentation, and persuasion. Reason is essential to the experience of tragedy and not some epiphenomenon to an allegedly more authentic experience of myth or ritual. Tragedy is not some Dionysian celebration of the power of ritual and the triumph of myth over reason. Such is the *doxa* that I am seeking to oppose in this book.

But what is the point of the elaborate, staged rational argumentation on display in tragedy after tragedy? Does it show, in some quaintly Habermasian manner, the force of the better argument? Sometimes this is the case, and as we have seen in Gorgias and Euripides, tragic language exhibits the power of the weaker to become stronger through argument. But might it not also show the limitation of rational argumentation? After the long back-and-forth of argument, most often in Euripides, a character or often the chorus will exclaim in a moment of complete disorientation, "What shall I do?" Rationality abounds in tragedy, but it is not as if reason solves anything or brings anything to a final resolution or reconciliation. And despite the extraordinary eloquence of Cassandra or Helen, they are still subject to desire, power, and violence. Might ultimately always seems to trump right.

Indeed, in Aeschylus's *Prometheus Bound,* there are two characters called Might and Violence, or *Kratos* and *Bia.* Although *Kratos* speaks in the opening scene of the play in a dialogue with

Hephaestus, who is charged with nailing Prometheus to his lonely rock for his transgressions, *Bia* remains mute throughout. Violence is present, but doesn't speak. In my view, the uses of rational argumentation in tragedy do not show the primacy of reason, but its limitation in relation to force, to mute violence. Reason is a fragile creature, and it is also easily corruptible through the stratagem of the persuasive lie. When reason confronts mute violence, even at its eloquent best, violence usually wins.

27

Plato's Sophist

What picture of the Sophist emerges in Plato's dialogues? This would appear to be an easy question to answer. It is clearly a negative image. Socrates relentlessly opposed the Sophists, and most of what we know about them comes from the caricatures we get in a large number of Plato's dialogues. Think of the many dialogues devoted to Socrates' debates with various leading Sophists (*Protagoras, Gorgias, Hippias Major, Hippias Minor, Euthydemus,* and the *Sophist,* of course). Sometimes, indeed very often, Plato reduced the enemy to the level of flat caricature. Elsewhere, as in the *Sophist,* where the philosophical authority is given to the Stranger from Elea and where Socrates is present but silent after some opening remarks, the final—rather abstruse—definition of sophistry runs as follows:

> Sophistry is a productive art, human, of the imitation kind, copy-making, of the appearance-making kind, uninformed and insincere in the form of contrary-speech-producing art. (268 c–d)

The contrary-speech-producing art refers to the sophistical practice of *antilogia,* which proceeds by antithesis. We find a cruder definition in the *Protagoras:* "a Sophist is really a merchant or peddler of goods by which a soul is nourished" (313c). Once again, we go back to the idea of the Sophist as a wisdom whore turning cheap rhetorical tricks for rich young men that gives them the patina of virtue without any real knowledge. For Socrates, by contrast, virtue cannot be taught. It cannot be sold in a neat financial parcel. A similar view can be found in Aristotle's *On Sophistical Refutations*. The point of this short, polemical text is to show that the arguments provided by the Sophist, of the kind we saw in Gorgias's fragments, *appear* to be refutations, but they are merely superficial fallacies. Aristotle claims, "The art of the sophist is the semblance of wisdom without the reality" (165a). Such an art is an excellent acquisition for people who want to appear to be wise without being so. In other words, sophistry is bullshit, and we dearly love declaring that things are bullshit.

But there is a more interesting and complex way of answering the question about the relation of Socratic dialogue to sophistry. I'd briefly like to consider two dialogues: *Phaedrus* and *Gorgias*. These dialogues are strongly related in that they deal with the same topic, broadly speaking the relation between philosophy and rhetoric, as exemplified in sophistical practice. But they deal with the topic in surprisingly contrary ways, where one dialogue is a stunning success and the other is arguably an abject failure. We will proceed, then, in the manner of *antilogia,* balancing affirmation and negation, success and failure. Let's begin with the success.

28

Phaedrus, *a Philosophical Success*

There appears to be something enigmatic about Plato's *Phaedrus*.[1] It seems to discuss two distinct topics, rather than one: *eros* and rhetoric. The first half of the dialogue culminates with Socrates' Second Speech on *eros,* which many readers appear to like and find memorable. But it is followed by a long forensic discussion of rhetoric that readers tend to find rather dull and forget about. But this is a profoundly mistaken impression of the *Phaedrus:* the twin themes of *eros* and rhetoric are really one.

The purpose of the *Phaedrus* is to induce a philosophical *eros* in the rather unphilosophical Phaedrus. Phaedrus is not the kind of feisty, angry, and highly intelligent opponent that Socrates finds in the Gorgiastic Callicles, or even in Thrasymachus in the *Republic,* let alone the superior intellect of the Stranger from the *Sophist.* Phaedrus is a simpler soul. We might define him as a being who lives in order to receive pleasure from listening to speeches, sophistical speeches. So Socrates gives him that pleasure in order both to please and to persuade him. Not just once, but twice. Indeed, the sheer length of the Second Speech on *eros* might arouse our suspicion, for we will see in the *Gorgias* that Socrates hates long speeches, even delivered by the most eloquent of Sophists. Why is Socrates doing what he hates?

He is doing it in order to engender philosophical *eros* in Phaedrus. And this requires rhetoric. That is, rhetoric is the art by which the philosopher persuades the nonphilosopher to assume philosophical *eros*, to incline their soul toward truth. But to do this does not entail abandoning the art of rhetoric or indeed sophistry, which teaches that art, although it does so falsely, according to Socrates. Philosophy uses true rhetoric against false rhetoric. The philosopher is not just the anti-Sophist, but the *true* Sophist. This is a terribly important point. There is no philosophy without rhetoric and thus without the passage through sophistry. Does philosophy pass beyond what it sees as sophistry? Such is the question.

I am not suggesting that Phaedrus is stupid, but he's perhaps not the brightest spark in Athens, which was a city with many bright sparks. He keeps forgetting Socrates' argument and needs constant reminders: "So it seemed," he says late in the dialogue, "but remind me again how we did it" (277b). And this is during a discussion of recollection versus reminding. Phaedrus forgets the argument during a discussion of memory! Much of Socrates' rather obvious and extended passages of irony in the dialogue also seem to pass him by completely. Occasionally, Phaedrus will burst out with something like, "Socrates, you're very good at making up stories from Egypt or wherever else you want" (275b). Phaedrus is nice but a little dim.

Rehearsing a definition itself given by Gorgias in Plato's dialogue (*Gorgias,* 452e—it would appear that *Gorgias* was written prior to *Phaedrus*), rhetoric is defined as inducing persuasion in the soul of the listener. Socrates goes further and defines rhetoric as a *techne psychagogia,* an art of leading or directing the soul, a kind of bewitchment that holds the listener's soul spellbound (261a). Of course, the irony here is that it is precisely in these terms that Socrates criticizes the effects of tragic poetry in the *Republic,* which is why all forms of poetic *mimesis* cannot be admitted into a philosophically well-ordered city.

We have to keep this irony in mind because Socrates' speeches in the *Phaedrus* are precisely the kind of *psychagogia* of which he is apparently so suspicious in the *Gorgias*. Phaedrus, who loves speeches, is completely entranced. His soul is conjured by Socrates with complete success. The dialogue brings Phaedrus to love philosophy by loving philosophically. It might appear on a superficial reading that the question of *eros* disappears in the second half of the *Phaedrus*. But this is deceptive, for the forensic discussion of Lysias's speech on *eros* leads to a definition of artful or true speech that we will see presently. The dialogue culminates in a definition of the philosopher as the true lover or lover of truth (278d), by which point Phaedrus is completely persuaded by Socrates.

The intention of the *Phaedrus* is thus to persuade Phaedrus. Nothing more. Someone like Phaedrus. Someone not supersmart. The purpose of the dialogue, as Alexander Nehamas has persuasively suggested, is to inflame a philosophical *eros* in him that gives him the ability to distinguish bad rhetoric, of the kinds found in Lysias's speech and in Socrates' First Speech (and, by implication in Sophists like Gorgias), from true rhetoric, of the kind found in the Second Speech and then analyzed in the second half of the dialogue, using the techniques of division and collection that are extended in intricate detail in the labyrinthine discussions of the *Sophist*.[2] True rhetoric passes over into dialectic. Sophistry becomes philosophy.

The sheer reflexivity of the *Phaedrus* is astonishing. It is not only a piece of the most beautiful writing that, in the concluding pages, denounces writing. It is also an enactment of the very conditions of the true philosophical rhetoric theorized in the dialogue. It is the enactment of theory as practice. The opposite of a self-contradiction, the *Phaedrus* is a performative self-enactment of philosophy. The subject matter of the *Phaedrus* is rhetoric, true rhetoric. Its intention is to show that true *eros,* as opposed to the kind of vulgar pederasty that Socrates criticizes and that was the Athenian specialty of the time, is both subject *to* true rhetoric and the subject *of* true rhetoric. Philosophical *eros* is the effect of rhetoric, of language used persuasively.

Consider Socrates' conclusion about the nature of true or artful speech, which allows an interesting and possibly troubling question to be raised about the relation between philosophy and sophistry. Socrates says, toward the end of the *Phaedrus,* in an anticipation of the description of the method of division and collection,

> No one will ever possess the art of speaking, to the extent that any human being can, unless he acquires the ability to enumerate the sorts of characters to be found in any audience, to divide everything according to its kinds, and to grasp each single thing firmly by means of one form [*idea*]. And no one can acquire these abilities without great effort—a laborious effort a sensible man will make not in order to speak and act among human beings, but so as to be able to speak and act in a way that pleases the gods [*theois*]. (273e–74a)

To which the ever-so-slightly-dull Phaedrus exclaims, "What you've said is wonderful, Socrates—if only it could be done" (274a). But what needs to be emphasized here is that the huge effort involved in speaking well is not made, as it is with Sophists or with people who speak in a law court or public assembly, in order to please human beings, but in order to please those who are truly wise, namely the gods.

We are here brought face-to-face with a persistent theme in Plato, which was mentioned above and which also appears elsewhere in ancient Greek philosophy (Empedocles), the Hellenistic schools (Epicurus), neo-Platonism (Plotinus), and which could be said to resurface in modernity in Spinoza and when Hegel defines Spirit in the *Phenomenology of Spirit* as "God manifested in the midst of those who know themselves in the form of pure knowledge."[3] Against Protagoras, man is not the measure of all things. Such is sophistry. The philosophical measure—i.e., the measure *of* philosophy—is divine. Philosophy's highest ambition is the life of the gods or the divine life. Such is what Aristotle calls at the end of the *Nicomachean Ethics* (1177b–78a) *ho bios theois*, the life of the gods. In the famously enigmatic "digression" in the *Theaetetus*, Socrates says that the philosopher's body alone dwells within the city's walls. In thought, they are elsewhere. The philosopher lives by another measure, what Plato calls a divine measure, the life of the gods (172c–78c).

I am making this point in order to underline an essential distinction between philosophy and sophistry. If philosophy promises the life of the gods or some kind of blessedness that is more than human, then sophistry is resolutely human all too human, and confines itself to human affairs and expresses not disbelief but simply skepticism about the gods. The choice between philosophy and sophistry is a choice between the divine and the human. Which should one choose? It's hardly for me to say. The point is that one has to make a decision.

29

Gorgias, *a Philosophical Failure*

If the *Phaedrus* is a glorious success as a dialogue, then the *Gorgias* is an abject failure.[1] Socrates is peculiarly irritating throughout this dialogue. Before the action of the dialogue begins, Gorgias has been declaiming eloquently and extremely effectively in the house of Callicles. But Socrates doesn't want to go and hear Gorgias's speech, because he hates long speeches unless he gives them himself, as he often does, for example in *Phaedrus,* at the end of the *Gorgias* itself and with the myth of Er at the end of the *Republic,* which we will turn to in Chapter 38. Instead Socrates catches Gorgias at the end of his speech, when he is already tired. He then begins to badger him with questions.

Socrates stubbornly persists in asking what it is that Gorgias teaches. What is his art? Gorgias says he teaches the art of rhetoric, and he offers to make other people rhetoricians too. Rhetoric is the art of persuasive speech. If someone is taught rhetoric, then they possess a powerful weapon that can be used to persuade judges in the law courts and citizens in the assembly (452e). Led on a little deceptively by Socrates, Gorgias claims that rhetoric is not a particular art, but embraces all the other arts and is more powerful than medicine (456a–c).

Then something entirely predictable happens. When Gorgias says that this prodigious art of rhetoric must be used justly, Socrates seizes on the opportunity to interrogate him about the nature of justice and the good. Can rhetoric teach virtue? Gorgias declines to accept that virtue or excellence is anything in itself as distinct from the displays of excellence in specific practices. In the *Meno*, Socrates calls this position "a swarm of excellences" and demands, as ever, a single definition, a unique *eidos* or *idea* (72a). Incidentally, Aristotle, in the *Politics*, sees things differently and opposes those who seek a single, general definition of excellence, saying, "Far better . . . is the simple enumeration of the different forms of excellence, as followed by Gorgias" (1260a). Unlike Protagoras, Gorgias did not claim to be able to teach virtue. Rhetoric must be used justly and judiciously, but the teaching of the art of rhetoric does not make people good.

Socrates is having none of this, and while Gorgias is sidelined in the dialogue his place as interlocutor is taken by his acolyte Polus, and things begin to take a turn for the worse. Socrates refuses to accept that rhetoric is an art and calls it instead a knack, and then insists that it is the knack of flattery that is itself a branch of politics. Socrates says, "I call it [i.e., rhetoric] foul, as I do all ugly things" (463d). Matters deteriorate even further when Polus's place is taken by the tough and unforgiving Callicles. Now, I find Callicles very funny, a kind of fifth-century version of Nietzsche. Where most of Socrates' opponents, like Thrasymachus, eventually roll over and play along with his endless questions, Callicles refuses to play the game. Philosophy, Callicles insists, is nice enough to engage in when you're young, "But if one grows up and becomes a man and still continues in the same subject, why, the whole thing becomes ridiculous, Socrates" (485c). Philosophy is unmanly, "skulking in corners, whispering with two or three little lads, never pronouncing any large, liberal or meaningful utterance" (485d). "Such a man," Callicles goes on, "is one you can slap in the face with impunity" (486c). Socrates doesn't forget this insult. He can clearly bear a grudge. When the philosopher is fully grown, he should abandon his childish ways and take up "the fine art of business" (486c), make some money, and contribute to the life and upkeep of the city. Callicles sounds rather like my dad— God rest his soul.

For Callicles, justice is merely the set of conventions and customs that keep the strongest in check. Instead, we should follow what is naturally good, namely that which accords with power and strength. In other words, morality is the consequence of a slave revolt and is a consequence of *ressentiment* as Nietzsche will argue in *The Genealogy of Morals.* The only moral code is that which corresponds to our desire, and "A man who is going to live a full life must allow his desires to become as mighty as may be and never repress them" (491e–492a). Callicles is not just the progenitor of Nietzsche, he is also the precursor of Spinoza, Deleuze, and, on a certain reading, Lacan, where the ethical demand of psychoanalysis is not to give way to one's desire.

What is so fascinating about this dialogue is that Socrates can get no grip on Callicles because he refuses to share any common ground with him. At one extraordinary moment, Callicles simply refuses to answer Socrates' endless and, for him, endlessly piffling questions. At which point, after the final intervention of Gorgias himself (who is a model of decorum and even manners throughout the dialogue), Socrates simply starts to speak to himself and answer his own questions. Indeed, this goes on for several pages (506–509). Callicles quips to Socrates, "Go on and finish up by yourself, friend" (506c). Socrates talks to himself like a crazy person in the street.

The *Gorgias* perhaps shows the limits of Socratic dialogue, which makes one wonder what Plato was up to in writing it in the first place. What is the point of the dialogue? It is unclear. At the very least, in stark opposition to the *Phaedrus,* the *Gorgias* is a powerful example of how philosophy can go wrong when rhetoric is not used effectively or persuasively. Rather than bringing his interlocutor around to his point of view, all that Socrates does in the *Gorgias* is alienate his audience and show what a painful irritant he can be. Happily or unhappily, Callicles does not punch Socrates in the face, but allows him to drone on until he is finally done. The *Gorgias* is a fascinating failure. But what does it reveal?

The usual way the exchange between Callicles and Socrates is discussed in philosophy classes is to say that the example of Callicles shows how difficult it is to refute a determined immoralist. But it is not clear to me that Callicles is the immoralist in the *Gorgias*. This becomes clear, I think, in the final stages of the dialogue, when Callicles rejoins the discussion and matters turn to politics. Socrates asks Callicles whether there are any good statesmen in Athens. Callicles thinks for a moment and says that while there are none that he knows of that are still living, there are the examples of Themistocles, Cimon, and, most interesting, Pericles, who is said by Callicles to have died "only recently" (503c), which means that the dramatic date of the dialogue could be around 425 BCE, as Pericles died from the effects of the plague in 429 BCE.

Socrates vigorously denounces Pericles and his democratic reforms in Athens with the words "Pericles made the Athenians idle and cowardly and loquacious and greedy by instituting the system of public fees" (515e). To be clear, these were the fees that were provided to working citizens that enabled them to engage in the democratic practices of Athens, such as the assembly and council, but also to participate in the theater of the City Dionysia through the "Theoric Fund," which was given as a dole to enable citizens to pay the theater entrance fee. For Socrates, Pericles was a bad man and a pernicious influence in political life. And the same goes for Themistocles and Cimon: "Men say that they made our city great not recognizing that it is swollen and ulcerous" (518e). The inference is clear: Periclean democracy has corrupted the virtue of Athens, and this corruption has been aided and abetted by "those who call themselves Sophists" (519c).

Two striking things happen before the end of the dialogue, both of them very revealing. Firstly, Plato exploits the *anachronism* of a dialogue that is staged nearly thirty years before Socrates' trial and execution but is written long after it, to anticipate Socrates' condemnation by the city of Athens. If Attic tragedy uses the anachronism of Mycenaean Bronze Age past by juxtaposing it with the present of the Athenian *polis,* then Platonic dialogue exploits the more minimal, but still significant, time lapse between the date of the staging of the dialogue and the moment of its literary composition by Plato (it is a little like writing a dialogue now that is set in the 1960s, where everyone knows that the main protagonist was put to death by the state in the late 1980s). In response to Callicles' teasing that Socrates might well end up being dragged into court for his heretical views, Socrates grows morally indignant and wildly arrogant. He defensively declaims,

> In my opinion I am one of the few Athenians (not to say the only one) who has attempted the true art of politics, and the only one alive to put it into practice. (521d)

Socrates thinks he is entitled to this view because he does not have his eyes on personal gratification, but only on "the highest good, not on that which is merely pleasant" (521e). At this moment, in my view, Socrates is revealed as a moral absolutist where Plato anachronistically exploits the foreknowledge of Socrates' demise at the hands of the Athenians in order to justify the dogmatism of his position. And if politics is the life of the city's institutions, like the assembly and the council, then it is clear that the true art of politics is antipolitical.

Not only that. What is going on here is a massive idealization of the figure of the morally righteous but deathbound and solitary philosopher. This view finds its final vindication in a second feature, namely a story about the afterlife, which is how the *Gorgias* ends. Socrates recounts the myth of the judgment of souls in the afterlife in Hades by King Minos, who holds the urn of doom. At this moment of the last judgment, the final reckoning, "the philosopher, who has kept his own business and has not meddled with others' affairs during his lifetime" (526b), will be judged well and granted immortal life, Socrates says. By contrast, when Callicles—and by implication Gorgias—awaits the judgment on the state of his soul, he will be judged severely: "You will stand there with gaping mouth and reeling head no less than I here; and it will be you, perhaps, whom they will shamefully slap in the face and mistreat with every indignity" (527a). The Sophist may well slap the philosopher's face here in the city, but the Sophist's face will be slapped in the afterlife for eternity. Here, then, is the final refutation of sophistry, in the afterlife when all are judged according to their merits. From the standpoint of eternity, philosophy will finally be vindicated. From the standpoint of the divine life, the immortal life that is the philosopher's goal, the Sophist will appear to be the fool and the philosopher will be judged to be wise. As to the wisdom or folly of Socrates' case against Gorgias, I suppose we will find out the truth in the hereafter, if there is anything after here.

In case it might be thought that the *Gorgias* is an aberration, we should recall that the *Republic* also ends with a story about the immortality of the soul and the rewards of virtue in the afterlife. Philosophers might get killed here below, but they will be forever vindicated in the afterlife. At this point, we are now ready to turn to Plato's *Republic,* which I would like to read more carefully and in close detail, for it is here that the philosophical case against tragedy finds its full expression.

PART IV

Plato

30

Indirection

Tragedy presents a conflictually constituted world defined by ambiguity, duplicity, uncertainty, and unknowability, a world that cannot be rendered rationally fully intelligible through some metaphysical first principle or set of principles, axioms, tables of categories, or whatever. Tragedy is the experience of transcendental *opacity*. As such, the experience of tragedy poses a most serious objection to that invention we call philosophy. It is not surprising, then, that the best-known example of Plato's philosophical invention that we possess—the *Republic*—should turn on a refutation and refusal of tragedy.

*

Once again, it is important to note the deliberate anachronism of Plato's dramatic technique, where the staging of the dialogue and its composition are articulated around the hinge of Socrates' trial and execution in 399 BCE. Allusions to trials, threats of execution, and legal processes abound in the *Republic* and elsewhere in Plato. Estimates vary as to the dating of the setting of the dialogue (possibly 411 or 410 BCE, or even earlier, up to 422 BCE) and its writing (somewhere in the so-called Middle Dialogues, possibly around 380 BCE). It is a matter of much scholarly debate, but it is reasonable to say that the *Republic* is staged late in the Indian summer of Attic tragedy, and both Sophocles and Euripides would still have been alive. Plato would have been rather young at the time when the dialogue is set, and it is a matter of great interest that Socrates' main interlocutors are his brothers, Glaucon and Adeimantus, and Socrates alludes to Plato's father, Ariston, in his opening words (327a) and on three other occasions.

To reiterate the obvious point made above, Plato writes dialogues. He does not speak in his own voice—"Plato" is mentioned only twice in the dialogues. We don't know how to understand the use of dialogue, or even why the dialogues, which so clearly emphasize living speech, as in the closing pages of *Phaedrus*, were written down in dead letters. To label such a procedure a performative self-contradiction is seriously to underestimate Plato's artfulness. Are the written dialogues meant to be instructive pedagogical tools intended to be used inside Plato's Academy? Or were they intended to be used outside the Academy's walls in order to facilitate the dissemination of its teaching? We don't know. Are we to take seriously or literally everything that is written in the dialogues? Clearly not. Very early in the *Republic,* Thrasymachus bursts out with scornful laughter and says, "Here is that habitual irony of Socrates" (337a). Examples of such irony are legion in the dialogues, and it is unclear what, if anything, is to be accepted at face value. There is irony everywhere, but its depth is immeasurable and its relation to the apparent surface teaching of the dialogues is completely unclear.

In Plato, the discursive invention that is called philosophy, for reasons that we can only surmise, does not begin with direct discourse, but with indirect communication. That is, it is mimetic. It is an imitation of imagined or possibly real dialogues with Socrates. Platonic dialogue, as we will see, is *mimesis* against *mimesis*—a kind of meta-*mimesis*, an imitative antidote to imitation. If *mimesis* is poisonous, as Socrates will insist, then the cure is another *mimesis*, another poison, what Plato calls in *Phaedrus* a *pharmakos*. This might give the dialogues a homeopathic function—curing like with like—or indeed they might have an apotropaic effect, warding off certain perceived evils, perhaps especially political evils. But why does philosophy employ indirect communication and indeed drama in its refusal of tragic and comic drama? We don't know and can only guess. Is the extremity of Socrates' treatment of drama in the *Republic* caused by the proximity of the Platonic dialogues to the much better known and essentially public form of indirect communication they are seeking to displace? Attic drama is the competitor discourse that philosophy is seeking to echo, trump, and usurp. And if tragedy often turns upon the death of a hero, then the anachronism of Platonic dialogue, hinged around the historical fact of Socrates' trial and execution, works as dramatic irony, where the audience for the dialogues knows that the city where Socrates lives, breathes, and talks will be the very place that will soon condemn him to death. Indeed, in the *Republic,* Socrates repeatedly refers to his interlocutors as arresting him and placing him under a trial. As Hegel says, the death of Socrates replaces the death of the tragic hero, and drama comes off the stage to become the drama of civic life as such, as Athens declined from imperial hegemony to war-hungry populist democracy until it eventually submitted to the Macedonian pike and became a college town (which is the historical fate of many an erstwhile imperial metropolis).[1]

But Plato's lesson in indirection was not lost on various thinkers who came after him. Think of the pseudonymous indirection of Kierkegaard's authorship. And it should not be lost on us. Why do we privilege the idea of the philosopher speaking directly and apparently sincerely over the staging of an indirect and ironic drama? Why do we value monologue over dialogue or polylogue in philosophy?

Every few years, someone will claim to have discovered the key to Plato's dialogues, either with reference to some new philological or archeological discovery, some esoteric or secret doctrine, often Pythagorean, some mathematical and arithmetical pattern or code or even through the use of psychedelic drugs (a few years ago, I met a man in New York in a bar who called himself a shaman and told me he had discovered the secret to Plato while taking LSD). But there is no key, and anyone who claims to have found the key to understanding Plato is misguided. What we have are the texts, and our business is a hermeneutical work of interpretation. Although many very clever people, with much better Greek than I, have claimed to find a hidden doctrine in Plato, I remain rather skeptical. In what follows, I will offer a nakedly textualist reading of the *Republic* by looking simply at the words on the page.

31

A City in Speech

What does the title *Republic* mean? In Greek, it is *Politeia,* "on politics," or better, "on the order of human things in the city-state," where "city-state" translates *polis.* For Bloom, whose translation I will follow (but not his interpretation), *polis* is "city" and *politeia* is translated as "regime," in the sense of *ancien régime,* where the issue becomes one of imposing the right form on the matter of the city, and the regime is formed by the group that conducts that imposition and protects the city: the guardians. The *politeia* is the organizing form or essence of the *polis.*[1]

Now, how should the city be structured or ordered? (And what we are dealing with here is obviously modest by modern standards, perhaps 100,000 citizens or so, but this is not a small city, and early in Book II, Socrates variously calls the city "healthy," "luxurious," and even "feverish" [372e]). Well, it should be ordered rightly. It should be ordered around the right, the just, *dike,* that thing that twists and divides into its opposite in Attic tragedy. In tragedy, justice is divided between claim and counterclaim. In philosophy, justice is one; in tragedy, it is at least two. The *Politeia* is concerned with the just ordering of human things in the city-state.

The question that this raises, which is the main topic of the *Republic,* is: What is the right? What is justice? Justice is *dikaiosune,* which is closer to righteousness as a personal virtue than justice as the purported frame of an impersonal legal apparatus. The main topic of the dialogue concerns the nature of what is right, of *dike*. In Book I, after showing his characteristic reluctance to talk because he claims he doesn't know anything, Socrates philosophically cross-examines the conventional views of justice. For example, Polemarchus cites the poet Simonides' view that justice consists in giving to everyone what is fitting, giving them their due (332c). Socrates elegantly and swiftly inverts Simonides' view, at which point another of the auditors of the dialogue, Thrasymachus, who is "hunched up like a wild beast" (336b), bursts into life. He denounces what Socrates is saying as nonsense and sycophancy, and proposes another view of justice, which was associated with the teaching of the Sophists in Athens. For Thrasymachus, justice is simply the advantage of the stronger over the weaker, or, in looser terms, right equals might. On this view, all abstractly benevolent considerations of justice dissolve into assertions of strength, which can as readily be maintained by the unjust man as by the just, in fact more readily.

Although he admits to being terrified by Thrasymachus, Socrates unravels his argument in a few pages and shows that the just man is good and wise, and the unjust man unlearned and bad (350d). Therefore, justice cannot consist in strength or the assertion of advantage. At this point, Thrasymachus is described as producing "a wonderful quantity of sweat, for it was summer" (350d), and he blushes. It is an odd and touching moment. From this point on, Thrasymachus gives way to Socrates, saying repeatedly that he will let him feast on the argument: "Let that be the fill of your banquet" (354a). Socrates inverts Thrasymachus's claim, showing that the just man must be happier than the unjust man; he has *eudaimonia*, which means something much closer to flourishing or blessedness than the more modern pursuit of happiness. Socrates argues that whatever justice might be, it must consist in something functioning in terms of its excellence, its *arete,* its virtue. The examples Socrates uses here as elsewhere are always artisanal: when a carpenter makes a table and it performs its function, then this is an excellence, the excellence of tableness and so forth (Socrates admires people with practical skills, although he had none himself). So, justice is a kind of excellence, when a human being is functioning in the terms that are proper to it, but Book I ends with Socrates asserting that we are no closer to understanding justice "so long as I do not know what the just is" (354c). Socrates concludes, "As a result of the discussion I know nothing."

Picking up on the freighted legal metaphor of being arrested by his interlocutors, Socrates very much hopes that the discussion might now be at an end and he might be "freed from argument" (357a). But at that precise point, Plato's brothers step forward to arrest Socrates, deeply unsatisfied with the way in which Thrasymachus had given up his argument in a blush of shame. First Glaucon and then—even more vehemently—Adeimantus seek to restate Thrasymachus's argument in order to provoke Socrates into a response. What is particularly fascinating is the way in which Adeimantus offers a series of citations from Homer, Hesiod, and other poets that show what a confusing picture of virtue and vice is offered by the Greek myths, particularly when it comes to the aberrant behavior of the gods (362c–68a). Indeed, the whole argument about poetry in Books II, III, and X that we will consider in detail is a direct response to Adeimantus's argument that if the myths of the Greeks present such a confused picture of virtue and vice, then "What do we suppose they do to the souls of the young men who hear them?" (365a).

Eventually, Socrates submits to the pleading of Plato's brothers and says simply, "So I spoke my opinion." The entire remaining argument of the *Republic* kicks off from this point. It turns out that Socrates has quite a lot of opinions. His first move is very interesting. He compares justice in one man with justice in a city and asks, "Is a city bigger than one man?" At which point, the dialogue turns to the nature of justice in cities and Socrates begins to build his city in speech that is the vision of the *Republic*: " 'If we should watch a city coming into being in speech,' I said, 'would we also see its justice coming into being, and its injustice?' "(369a).

The question of justice becomes the question of the nature of the city, and the *Republic* is the upbuilding of a city in speech. As Socrates coyly and reluctantly reveals at the end of Book V, in an admission that he expects to be drowned out with laughter, in order for a city to be just, it must be governed by philosophers, where political power and philosophy coincide (473d). The question whether such a city can ever come into being is persistently raised by Plato's brothers, but the response to the question is always deferred or Socrates uses irony to demur. The question is whether the many, the *hoi polloi* who make up the body of the existing city, can ever be philosophical. The stark conclusion that is reached in Book VI is that this is impossible (494a). The inference from this conclusion is that the few, namely the guardian-philosophers, must govern the just city.

One more detail is important. The setting for the *Republic,* as is the case with many of the dialogues, might appear to be incidental, but is strangely revealing. It takes place at the Piraeus, the port of Athens, which is six miles from the Acropolis. Although some distance away, Athens was connected to the Piraeus by "the long walls" and was technically and legally still part of the city. Socrates and Glaucon had gone down to the Piraeus to observe the festival of Bendis, a female goddess, possibly Thracian, and newly imported. Ports, then as throughout history, are locations for novelty, even religious innovation. Also, the dialogue takes place in the home of Polemarchus, son of Cephalus, an extremely wealthy metic, a resident alien, an Athenian green card holder. Cephalus is described as "very old" (328c), and Socrates has not seen him for some time, as the latter very rarely visited the Piraeus. The initial discussion of justice between Cephalus and Socrates turns on moneymaking and what the greatest good might be that accrues from wealth. Cephalus says that the possession of money is most worthwhile for the "decent and orderly" man, namely the just man. After this brief opening exchange, Cephalus excuses himself, for he has to go and make sacrifices, and he hands down the argument—like a trust fund—to his heir, Polemarchus (331d).

So, the *Republic* takes place officially within the city of Athens, but at a certain crucial distance from the center, during the festival for a new foreign goddess, in the house of a very wealthy metic. Only men engage in the dialogue. And there is an audience, who are pointedly and individually named (328b). Eleven men are present in the house, a soccer-team-sized number, although five of them do not speak. And here the technique of anachronism expresses a deeper but darker and more mysterious purpose. Some years after the dialogue was set, in 404 BCE, Athens suffered defeat and humiliation by Sparta at the end of the long Peloponnesian Wars. Democracy was suspended, and an oligarchy was established in Athens, with the rule of the "Thirty Tyrants." Polemarchus was executed during the oligarchy, presumably because he was judged an enemy of the regime. And a few years after democracy was restored in 403 BCE, Socrates was tried and executed. One of the accusations made against him was that some members of the oligarchy had been followers of Socrates, which would indeed appear to be true. Given the very clear arguments against democracy in the *Republic,* but also his critiques of oligarchy and tyranny, Socrates' building of a city in speech where political power and philosophy would coincide expresses a clear, contrary intention. The practicability of such an intention is left, like speech itself, expressing itself emptily into the air.

32

Being Dead Is Not a Terrible Thing

In Book II, Socrates and Plato's brothers begin to color in the contours of their imagined city. It becomes more and more elaborate, with relishes, perfume, incense, courtesans, and cakes, and with rhapsodes, actors, choral dancers, swineherds, and servants, not to mention doctors, who are required to treat the effects of such urban excess (373a–c). Socrates then assumes as a simple statement of fact that such a city will eventually go to war (373e). It is not a question of the good or evil of war, but rather that when war happens—as it will—who will protect the city? Who will be the guardians of the city? Such guardians must possess the apparently contrary virtues of kindness and cruelty: kindness to their fellow citizens and cruelty to the city's enemies. Socrates makes the interesting comparison with "noble dogs" (375d), tail-waggingly nice to their familiars while barking frighteningly at people they don't know. Socrates stresses that such canine virtue is a learned response, which the guardians must also acquire. So, the guardians, like dogs, must be lovers of learning.

It is on this basis that the argument moves swiftly to the nature of learning and the precise content of the guardians' education, or *paideia*. For the Greeks, education was the rearing or bringing up of a child, which is teaching, but also discipline, training, and correction. For the Athenians, it was restricted to boys, although in Book IV of the *Republic* Socrates will challenge this practice by extending it, in a more Spartan fashion, to girls as well. So, the question to be considered is the content of education into what is right or the just. As will become clear in the later books of the *Republic,* what the interlocutors in the dialogue are imagining is the formation of a protective, governing class of the city, where the major task of education is turning the guardians into philosophers, philosophers who would govern, namely philosopher kings.

Socrates asks Plato's brothers, "Come, then, like men telling tales in a tale and at their leisure, let's educate the men in speech" (376d). And then he immediately adds, "What is the education?" We should note that the entire itinerary of the analysis of poetry and drama in Books II, III, and X, and which will be followed in this chapter, arises in the context of education, and it recognizes itself to be mythic, to be telling tales in a tale. The question of which myths we should admit into a just city is itself mythic. With this awareness of intense self-reflexivity, or what we might today call metafiction, the question of Socratic irony pops up its head once again: Is this discussion of education ironical? Are we meant to take Socrates' proposals seriously or is there a massive, unspoken but implicit irony at work in the text, where its explicit, exoteric arguments disguise a hidden, esoteric intention? We simply don't know, and we can never truly give the answer to such a question because the only evidence we have is the dialogues themselves. Once the question of irony is raised in Plato's dialogues—and it is suggested everywhere—then a vertiginous, infinite, and irresolvable process of doubt insinuates itself in the reader. It is like climbing quickly to the top of a long spiral staircase in a tall building and turning around, slightly out of breath, to see the floors beneath slide out of focus and the ground far below fall away. All we can do is to hold on tight to the banisters and try and maintain our balance.

The first business of education becomes the supervision of the production of stories, in other words, censorship, of what sorts of poetry are to be allowed in the city. The stories in view are principally those of Homer and Hesiod (377d), which provided the core to a classical Greek education and were, of course, the primary sources for the stories in Attic drama. It is difficult to overstate the radicality of Socrates' gesture here. Nothing in our world, with the possible exception of Shakespeare in certain corners of it, has the canonical status that the Greeks assigned to Homer in particular. The way in which Socrates censors Homer and the rest must have been truly shocking to Athenian ears. Socrates says, "Adeimantus, you and I aren't poets [*poietai*] right now but founders of a city" (379a). The judgments made about poetry are not, then, "aesthetic" in our modern sense, but political. The chief objection to poetry, particularly tragedy—which is first explicitly mentioned on 379a, and Aeschylus's no longer extant "Sorrows of Niobe" is quoted on 380a—is that it misrepresents or "images badly" the nature of the gods and heroes. The claim is that poetry that does this will have to be excluded from a philosophically well-ordered *polis*. Socrates says that god must always be represented truthfully, "such as he is" (379a). Why? The answer is simple: a god is the cause only of good things, not of bad. To which Adeimantus dutifully replies to Socrates, "What you say is in my opinion very true" (379b).

A god doesn't tell lies and is wholly free from falsehood (*apseudos*) (382e). If this is the case, then dramatic representations that show the gods lying or deceiving human beings, which are abundant in epic and tragic poetry, are misrepresentations and must be excised from the educational matter given to trainee guardians. At which point, Socrates presses the delete button on Homeric epic poetry (379d–e). But the wider theatrical context is also clear from the quotations from Aeschylus and the allusion to the misrepresentation of gods in tragedies (381d). Book II finishes with Socrates saying that although there is much that can be praised in Homer or indeed Aeschylus, such misrepresentations will not be allowed. If such a thing happens, Socrates says in a direct allusion to the practice of the *choregos,* the sponsor of dramas at festivals, then the consequence is clear and severe:

> "When someone says such things about the gods, we'll be harsh and not provide a chorus, and we'll not let the teachers use them for education of the young, if our guardians are going to be god-revering and divine insofar as a human being can possibly be."
>
> "I am in complete agreement with these models," Adeimantus said, "and would use them as laws." (383c)

Having established the framework for the argument, Socrates goes on in Book III to draw the consequences by establishing the rules for poetry in the just *polis.* Poetry must guarantee bravery in the guardians, which means that they should not fear death. To achieve this, all gloomy depictions of the afterlife, for example Odysseus's descent into the underworld, must be excised. "They must be deleted?" Adeimantus asks, to which Socrates calmly replies, "Yes." Here Socrates introduces the theme of the "decent man," the gentleman, the *epiekes,* who will reappear throughout the dialogue: "We surely say that a decent man will believe that for the decent man—who happens to be his comrade—being dead is not a terrible thing."

In addition to believing that death ain't really so bad, Socrates introduces another key stipulation that will grow in importance throughout the *Republic,* the need to eliminate all excessive lamentation (387e). This is a clear attack on tragedy, where there is very much lamentation, as we have seen in earlier chapters. Think back to what was said about rage, grief, and war, and it is clear that tragedy is the art of lamentation, whether we think of the entirety of Aeschylus's *Persians* and *The Suppliant Maidens,* Sophocles' *Ajax,* or the last third of *Oedipus the King.* Many other examples could be given. Socrates is against lamentation.

It is effeminate and the sort of behavior carried out by foreigners and women, occasionally even by foreign women like Hecuba, Medea, or Atossa. Socrates underlines the gender dimension of lament: "So, we'd be right in taking out the wailings of renowned men and we'd give them to women—and not to the serious ones at that" (388a).

Socrates presents a similar argument about laughter. The guardians must not be lovers of laughter, "For when a man lets himself go and laughs mightily, he also seeks a mighty change to accompany his condition" (388e). And although Socrates knows that he is "telling tales in a tale" and basically lying, the same argument is made about lies. Amazingly, Socrates says that he will regard as untrue stories that do not represent the gods properly or that represent heroes in a poor light, such as Achilles dragging the body of Hector around the tomb of Patroclus: "It must not be believed that he did" (391b), "We'll deny that all this is truly told" (391b), "Then let's not believe it" (391c). Namely, that if Homer says that Poseidon's son and Zeus undertook terrible rapes, then we will simply deny it. The argument here tends toward craziness. Just try to imagine Homer's *Iliad* without Achilles' rage or the stories of the gods without their numerous sexual indiscretions, such as Zeus raping Leda and then Ganymede to show that boys are just as good rape targets as girls. All such stories must simply be excised from the guardians' education in order to avoid any kind of excess and encourage self-control and the moderation of desire, the famous virtue of *sophrosune*. After filleting a passage from the *Odyssey* that simply describes a banquet table covered with bread, meat, and wine, Socrates says, "Do you think that's fit for a young man to hear for his self-mastery?" (390b–c). The aim of the guardians' education, which will later be revealed to be the key to a philosophical education, is to produce self-mastery. The moderate virtue of the decent man requires the elimination of lamentation and laughter in equal measure, for they both threaten mastery of self with an emotional excess.

33

The Moral Economy of Mimesis

In a swift transition that will prove to be determinative for the entire subsequent argument of the *Republic*, especially Book X, Socrates switches from the content of stories to their form or style (*lexis*) (392c). It is here that Socrates introduces the distinction between narrative and imitation, or *diegesis* and *mimesis*, a point that takes a little while to sink in with Adeimantus. *Diegesis* is pure narration, that is, it describes events in one's own person. *Mimesis* is a narration that proceeds by imitation, not by speaking in one's own voice, but speaking in the voice of another, as with mimicry.

> "But, when he gives a speech as though he were someone else, won't we say that he then likens his own style as much as possible to that of the man he has announced as the speaker?"
> "We'll say that, surely."
> "Isn't likening himself to someone else, either in voice or in looks, the same as imitating the man he likens himself to?"
> "Surely."
> "Then, in this case, it seems he and the other poets use imitation in making their narrative." (393b–c)

Socrates' point is that whereas narration is admissible in the just city, some *mimesis* should not be admitted because the guardians might seek to imitate bad characters and become bad themselves. The question then immediately becomes—this is our question—

whether tragedy and comedy should be admitted into the city. Socrates gives a strangely expurgated and rather dull third-person rendering of the opening of Homer's *Iliad,* revealingly adding, "I'll speak without meter; I'm not poetic" (393c–394b). Such, he says, is narrative without imitation. The opposite of the latter is imitation without narration, and Adeimantus then gets the point and understands the payoff, "That I understand too . . . that's the way it is with tragedies" (394b). To which Socrates replies, "Your supposition is most correct."

The whole matter of education becomes a question of the *economy of mimesis,* which cuts through the three classical genres. If drama is pure *mimesis,* and lyric is pure *diegesis,* where the poet (Pindar, Sappho, or whoever) speaks in their own person, then epic employs a mixture of *diegesis* and *mimesis.* Adeimantus goes on,

> "I divine," he said, "that you're considering whether we'll admit tragedy and comedy into the city or not." (394d)

To which Socrates replies with insouciance,

> "Perhaps," I said, "and perhaps something more than this. You see, I myself really don't know yet, but wherever the argument, like a wind, tends, thither we must go." (394d)

So, the question of style leads immediately to the question of whether tragedy and comedy will be admitted into the city. At this point, the economy of *mimesis* becomes a *moral economy.* The guardians are permitted to mimic the good and can use a mixture of *diegesis* and *mimesis* for this purpose. But the guardians should never mimic the bad, and they must always speak in their own voices. There then follows a rather long and slightly absurd list of items that the guardians must not imitate. They must not mimic women, "either a young woman or an older one," and especially not tragic women, who are "caught in the grip of misfortune, mourning and wailing" (395d–e). They must not imitate slaves, or cowards and criminals. And it goes without saying that a guardian cannot in any circumstance be an actor, especially when they liken themselves to the mad, as with someone playing, say, Heracles. They also should not imitate blacksmiths, craftsmen, or men rowing triremes (396a). Nor must they imitate the neighing of horses, the bellowing of bulls, or the roaring of the sea and thunder. At this point, the list of things to avoid mimicking becomes slightly ridiculous: wind, hailstorms; the noises of axles and wheels; trumpets, flutes, and all musical instruments; the barking of dogs, the bleating of sheep, or the singing of birds (397a–b).

The assumption that is driving the moral economy of *mimesis* is that in the just city it is a question of one man, one job. A shoemaker is just a shoemaker and not a part-time ship's pilot. A farmer is a farmer and not a judge along with his farming, a data analyst cannot be a professional juggler along with his analyzing, and so on. In the regime described by Socrates, "There's no double man among us, nor a manifold one, since each man does one thing" (397d–e). It is this refusal of the double man that prepares the ground for the initial exclusion of the poet from the city, for the poet is a mimetic artist whose skill derives from imitating many kinds of things. Socrates says, and note the well-mannered but biting irony of these lines,

Now, as it seems, if a man who is able by wisdom to become every sort of thing and to imitate all things should come to our city, wishing to make a display of himself and his poems, we would fall on our knees before him as a man sacred, wonderful and pleasing; but we would say that there is no such man among us in the city, nor is it lawful for such a man to be born there. We would send him to another city, with myrrh poured over his head and crowned with wool, while we ourselves would use a more austere and less pleasing poet and teller of tales for the sake of benefit, one who would imitate the style of the decent man and would say what he says in those models that we set down as laws at the beginning when we undertook to educate the soldiers. (398a–b)

Behind the politeness of these words is the quiet ferocity of a confident moral conviction that the arguments about poetry set out in Books II and III have the status and force of binding civic law. What is being excluded from the city is the person who can display or mimic a multiplicity of roles, who can become one thing and now another (which is precisely what, for example, Arendt praises about Athenian democracy in *The Human Condition*).[1] Plurality in the city is a corrosive evil that is inflamed by the plurality in the self that imitation ignites. In the just city, there will be no double man, and the doubling over of the self and the city that is definitional of drama can have no place in education.

34

Political Forms and Demonic Excess

Having followed closely the line of Plato's argument in the opening books of the *Republic*, I now want to make a large leap toward the end of the dialogue and focus closely on Book X, where Socrates will return to his claims about poetry with a more far-reaching and violent metaphysical and moral insistence whose target is tragedy. Indeed, although there is a clear, developing line to the argument of the ten books of the *Republic,* the argument is not simply linear. The dialogue is more rounded or spherical like an onion, with multiple layers, whose metaphysical core is the idea of the good. If justice is a virtue or excellence, then it consists in the soul orienting itself toward the good. The highest form of knowledge and its object is the good, which is approached in the argument of Book VI. But, crucially, the good is not directly defined. When Socrates is pressed by Glaucon to define the good, he refuses, confessing his usual ignorance. The good is the source of all things that are, which are in being. But the good itself is not being or existence since it is the cause of being. Socrates says that the good is "beyond being [*epekeina tes ousias*], exceeding it in dignity and power" (509b). To which Glaucon rather ridiculously replies, "Apollo, what a demonic excess" (509c). If the good is the core of the *Republic,* then it is a divine excess that cannot be caught directly in speech, but only approached indirectly through myth. Instead of defining the good, Socrates tells Glaucon that he will describe children of the good, in the three famous analogies that fill the center of the *Republic:* the sun, the divided line, and the cave.

The purpose of education is to orient the soul toward the good, which is also the goal of philosophy. The obvious inference from that claim, which emerges gradually in Book V and gathers momentum from that point on in the dialogue, is that the guardians must be philosophers. In Book VI, Socrates finally confesses to Adeimantus,

> "My friend, I shrank from saying what has now been dared anyhow," I said. "And let's now dare to say this: philosophers must be established as the most precise guardians." (503b)

The education whose content and form have been the focus of the early books of the dialogue becomes more and more clearly an apprenticeship in philosophy. If the guardians must be philosophers, then the inverse is also true: philosophers must be guardians. Namely, the philosopher must be compelled to govern the just city because he is acquainted with the form of the good. The real virtue of this claim, to my eyes, is that a philosopher by definition wants to study philosophy and focus on the divine things, and not be involved in the day-to-day, dirty human business of government. And this is the reason why philosophers *should* govern, because they have the least enthusiasm to do so. The city with the most eager rulers is the worst, and political power should never be given to those who want it most. Once the philosopher has completed the ascent out of the cave and toward the light of the good, then he must be compelled to go back down into the darkness and govern, even if the people might kill him, as they do Socrates (517a). The inhabitants of the cave are living through a dark dream, and the ascent toward the good is described in Heracleitean terms, as a process of awakening (520c). If those who have awoken are compelled to govern, then there is a chance that the city will not be full of factions fighting over shadows, but will be a just city whose foundation is knowledge of the good.

Once the form of the just city has been established in speech— and this is a city of speech that exists in language alone and not in reality—the question that is raised is how it compares with really existing political forms. Such is the topic of Book VIII, where Socrates and Plato's brothers engage in a critical taxonomy of regimes based on honor, money, equality, and raw political power: timocracy, oligarchy, democracy, and tyranny. Indeed, in dissecting the flaws of these four political forms, Socrates compares himself to a judge in a theatrical *agon,* reviewing various dramatic choruses (580b). What is particularly important for our purposes is the way in which democracy slides into tyranny and the role that theater plays in this transition.

In many ways, the argument of Book VIII turns on the question of excess. An excessive desire for honor gives way, in the transition to oligarchy, to an excessive love of moneymaking, which produces vast inequality between the rich and the poor. Democracy comes into being as a bloody rebellion of the poor against the rich (557a). It is founded on equality, and Socrates admits that "It is probably the fairest of regimes . . . just like a many-colored cloak." In other words, democracy looks great. It is like an old Benetton advert resplendent with brightly colored diversity. It is particularly attractive, he adds, to "boys and women," who enjoy looking at "many-colored things." But the excess within democracy is freedom, which is held to be the highest political good. The problem with freedom is that it encourages the license to do whatever one wishes, and this leads to a systematic confusion of public goods with private pleasures. In democracy, as a consequence, freedom rapidly descends into licentiousness and the gratification of private desires.

In other words, democracy leads to anarchy (562e), and out of this many-colored populist chaos of desire emerges the figure of the tyrant, for whom political power and excessive private desire coincide. Tyranny flows from democracy because the tyrant is voted into office as he seems to offer everyone what they want. Indeed, Socrates slyly insists, at first the tyrant doesn't appear at all tyrannical because he smiles and greets everyone he meets (566d). He grants freedom from debts, appears to distribute land to the people, and pretends "to be gracious and gentle to all" (566e). It is in this subtle way that excessive license dialectically inverts freedom into slavery, and the very people who welcomed the tyrant into power are shackled into subjugation to him.

This is where tragedy becomes politically hugely important. Tragedy deforms democracy into tyranny. Such is the force of Plato's critique of theatrocracy. At the end of Book VIII, in the only *explicit* reference to Euripides in the *Republic* (there are many implicit allusions), Socrates says with a huge dose of irony,

> "It's not for nothing," I said, "that tragedy in general has the reputation of being wise and, within it, Euripides of being particularly so."
> "Why is that?"
> "Because, among other things, he uttered the phrase, the product of shrewd thought, 'tyrants are wise from intercourse with the wise.' And he plainly meant that these men we just spoke of are the wise with whom the tyrant has intercourse."
> "And he and the other poets," he said, "extol tyranny as a condition 'equal to that of a god' and much else too."
> "Therefore," I said, "because the tragic poets are wise, they pardon us, and all those who have regimes resembling ours, for not admitting them into the regime on the ground that they make hymns to tyranny." (568a–b)

Tragedy is not to be admitted into the just city described in the *Republic*. The tragic poets are the lackeys of tyrants who receive huge wages and honor for their corrupt labor. In "gathering crowds, and hiring fine, big and persuasive voices, they draw the regimes toward tyrannies and democracies" (568c). Tragedy is the art form of tyranny that, through its very popular appeal and by *appearing* to satisfy the free desires of its spectators, enslaves citizens and turns them into subjects of spectacle. With the sound of Socrates' savage critique of tragedy ringing in our ears, let's turn in detail to Book X.

35

What Is Mimesis?

Let's begin with a metaquestion. With the confrontation of the philosopher with the tyrant and the victory of the former over the latter at the end of Book IX, at least in the imaginings of the three interlocutors, the argument of the *Republic*, namely the apology for the philosophically well-ordered city, would appear to be at an end. In sharp contradistinction to the excess that marked each of the four political forms, the philosopher-guardian maintains moderation of soul and body and keeps his eye "fixedly on the regime within him" (591d). By maintaining attention on the just city that lives in the soul and whose outlines are described in the speeches of the *Republic*, he won't mind the corruption and excess that characterize what Socrates calls "the political things" of life in his "fatherland" (592a). Glaucon replies,

> "I understand," he said. "You mean he will in the city whose foundation we have now gone through, the one that has its place in speeches, since I don't suppose it exists anywhere on earth." (592b)

To which Socrates says, in the last words of Book IX,

> "But in heaven, perhaps a pattern is laid up for the man who wants to see and found a city within himself on the basis of what he sees. It doesn't make any difference whether it is or

will be somewhere. For he would mind the things of this city alone, and of no other." (592b)

It doesn't matter whether the just city described in the *Republic* exists anywhere in the world. What is important is that the city has been inscribed onto the structure of the soul of the philosopher by following a pattern in heaven. With these remarks, the dialogue about the city that takes place at its portly outer reaches in the private house of a rich metic merchant would appear to be at an end.

And yet, the dialogue is not over. We turn to Book X and return to the argument about poetry. Book X is thus a kind of appendix. But—and here's the metaquestion—why does this appendix to the *Republic* exist at all? What purpose does it serve, given that it only restates the arguments of Book III and the initial exclusion of the poets from the philosophically well-ordered city? Might it not, at the very least, underline the importance of those arguments to the overall vision of the *Republic*? I think so. It might also serve another purpose, about the possible rewards of a just and moderate philosophical life, but we will come back to that.

Allan Bloom claims that Socrates returns to the argument of Book III because the latter dealt only with the uses and abuses of poetry in the education of the warrior-guardians. Yet Homer is teacher of all the Greeks, and the legitimacy of the claims of Book III needs to be extended into a more general attack on Homer and the tragic poets. Bloom writes, rightly, "Poetry is *the* opponent," and "Homer and the other great poets constitute the respectable tribunal before which philosophy is tried."[1] In a sense, then, the trial and execution of Socrates is a trial by poetry, by a dramatically legitimated city, a theatrocracy, the tattered remnants of the democratic regime restored after the humiliation of Athens by Sparta at the end of the Peloponnesian Wars and the rule by the Thirty Tyrants. Perhaps the ultimate dramatic irony of the *Republic* is that rather than Socrates having to make an apology to the theatrically legitimated (and hence illegitimate) city, the poets or the poetry's defenders should make an apology to him if they want to be let back in the city. The philosopher, as we saw in the *Gorgias,* is someone who can bear a grudge.

Socrates begins by suggesting that although he and Plato's brothers were right in the way in which they founded their city, they were particularly right in their reflection on poetry, namely the exclusion of *mimesis.* "Between us," Socrates insinuates, as if he were speaking in confidence, which in a sense is true, as they are talking in a private house (595b). Socrates' fear here is that his interlocutors will betray his confidence and give his argument away to the *mimetikous,* "the mimetic tribe," the imitators, the tragic poets (595b). His claim is that such imitations maim the thought of those that experience them, unless they have a remedy, and the Greek word is *pharmakon* (595b), a poison that is also a cure. Socrates speaks of his friendship for Homer and a shame that he feels before him, "which has possessed me since childhood" (595c), doubtless because of the nature of Greek education. He asserts that Homer is "the first teacher and leader of all these fine tragic things" (595c), a claim that is reiterated a few pages later when Homer is described as the "leader" (598d) of tragedy. Two things should be noted here: firstly, the clear linking and direct lineage between Homer and tragedy, between epic and dramatic poetry; and secondly, the massive irony of Socrates' sentiments, where the reference to "fine [*kalon*] tragic things" should be put alongside his biting remarks on the fine democratic regime of the city of Athens, the very city that would kill him. "Still," Socrates says, although Homer is truly fine, "a man must not be honored before the truth" (595c). At which point, Socrates bluntly demands of Glaucon, "Then listen, or rather, answer."

At which point, we get a rare and explicit statement of Socratic dialectical method. Socrates asks his characteristic *ti estin* question, namely "What is *x*?": "Could you tell me what imitation in general is?" (595c). Socrates is not concerned with any relativity of judgment with regard to some matter, namely what something might be for the Athenians or the Spartans or indeed the Barbarians, but with what that matter is as such, universally, or in its being. Socrates then says that this question that asks after a universal form has to be pursued by "our customary procedure" (*methodou*) (596a). *Methodos* bears within it a *hodos,* a path, way, or road. The method consists in postulating a single form or idea (*eidos*) for each set of particulars, each of the "manys" to which we apply the same name, requiring one form or idea from the many things, as we saw already in *Phaedrus.* Immediately, Socrates invokes one of his trademark artisanal examples. When a craftsman builds a couch or a chair, he fabricates it not by looking at the appearance of such an object, but by intuiting the idea or form. On this basis, Socrates makes the distinction, to which he will repeatedly refer, between appearances or things that look like they are (*phainomena*) and beings (*onta*) as they are in their truth (*aletheia*) (596e).

The claim is that the mimetic artist cannot attain to the being of the thing that is depicted, its *eidos,* and consequently because that which is true is only that which has being, the artwork is untrue. In this way, what Heidegger describes in his *Nietzsche* as "the raging discordance between art and truth" opens up.[2] The discursive invention that Plato calls philosophy creates a discord between the realm of appearances or phenomena and that of truth and being. Metaphysics is this gap between being and appearance, the division of the one world of experience into two domains.

Socrates then asks Glaucon to imagine another kind of craftsman. Not one who, like the carpenter, expertly makes particular entities like couches and chairs by following their forms, but someone who can make everything under heaven, earth, and even below in Hades. Glaucon exclaims, ironically, "That's a clever and wonderful man you speak of. . . . That's quite a wonderful Sophist" (596c–d). This sophistical, übercraftsman is the mirror man, who can create images of everything by simply holding up a mirror and carrying it around with him everywhere. To which Glaucon replies, "Yes . . . so that they look like they *are;* however, they surely *are* not in truth" (596e). The craftsman is then revealed to be the painter, the mimetic artist, who creates images of all things, but not the appearances of things or the things themselves in their being. On this basis, Socrates returns to his furniture maker example and postulates three different orders of couch (Socrates, like most philosophers who come after him, likes to give examples with medium-sized dry goods like furniture. He really likes couches, carpentry, and craft. Philosophy with its IDEA is often like a trip to IKEA):

1. The form of the couch in its being or truth, "Which, we would say, I suppose, a god produced" (597b);
2. The couchmaker's or carpenter's couch, which is in the realm of appearance;
3. The painter's or mirror man's couch, which is *mimesis.*

The claim is that both the god and the couchmaker make things, either the form of a thing or its appearance, but the painter or mirror man just imitates. Therefore, the work of the artist is at a third remove from being or that which is.

Socrates then immediately draws the inference from this argument to reveal the true target of the critique: "Therefore this will apply to the maker of tragedy [*tragodopoios*], if he is an imitator; he is naturally third from a king and the truth" (597e).

Having reached agreement about the nature of imitation and its relation to appearance and being, Socrates returns, with what can only be described as obsessiveness, to the charge against tragedy and Homer, as the tragedians' alleged chief. Homer is meant to be the educator of vice and virtue among the Greeks because he is supposed to have and offer knowledge of such things. Yet, if the metaphysical argument that Socrates has just offered is true, then Homer is like a mirror man, at a third remove from truth. He is an imitator and "Such a man makes what look like beings but are not" (599a). In a revealing formulation, Homer is described as "the craftsman of a phantom" (*eidolon*) (599d). This language recalls the allegory of the cave, namely that what Homer makes are idols, the kinds of things paraded behind the wall in the cave, whose shadows the captives are bound to see. Cranking up the attack even further, Socrates pretends to address Homer directly and asks him which cities have been reformed on the basis of his poetry. Has Homer ever produced a system of legislation, such as Lycurgus did for Sparta or Solon produced for Athens? Indeed, in seeming indifference to the lessons of the *Iliad,* Socrates asks, What war has been fought on Homeric principles? Unlike Thales, whose discoveries could mathematically predict eclipses and solstices, Homer produced no inventions of any use (599d–600b).

The conclusion is that Homer had no practical skills. Of course, this raises the fascinating further metaquestion: Does Socrates have any practical skills? There is a peculiar reflexivity to Socrates' critique of Homer. Socrates claims that Homer is not a reliable teacher of the most important human things, the implicit assumption being that it is better to be a doer than a knower or that the test of knowledge is action. In passages like this, Socrates begins to sound like some kind of pragmatist. But, as Bloom points out, "a moment's reflection makes one aware that these charges against Homer apply at least as well to Socrates. He was not a lawgiver, a leader in war, an inventor, or a professor in the manner of Protagoras."[3] Socrates had no practical skills, but just liked thinking about carpenters. Socrates calls Homer "an imitator of phantoms of virtue" (600e), but might not the same accusation be made about Socrates? He creates phantoms of virtue in speech that are, as he says, true in heaven, but not in the world. This metaquestion is compounded by the obvious fact that if Homer is an imitator, then so is Plato, who writes mimetic dialogues, sometimes even featuring members of his own family. The reflexivity of the critique of Homer also reflects on the mimetic procedure in which

Plato was engaged. It has to be asked: What cities did Plato successfully found? What practical inventions did his dialogues produce? What wars were waged on Platonic principles? Socrates insists that the artist knows nothing and the art of imitation has no serious value, but is "a kind of play and not serious" (602b). But is not Plato also an imitator, a mimic of Socrates? And if that is true, then by virtue of what exactly should we take seriously the Platonic dialogues? Are they not simply an extraordinarily interesting form of play, a dramatic antidrama?

36

Philosophy as Affect Regulation

At this point, the angle of Socrates' questioning changes importantly. We move from a metaphysical to a moral critique of *mimesis*. He asks, To which part of the soul does imitation appeal? (602c). It does not appeal to the calculating (*logistikos*) part of the soul, the logistical part, which is the "best part of the soul" (603a). Rather, imitation arouses the inferior part of the soul. It works, Socrates says, through the mimicry of various actions, whether voluntary or forced, and the imitator experiences either pain or pleasure as a consequence. Now, Socrates asks—returning explicitly to arguments about the refusal of the "double man" and the multiplicity of roles in Book III—in such mimetic activity "Is a human being of one mind?" (603c). Or is there not rather a war within the soul, where different factions contend with each other and do battle? Is it not rather the case that the mimetic soul is teeming with conflicts, with "ten thousand such oppositions arising at the same time" (603d).

Picking up on earlier arguments about moral psychology and the idea and ideal of psychical integration, we can restate the distinction between philosophy and tragedy. Philosophy is committed to the idea of a noncontradictory life, a psychic and political existence at one with itself, which can be linked to ideas of self-mastery, self-legislation, autonomy, and autarchy, and which inform the modern jargon of authenticity. As we have seen, tragedy is not committed to such a belief and the so-called tragic hero is shown to be essentially at odds with himself, doubled over and divided. Furthermore, the city of which the tragic hero is both the expression and symptom is also structured around essential conflict, ambiguity, and contradiction. The philosopher's city, the just city described in the speeches of the *Republic,* is premised upon the elimination of all such contradiction and therefore requires the excision of tragedy.

Matters then turn, importantly for our purposes, to the proper regulation of an affect like grief, the very emotion which is so central to the experience of tragedy. The decent man, the gentleman, Socrates says, will regulate the grief that he feels over the loss, say, of a son (603e). Whatever the decent man might be feeling privately, he will moderate any public display of pain and emotion. The error of the tragic poet, then, consists in publicizing what should be private and destabilizing the public/private distinction in a way that threatens a just city regulated by law: "The law presumably says that it is finest to keep as quiet as possible in misfortune and not to be irritated" (604b). Excessive grief and lamentation, what Socrates calls "taking it hard" (604b), never gets anyone anywhere. What should be cultivated instead, Socrates insists, is the capacity for deliberation (*bouleusis*), which is subject to the activity of *logos* and the calculating, rational part of the soul. What is clearly valued by Socrates is what he calls "the prudent and quiet character which is always equal to itself" (604e). Such a prudent man learns to "accept the fall of the dice and settle one's affairs accordingly" (604c). Adults should not behave like children who have fallen down and "spend their time crying out" (604c). On the contrary, after experiencing the loss of a child or some such, the decent man must set to work immediately to cure the soul as quickly as possible and set it right, "doing away with lament by medicine." The drug that is prescribed by Socrates is rational deliberation.

The dramaturgical problem with the behavior of the decent

man is that it is "neither easily imitated, nor, when imitated, easily understood, especially by a festive assembly where all sorts of human beings are gathered in a *theater*" (604e, emphasis mine). By its very nature, theater encourages excessive lamentation based on the perceived operations of fate, and discourages moral calculation based on accepting the nature of chance or luck or the force of circumstance. The quiet and prudent man is not a subject for the theater, which is drawn toward excess and the imitation of the vicious. Socrates' point is that it is hard to imagine a play called *The Decent Man Who Doesn't Show His Feelings* getting better reviews and bigger crowds than the sufferings of Hecuba, the wailings of Electra, or the railings of Antigone. But note here what this implies about the philosophical character. In a world governed by chance and randomness, where bad stuff happens, like the death of a beloved child, the point is to stay calm, remain focused, and think through your options rationally and deliberatively. And if you are going to weep, then be sure to do it in the privacy of your home. At the core of philosophy, in this picture, lies affect regulation, the rational ordering of emotion. Do we not glimpse here the cold, obsessional core of the philosophical personality?

Imitation is not aimed at the superior part of the soul that can withstand weal and woe through cool rational control. Its target is the soul's inferior part, which is deemed "irrational" (*alogiston*) (604d). *Mimesis* always imitates what is easily mimicked in us, what is worse in us, inflaming it with extreme, sham displays of emotion, making public what should be private. In so doing, the imitative poet destroys the calculating part of the soul. "And thus," Socrates concludes about the mimetic artist,

> we should at last be justified in not admitting him into a city that is going to be under good laws, because he awakens this part of the soul and nourishes it, and, by making it strong, destroys the calculating part. (605b)

Socrates and Plato's brothers are right in refusing to admit the mimetic poet into the philosophically well-ordered city because imitation causes the soul to be at odds with itself, at war with itself. By dividing the soul, imitation encourages the worst elements and denigrates the best. It introduces a bad regime, or *politeia,* into the soul and, given the basic analogy between the soul and the city that defines the argument of the *Republic,* drama makes the city vicious, factional, and warring. Drama is appropriate to the many-colored, multitasking horror show of democracy, but it has no place in the just city.

37

The Inoculation against Our Inborn Love of Poetry

The argument of Book X then turns toward the final exclusion of the tragic poets. What Socrates calls "the gravest accusation" against *mimesis* is that it succeeds in "maiming even the decent man" (605c). The most serious problem with imitation is simply that we enjoy it, that we give ourselves over to it. So when we hear, "Homer or any other of the tragic poets imitating one of the heroes in mourning and making quite an extended speech with lamentation" (605d), we cannot help ourselves. We suffer along with the suffering hero and then heap praise on the tragedian who is able to extract the most empathy from the spectator. The poet who wins the *agon* at the City Dionysia is the one who produces the strongest affective response. And yet, Socrates insists, in our private grief and sorrow, we pride ourselves on being able to keep quiet, "taking this to be the part of a man and what we then praised to be that of a woman" (605e). *Mimesis*, then, has two vicious effects:

(1) it threatens the distinction between the public and the private, by making public what should be private, namely lamentation and other extreme emotions; and,

(2) it threatens the economy of sexual difference that is organized along the lines of the public/private distinction. Imitation is womanish and effeminate.

Of course, this is precisely Rousseau's argument against theater in his *Letter to D'Alembert* some millennia later.[1] Theater is essentially effeminizing. It turns men into women. And here is the truth of the purported gender equality of Book IV of the *Republic*. The real purpose of extending education and the role of guardians to women as well as men is to turn those women into decent men, into facsimiles of moderate gentlemen.

What disgusts Socrates with tragedy is the fact that we enjoy it so much. It is tragedy's very attraction that repels Socrates. What is most dangerous about tragedy is the pity that we feel in watching the sufferings of the tragic hero. That which is "held down by force" (606a) in our private misfortunes and which "has hungered for tears and sufficient lament" is suddenly unleashed on the stage by the enjoyment we feel in watching tragic suffering. "What is best in us," Socrates goes on, "relaxes its guard over the mournful part because it sees another's sufferings" (606a). This is a fascinating claim. Socrates is acutely aware of the affective power of tragedy, namely its ability to cause a destabilizing emotional effect in us through imitation. But the pleasure that we feel in watching the heroes suffer is "shameful" (606b), for it gives free rein to that which should properly be held down by force, by the power of inhibition. Once enjoyment in suffering is admitted into the city, then the sexualized economy of public and private is ruined and there can be no possibility of justice. The political consequence is clear: tragedy is the government of the city by private pleasure, which leads ineluctably to tyranny.

And what goes for tragedy is also true of comedy. The obscene private jokes that one would be ashamed to tell in public are suddenly licensed by comic imitation, as with the plays of Aristophanes, who of course makes an important appearance in Plato's *Symposium*. The problem with comedy is that the buffonic sentiments that are properly "held down by argument" are unleashed, so that "you become a comic poet" (606c). In other words, the problem with watching comedy is that everyone thinks they are a comedian. For Socrates, a society full of stand-up comics would be doomed to viciousness. And the same argument is valid for sex (*aphrodision*) and all forms of spiritedness (*thymos*). Once these desires and their consequent pleasures become available to us, then we are no longer rulers of ourselves, but are tyrannically governed by private delight. Tragedy, comedy, and sex foster and water pleasures "when they ought to be dried up" (606d). Philosophy, then, might be described as an education in desiccation, where we learn to hold down effeminizing private pleasures through the force of argument.

At the end of this extraordinary line of reasoning, Socrates brings Glaucon to the final and definitive exclusion of tragedy from the just city. With all the reflexivity of this mimetic critique of *mimesis,* the layerings of irony continue to accrete. Socrates asks Glaucon to imagine meeting a eulogist of Homer who claims that he is the source for all moral and practical education. What would one say to such a person? The following, apparently:

> You must love and embrace them as being men who are the best they can be, and agree that Homer is the most poetic and first of the tragic poets; but you must know that only so much of poetry as is hymns to the gods or celebrations of good men should be admitted into a city. And if you admit the sweetened muse in lyrics and epics, pleasure and pain will jointly be kings in your city instead of law and that argument which in each instance is best in the opinion of the community. (607a)

Socrates is polite but firm: the only poetry to be admitted into the city are hymns to the gods (following the strictures on the representation of divinities discussed in Book II) and paeans to great men. This doesn't sound all that entertaining. All other forms of poetry must be refused because once the "sweetened muse" is allowed free rein in the city, then it will become a tyranny based on a metric of pleasure and pain. Using the legal language of the democracy that he despised and that would soon condemn him to death, Socrates says that this will be our "apology," our defense in court. He bluntly concludes, "The argument determined us" (607b). End of story.

Yet, if this apology appears too "harsh" (or sclerotic, *sklerotes*) (607b) or "rustic" (*agroikia,* which also means "boorish" and "countrified"), then something more cunning and diplomatic might be said to the defender of Homer and tragedy. For example, we could suggest that there is an ancient quarrel between philosophy and poetry (607b). This is a very interesting moment in Book X, which is often misunderstood. For those who do *not* believe that the argument against poetry is too sclerotic and too redneck, those who are not poetic—namely Socrates himself and his interlocutors—then there is no need to speak of any quarrel between philosophy and poetry. The suggestion that there is such a quarrel is merely hypothetical. It is a ruse, a rhetorical move in an argument that might persuade an opponent. But if it becomes necessary to employ this hypothesis in front of the defenders of poetry, then it might further be said that,

> If poetry directed towards pleasure and imitation have any argument to give showing that they should be in a city with good laws, we should be delighted to receive them back from exile, since we are aware that we ourselves are charmed by them. But it isn't holy to betray what seems to be the truth. (607c)

The rhetorical guile of these words is fascinating. Socrates suggests to Plato's brothers (and, one imagines—anachronistically— to Plato himself), that to avoid looking like a boorish hick, it is necessary to grant to poetry's defenders the charming power of imitation. The exile of poetry should not appear to be some brutal, philistine act of ostracism, and it is important that poetry's defenders see that people like Socrates and Glaucon understand the delights of verse. Socrates then makes the apparent concession that poetry might be welcomed back into the just city if an *argument* can be made for it. But this argument for poetry, Socrates insists, must not itself be poetic, but must be stated "without meter" (607d), namely in the rational prose of philosophical dialogue. Yet, we have just learned that the consequence of the long conversations in the *Republic* is the exclusion of poetry: "The argument determined us." Socrates therefore knows full well that poetry cannot make a convincing philosophical argument. It can work its charms only by seducing us with the rhetorical force of *mimesis*. This is why Socrates says that if the defender of poetry should try and make a philosophical argument in its defense, then "we shall listen benevolently" (607d). Such apparent benevolence toward poetry is a polite, diplomatic trick that conceals the moral ferocity of the philosophical position that Socrates has occupied in the course of the dialogue.

Giving up on poetry is like giving up on a love that is not beneficial, keeping away from it "even if they do violence to themselves" (607e). The violence here is an implicit reference to traditional forms of Greek education, largely based on the memorizing of Homer. Socrates and Plato's brothers are products of an educational system whose core has been judged illegitimate and radically undermined by the argument of the *Republic*. With biting irony, Socrates refers to "the inborn love of poetry we owe to our rearing in these fine regimes [*ton kalon politeion*]" (608a). The argument of Book VIII of the *Republic* has very powerfully shown that these Greek regimes are far from being fine or beautiful. The clear inference is that the love we feel for poetry is fake; it is the consequence of the bad education that Socrates has sought to put right. Unlike the future, imagined guardians, Socrates and his interlocutors have to inoculate themselves against the charms of poetry.

For as long as poetry cannot make its apology, and it is clear that it will not be able to make it in the required argumentative, nonpoetic, philosophical form, then Socrates says,

> We'll chant this argument we are making to ourselves as a countercharm, taking care against falling again into this love, which is childish and belongs to the many (*ton pollon*). (608a)

What is fascinating here is the acknowledgment of the seductive effects of poetry. The clear cause of this effect is the traditional Greek education system, which places such a high value on Homer and the rest. Such an education inculcates a childish sentimentality that belongs to the many, namely the citizens of the "fine regime" of democracy. Socrates is suggesting that he and the few who listen to his arguments in the house of Cephalus on that summer afternoon at the Piraeus must tie themselves, most Odysseus-like, to the mast of the argument of Book X and thereby prevent themselves from being seduced by the siren song of poetry. The argument against poetry has to be recited like a countercharm, or indeed a kind of mumbled mantra, against the charms of poetry. "For the contest is great, my dear Glaucon," Socrates says,

> greater than it seems—this contest that concerns becoming good or bad—so we mustn't be tempted by honor or money or any ruling office or, for that matter, poetry, into thinking that it's worthwhile to neglect justice and the rest of virtue. (608b)

The life of virtue, the life available only to the few, must be steadfastly maintained by an iron discipline. It must not be deflected by honor, money, or holding office, that is, by the lures of timocracy, oligarchy, or democracy, each of which is legitimated by poetry and descends toward tyranny.

38

The Rewards of Virtue, or What Happens When We Die

At which point, the argument takes what appears to be a sudden shift until the end of Book X and the final pages of the *Republic*. The talk of virtue leads Socrates to turn to the question of the possible rewards of a just life. This introduces, firstly, an argument for the immortality of the soul, and secondly, a vision of the afterlife: the myth of Er. "Haven't you perceived," Socrates says, "that our soul is immortal and is never destroyed?" To which Glaucon rather stupidly says, "No, by Zeus, I haven't" (608d). Now, probably because immortality and the afterlife are not such fashionable topics in philosophy and indeed might be judged to be slightly embarrassing, most discussions of Book X end with the final exclusion of the tragic poets and usual talk of the ancient quarrel between philosophy and poetry. But the discussion of immortality and the afterlife occupy as much space in Book X as the critique of poetry, and indeed this is how the long dialogue of the *Republic* ends. If, as I tried to show, the beginning of the *Republic* is such a carefully coded series of literary and political conceits, then by virtue of what argument is one entitled to ignore the book's conclusion?

What, then, is the connection between the two halves of Book X and the arguments for the exclusion of poetry and immortality and the afterlife? It is unclear, to say the least. Allan Bloom argues, cutely, that "Book X begins with a criticism of Homeric poetry and ends with an example of Socratic poetry" (page 427).

But we might recall that the *Gorgias* also ended with a discussion of the afterlife and the judgment accorded to the virtuous and the vicious in Hades, where the unjust receive a slap in the face for eternity. And Socrates famously argues for the soul's immortality in the *Phaedo* and elsewhere. So, we can't simply ignore these arguments because they do not suit whatever contemporary philosophical prejudices we might have.

Throughout the *Republic*, Socrates has emphasized the distinction between being and seeming. The philosopher's soul should be oriented toward that which truly *is* and not the realm of appearance, let alone imitation, which is the mere shadow of appearance. In Book X, he argues that the soul is akin to what *is* always and is therefore the same substance as the divine, which is by definition immortal (611e). The soul cannot be destroyed with bodily death and continues on in existence (610c). What Socrates calls the "wages" of justice and the rest of virtue "in their quantity and in their quality" are not just paid in life. Their real dividend is paid after death (612c). "Thus," Socrates says,

> It must be assumed in the case of the just man that, if he falls into poverty, diseases, or any other of the things that seem bad, for him it will end in some good, either in life or even in death. For, surely, gods at least will never neglect the man who is eagerly willing to become just and practicing virtue, like himself, as far as is possible for a human being, to a god. (613a–b)

As we saw in Chapter 28, the contrast between philosophy and sophistry turns on the issue of whether one judges that man is the measure of all things or not. Philosophers refuse the limitation of the human measure and orient themselves toward the divine and try, as far as is possible, to achieve *homoiosis theo,* likeness to a god. Having sought to achieve this likeness by living justly, the question at the end of the *Republic* is the nature of the "prizes" (613b) that the just man receives from the gods. Using the example of an athletic contest, which again has been emphasized throughout the dialogue with reference to the gymnastic education of the guardians, Socrates insists that the just win life's race and are garlanded and rewarded with prizes (613b). Even if the unjust—such as the tyrant—appear to get a head start in life's race or indeed seem to get away with murder, the just will win in the end. And what they win in life, in the austere moderation of the philosophical life described in the *Republic,* is nothing in comparison with what they receive in the afterlife. When they are dead, "each of these men will have gotten back the full measure of what the argument owed him" (614a). Again, the measure is divine and not human. If one allows one's soul to be determined by the argument of the *Republic,* then the reward of a life of virtue is eternal, godlike happiness.

"Do tell," says Glaucon, in the last words of any of Socrates' interlocutors in the *Republic* (614b). To prove his point about the afterlife, Socrates tells the myth of Er, "a strong man" (614b) who died in battle and who came back to life twelve days after his death to recount what he saw in the afterlife. It is a long speech, and we know that Socrates hates long speeches, unless he gives them himself. And it is a mighty strange speech, with millennial journeys lasting thousands of years, a vast vision of the entire universe as a mighty spindle of Necessity and a whorl of circles on which are perched Sirens and the Fates, the daughters of Necessity: past, present, and future; Lachesis, Clotho, and Atropos. There is even an account of reincarnation, where the just souls are each accompanied by a demon and allowed to choose the form in which they will return to life on earth. Er sees Agamemnon choosing to return as an eagle and Thersites as an ape, and so on. Each soul is led by its demon to the three Fates who make past, present, and future irreversible. At which point, the souls are led to the plain of Lethe to drink the waters of forgetfulness, which is why we have no recollection of the afterlife in our diurnal existence. For reasons that are not given, Er is forbidden from drinking the amnesiac waters and returns to life on his funeral pyre with a memory of what took place when he died and a tale to tell.

The moral of the myth of Er is brutally simple: the just get a beautiful afterlife and the unjust receive ghastly punishments. Consistent with the overall political argument of the *Republic,* tyrants are particularly nastily punished, and Socrates refers to their fate on several occasions in the final pages (615c, 615d, 618a, 619a, 619b). By contrast, the just man, the virtuous soul,

> Must go to Hades adamantly holding to this opinion so that he won't be daunted by wealth and such evils there, and rush into tyrannies and other such deeds by which he would work many irreparable evils, and himself undergo still greater suffering; but rather he will know how always to choose the life between such extremes and flee the excesses in either direction in this life, so far as is possible, and in all of the next life. For in this way a human being becomes happiest. (619a–b)

To live justly, therefore, is to be sure of the reward of eternal happiness. Socrates' final advice to Glaucon is that if we are persuaded by the myth of Er, then we shall make a good crossing of the river of Lethe and not defile our soul. If we are persuaded that the soul is immortal and "practice justice with prudence" (621c), then "we shall become friends to ourselves [*autois philoi*] and the gods [*tois theois*]" (621c).

Such, then, are the rewards of philosophy: endless rebirth in an ever purer and better soul and the guarantee of eternal bliss. It would be easy to dismiss the end of the *Republic* with some sort of ironic or even cynical shrug. But I think it must be taken seriously. I see no reason why one should work through the metaphysical and moral critique of poetry and then ignore the argument for the immortality of the soul and the afterlife. The two arguments are yoked together in Book X and indeed can be linked to the claim in Books II and III that the education of the philosopher-guardians should refuse gloomy, tragic pictures of Hades and the afterlife. If we live justly, if we live philosophically, then death is nothing to fear, for the soul is deathless and the reward for virtue is eternal bliss.

Socrates appears to be using the conceit of a myth to make the case for an analogy between the structure of the just soul and the cosmos, in a way that echoes and indeed amplifies the analogy between the city and the soul at the core of the *Republic*. Now, Plato's most extensive account of cosmology, which begins with an account of the "world soul," is presented in the *Timaeus*.[1] It is absolutely fascinating that, although the *Timaeus* was probably written some twenty years after the *Republic*, around 360 BCE, it is set dramatically on the following day. *Timaeus* is a continuation of the *Republic*, and it begins with a very selective summary of the arguments of the early books of the *Republic*. Indeed, it even rehearses the critique of poetry and imitation (19d–e). It is also curious that the teleological account of the shaping of the cosmos by the Demiurge ends with an account of reincarnation, where Timaeus of Locri, a Pythagorean from southern Italy, helpfully informs us that "Land animals, a brutish race, are reincarnations of men who never applied themselves to philosophy" (91e). But, strangest of all is the fact that although Socrates speaks at the beginning of the *Timaeus*, and is present throughout, the main body of the text is a monologue that continually refers to itself as only "a likely story." All that the usually fiercely critical Socrates says in response to the really quite bizarre cosmogeny of the *Timaeus*—whose most obscure core concept is the *chora*, or "receptable"—is the following: "Excellent, Timaeus! You're absolutely right: we must, as you suggest, be satisfied with that" (29d).

How are we to understand this? It is hard to say. The reflexive dramatic conceits of the *Republic* find their echo and complex continuation in the *Timaeus* and rebound across the other dialogues. What is clear is that there is an intrinsic connection between the political argument of the *Republic,* the exclusion of Homer and the tragic poets, the cosmological account of immortality and the afterlife, and the understanding of the nature and rewards of the philosophical life.

PART V

Aristotle

In the *Republic*, philosophy is staged dramatically as an exclusion of drama. It is a regulation of *mimesis* in mimetic form. Specifically, the *Republic* is a dramatized argument, elaborately staged in the form of indirect communication, for the implementation of a regime or *politeia* in the soul and the city, where the latter is the mirror of the former. And even if the city may not ever exist in reality, there is a pattern laid up in heaven whose dimensions can be discerned in the closing cosmological myth of Er that details the rewards of virtue. The core of the critique of *mimesis* is the call to control the excessive affect caused by dramatic imitation, particularly the extremity of lamentation and displays of grief in tragedy, but also the ridicule and risible laughter exhibited in comedy. To be a philosopher, then, is to control the excess of *mimesis* and the threat of affective *ekstasis* and self-division that it enacts. Imitation causes the soul of the philosopher-guardian to be teeming with conflicts, doubling, and self-division in a way that undermines the self-mastery and moderation that define the character of the decent man.

As we saw in Part 4, there are two major problems with tragedy. Firstly, it threatens the proper balance between the private and the public, by making public what should properly be private, the main example being the lamentation associated with the experience of grief. Secondly, tragedy disturbs and inverts the proper economy of sexual difference in the city by effeminizing men. With its endless displays of female grief, wailing, and lamentation, say in the sufferings of Electra or Hecuba, tragedy turns the men who watch it into women. The combined effect of these two problems is the following: dramatic *mimesis* leads the soul of the decent man into contradiction with itself, teeming with a thousand conflicts. The public institution of tragedy in the City Dionysia and elsewhere tips the licentious freedom that characterizes democracy into the domination of private pleasure, which defines tyranny. Both democracy and tyranny are regimes of theatricalization where drama legitimates the transition from the one to the other. Tragedy leads to theatrocracy and ruins the psychic economy and equilibrium of the city. This is why dramatic *mimesis* must be expelled.

39

What Is Catharsis in Aristotle?

Now, if philosophy is a practice of rational affect regulation and resistance to the forms of theatrical spectacle endemic to democracy and tyranny, then the question that is immediately raised is the following: What on earth is Aristotle up to in the *Poetics*? Possibly written around 335 BCE in the final phase of his career, a generation or so after the *Republic,* is the *Poetics* the kind of apology for poetry written in prose, in language without meter as Socrates stipulates, called for in Book X? It will be recalled that although Socrates has no need of a defense of poetry, he worries that his exclusion of Homer and the tragic poets might appear too sclerotic and countrified, too angry and rural. So, is Aristotle's *Poetics* the kind of calm and urbane philosophical defense of poetry that Socrates asks for?

This is obviously how the *Poetics,* written by someone who was a member of Plato's Academy for probably twenty years, has often been read. And it is not wrong. Not at all. But it might not be the whole story. The main genre of poetry examined in the *Poetics* is tragedy, and the latter is defined as the imitation of elevated action, produced in meter, that yields the affects of pity and fear in a way that accomplishes the catharsis of these emotions. The whole question of tragedy, indeed the whole question of poetry and its relation to philosophy, turns on how we understand the core concept of catharsis.

So, what is catharsis? The initial problem is that the concept is introduced in *Poetics* VI with no explanation or elucidation (1449b28). There is one further use of the related term, *katharseos,* in *Poetics* XVIII, but it sheds little light on the issue (1455b15). There is another famous occurrence of catharsis right at the end of the *Politics,* where catharsis is often translated as "purgation" (1341b37–39). Very curiously, Aristotle does not explain the meaning of the term, but promises to do so hereafter in his poetical works, which he either didn't do or it was included in work that has been lost. It is generally thought that the *Poetics* was written later than Aristotle's two no-longer-extant works on poetry, *On Poets* and *Homeric Problems,* because they are both alluded to in the former treatise.

Is catharsis, as is often claimed, best thought of as a kind of purgation? Is it a kind of emotional laxative, soul cleanser, or theatrical detox, where we purge the terrible passions of pity and fear that tragedy has inflamed in us and experience some sort of quasi-physical relief? Or is catharsis something closer to purification, with its religious and ritualistic connotations? Or, indeed, is catharsis closer to sublimation in the psychoanalytic sense, which we can think of as the transformation of passion? So, is catharsis either purgation, purification, or transformation? The problem is that we simply do not know for sure what Aristotle meant by catharsis. Therefore, it is hard to be able to judge the nature and force of the *Poetics* as a response to Socrates' call for an apology for poetry in prose. Indeed, Aristotle might not be responding to Plato at all.

The central concept of the *Poetics* forms, then, a kind of lacuna in the text, which scholars cannot but fill with meaning. Helpful here is Stephen Halliwell, whose excellent translation I will follow in this chapter. He claims that it is difficult to sustain what he calls "the modern view" that catharsis is simply a kind of purgation, emotional outlet, or release. While accepting there is no clear definition of the concept, Halliwell goes on to link catharsis to Aristotle's moral treatment of the emotions in the *Rhetoric* and elsewhere.

> While, in the absence of an Aristotelian elucidation of the term for tragedy, the significance of catharsis cannot be conclusively established, we are more likely to approximate to the truth if we keep in view the ethical importance of emotions for Aristotle.[1]

Halliwell goes on to say that tragedy revolves around the theatrical exhibition of suffering that stems from a profound and general sense of human fallibility, which is how he understands the key concept of *hamartia,* to which we will return in Chapter 45. In other words, the sufferings of the tragic hero invites pity or fellow feeling (*philanthropia*) from the spectator as well as fear, for we are not so different from him. By engaging the moral understanding and the emotions in the theatrical contemplation of suffering, tragedy "succeeds in affording an experience which deeply fulfils and enhances the whole mind."[2]

These are fine words and handsome sentiments, and the temptation to give an ethical significance to catharsis by linking the *Poetics* to Aristotle's moral views is very strong. But still, I am far from sure that Halliwell is right, particularly as it is completely unclear what "right" might mean in connection to catharsis. We might say that catharsis is an essentially contested concept. For example, Alexander Nehamas is also suspicious of what he calls the "current consensus" to understand catharsis as purgation, based on the passage from the *Politics* mentioned above.[3] To some extent following Martha Nussbaum in *The Fragility of Goodness,* Nehamas sees catharsis not as purification, but as a kind of "clarification."[4] But what Nehamas means by this is not some kind of moral clarity, but rather what we experience with the resolution, denouement, or solution to the tragic plot. Interestingly, Nehamas sees this experience of catharsis not as any kind of response to

Plato's argument in the *Republic,* which he thinks it is not, but simply as the effect aroused in the spectator by the drama itself. It is as if we reach the end of watching a play and say to ourselves, "Ah, that's how it ends!"; and this is catharsis.

A somewhat related and fascinating analysis of catharsis is presented by Jonathan Lear in a peculiarly sober and pathos-free paper.[5] Lear skillfully and unsentimentally unravels the many assumptions and misunderstandings connected with catharsis. In particular, he picks apart the view—very attractive to contemporary philosophers and literary critics, not to mention actors and movie directors—that catharsis is some kind of moral education of the emotions. Lear shows, to my mind convincingly, that such a view has no foundation in Aristotle's writings. Education into a life of virtue was obviously very important for the formation of Greek male children and young boys, but not for the adult citizens who went to the theater. They were obviously already educated and therefore did not need to go to the theater in order to find out about virtue. They already knew. They were hardly morally ignorant.

In strictly Aristotelian terms, tragedy induces the emotions of pity and fear. It does not seek to persuade its audience of anything or educate them into the way things are or, indeed, how they might be on some alternative view of matters. The experience of tragedy yields affects, but the goal or *telos* of drama is not just to inflame the passions or produce some overwhelming affective response. Pity and fear are raised only *in order to* bring about a catharsis of those emotions. Now, it is the precise nature of such catharsis that remains unclear and undefined. Lear's view, with which I see no reason to disagree, is that, for Aristotle, the world is "a rational, meaningful place in which a person can conduct himself with dignity."[6] That is, for the adult male citizen of a city with a clear understanding of virtue, the rationality that governs their worldview before visiting the theater remains intact after the play has finished. Nothing really changes. This is why Aristotle is so insistent in the *Poetics* that a tragic plot should be plausible and its events convincing. It must have an inherent rationality because the spectators are inherently rational.

So what, then, is going on in tragedy? Lear's view is that tragedy provides a safe environment in which emotions are raised and then relieved. But this relief is nothing as dramatic as a sudden release of dark, repressed, pent-up passions, let alone their quasi-religious purification or moral transformation. No, we go to the theater, we see characters completely unlike us, mythical characters from the ancient past, but with whom we can rationally experience fellow feeling for their suffering. The emotions of pity and fear are raised in us and then they disappear when the play finishes. At which point, we leave the theater and go and have dinner, attend to our business, give some instructions to our slaves, talk with the wife, and enjoy a good night's sleep as usual. We are not transformed by theater, because we do not need to be changed. As rational, virtuous, adult, male citizens of the city, we are what we are. Tragedy entertains us, it provides a particular experience of pleasure, and then the whole thing is over. Lear concludes, "Even in tragedy, perhaps especially in tragedy, the fundamental goodness of man and world are reaffirmed."[7] On this view, Aristotle is not in the slightest way concerned with responding to Plato's arguments in the *Republic*. He is simply giving an account of what he thinks happens when we go to the theater and see a tragic drama.

I find this minimalist understanding of Aristotelian catharsis compelling because of the deflationary effects it has on any moralistic or pedagogical conception of the purpose of tragedy in particular and art in general. Art is not moral tutorial. Perhaps the most disturbing thought one can have about tragedy is that it does nothing much. It leaves us in the same condition in which it finds us. In between times, we feel something, what Aristotle calls pity and fear. Catharsis, on this view, would be the experience of no longer entertaining such feelings. To be clear, I think that Lear gives us a plausible account of what Aristotle may think about tragic catharsis, and I'd like to keep it in mind in what follows. However, although I would like to hang on to aspects of this deflationary, antimoralistic understanding of tragedy, I do not think that it accounts for what takes place in tragedy, as I have sought to show earlier.

40

More Devastating

Matters are further complicated by the fact that if one peruses the extraordinary online tools that classicists have at their disposal these days, such as *Perseus* (http://www.perseus.tufts.edu /hopper), the research results are rather revealing. There are sixty-four uses of the term *katharsis* in the Aristotelian corpus. It occurs twenty-six times in *De Generatione animalium* and twenty-five times in *Historia animalium,* namely in Aristotle's substantial biological texts. This might perhaps come as no surprise, as Aristotle was, first and foremost, a naturalist, an ancient proto-Darwinian, and what naturalists always seek to do is to categorize matters neutrally, dispassionately, and in great detail, even when it comes to phenomena like theater. In Aristotle's biological writings, catharsis refers to such matters as seminal discharge, urination, and even the evacuation of the bowels. But the preponderant use of the term describes menstrual discharge in women. In the first paragraph of his paper, Jonathan Lear floats the following interesting thought:

> As far as I know, no one in the extended debate about tragic katharsis has suggested the model of menstruation. But why not? Is it not more compelling to think of a natural process of discharge of the emotions than of their purging?[1]

Why not, indeed? If the overwhelming majority of the uses of catharsis in Aristotle refer to physiological functions such as menstruation, then by virtue of what is one entitled to eliminate this meaning of the term in favor of purgation, purification, or transformation? Perhaps tragic catharsis should be thought of on the model of physiological discharge, a natural process, a simple clearing away of what Galen would much later call the morbid humors from the body. Perhaps going to the theater is more like going to the toilet than some sort of religious ritual or moral edification.

The point I have been trying to make in these introductory remarks is that the meaning of catharsis is unclear. The lexical definition of the word has shades of physiological and ritualistic meaning, although the attempts to understand Aristotelian catharsis exclusively as either purgation or purification, let alone moral education and edification, are at the very least questionable. The problem is that if catharsis is the central concept of the *Poetics,* and if we don't know what the concept means, then we have no idea of what effect poetry or indeed art was considered to have for Aristotle and for the tradition that he inaugurates, namely the entire, long history of aesthetics. In a dialogue with Anne Carson, I made the suggestion that it might be desirable to free the experience of tragedy from the Aristotelian framework, in particular the way in which catharsis tends to dominate the discussion. To which Carson suddenly responded, "I've never understood catharsis."[2] When I suggested that tragedy was a much more curious art form, she agreed and added simply, "More devastating." It is toward this more devastating view of the nature of tragedy that I would like to make my way in what follows.

That said, I find the *Poetics* to be completely fascinating, and the more I have reread the text over the years, the more compelling it becomes. What is so impressive about Aristotle is the compression and detail of his analysis of poetry. Into this short treatise of merely ten thousand words or so, Aristotle packs a vast number of examples, which function almost like botanical specimens that he categorizes and deploys to make broader distinctions and formal definitions. Aristotle is clearly someone who went to the

theater a good deal and both saw and was able to read a significant number of plays. Rather than any speculative philosophy of
the tragic, based on one or two privileged examples (usually the
Antigone), Aristotle provides a theory of tragedies. And although
some of what he says is uncertain, as many of the plays he refers
to have been lost, the formal, categorical points are always crys-
tal clear even when the meaning of central concepts like catharsis
might be cloudy.

41

Reenactment

Aristotle begins his discussion of poetry by going back, as is natural (*kata physin,* 1447a12), to first principles. The first principle is *mimesis,* Socrates' word, which is largely left untranslated by Halliwell, although he sometimes uses "representation." This is a perfectly fine choice, although it sets off all sorts of unfortunate echoes with Kantian and post-Kantian epistemologies and Hegel's idea of representation as mere "picture thinking." Perhaps "imitation" is a better rendering. All forms of poetry—epic, tragic, and comic—are mimetic, and there are many different media for *mimesis,* produced by rhythm, language, and music, "for aulos and lyre," as Aristotle repeatedly says in the opening pages of the text. We might immediately note the stark difference between Plato and Aristotle: *mimesis* is not a threat to the moral self-mastery of the "decent man." Rather, imitation is "what comes naturally to us"(1448b19). For Aristotle, as for Darwin, human behavior is imitative *kata physin:* it is based on action, reaction, repetition, and adaptation through behavioral memes. Without ever, perhaps wisely, offering a definition of the term, *mimesis* is, in Halliwell's words,

A supple concept of the human propensity to explore an understanding of the world—above all, of human experience itself—through fictive representation and imaginative "enactment" of experience.[1]

"Supple" is a very useful way of describing the elasticity of *mimesis*. Imitation is best thought of as *enactment,* and, in the final words of his discussion of tragedy in *Poetics* XXIII, Aristotle even speaks of *to prattein mimeseos,* enactive imitation (1459a16). This is extremely interesting, for if human behavior is by nature mimetic, then tragedy in particular and art in general are forms of *reenactment,* the repetition through action of a previous action. Art, then, is a double, supple activity: it is action upon action. This also implies, as will become clear later in the *Poetics,* that imitation cannot be subordinated or judged inferior to narration or *diegesis,* as we saw in the *Republic. Diegesis* is also a form of *mimesis,* namely the imitation of narration, the retelling of stories that were previously told, which is indeed one plausible way of approaching the origins of epic poetry.

Having introduced his elastic first principle, Aristotle then draws a major distinction: if the mimetic arts imitate people in action, then such people are either virtuous or vicious, and the imitation will therefore either be elevated (*spoudaios*) or base (*phaulos*) (1448a2–5). It is this distinction between the elevated and the base that is the criterion for the separation of tragedy from comedy. Yet, despite this separation, what tragedy and comedy have in common is what distinguishes them both from epic poetry. If the latter, in Homer, say, proceeds by narration or by the narrative impersonation of a character like Achilles, then what Sophocles (who is mentioned for the first time on 1448a26) and Aristophanes have in common is the imitation of people in direct action without narration. "Hence," Aristotle says, "the assertion some people make that dramas [*dramata*] are so called because they represent people in action [*drontas*]" (1448a28–30). We then get a fascinating account of a dispute about the origins of drama, and whether tragedy and comedy are Dorian (roughly speaking, the Peloponnese and northern Greece) or Attic (the region on the Greek mainland whose principal city was Athens).

The Dorian case is supported by a curious etymological argument: namely, that they call their villages *komoi,* and the comic performers (*komodoi*) allegedly got their name from reveling (*komazein*) in villages when banned from the city. Furthermore, the Dorians contend that their word for acting is *dran,* which is closer to *drama* than the Athenian *prattein.* Aristotle doesn't tell us which origin story he thinks is correct, but what is fascinating here is his interest in and knowledge of the history of drama. The *Poetics* is our main source for any speculation on the birth of tragedy, and it is revealing that there is no mention of the he-goat (*tragos*) or of drama originating in goat song, whatever that might be. However, what both the Dorian and Attic origin story of theater have in common is the intrinsic connection between drama and action.

42

Mimesis Apraxeos

This is where I'd like to open a first window in the commentary on Aristotle. Is the identification of drama with action as self-evident as it would seem? In a very late and polemical text by Nietzsche, *The Case of Wagner,* written in Turin in 1888 shortly before his final collapse, he writes the following footnote:

> It has been a real misfortune for aesthetics that the word drama has always been translated as action [*Handlung*]. It is not Wagner alone who errs at this point. The error is world-wide and extends even to the philologists who often know better. Ancient drama aimed at scenes of great *pathos*—it precluded action (moving it *before* the beginning or *behind* the scene). The word *drama* is of Doric origin, and according to Doric usage it means "event," "story"—both words in the hieratic sense. The most ancient drama represented the leg-end of the place, the "holy story" on which the foundation of the cult rested (not a doing but a happening: *dran* in Doric actually does not mean "do").[1]

Nietzsche is here taking direct aim at Aristotle's *Poetics* and questioning the identification of drama with action and the idea that tragedy is *mimesis praxeos,* imitation of action. The claim is that this identification is a huge error in Aristotle and damaging to the subsequent history of aesthetics. The Doric word *drama* is not a cognate for the Attic *praxis*. It means rather an event or story that is related to *hieros*, namely the priestly or sacred. Drama, then, is the imitation of a holy story.

Nietzsche's point is powerful and obvious: If drama in general and tragedy in particular were about action, then there would be action in tragedy, right? The problem is that there isn't much if any action. Drama presents scenes of great pathos or suffering, but the *praxis* occurs either before or behind the scenes. The action has either occurred before the play begins, say, with Oedipus's murder of his father or Agamemnon's slaughter of his daughter, or it takes place offstage, as with the blinding of Oedipus, the suicide of Jocasta, or the murders of Agamemnon and Cassandra. Nietzsche's compelling thought here is that Aristotle's definition of tragedy as *mimesis praxeos* should more properly be reconceived as *mimesis apraxeos*, imitation of inaction. Drama is an event or a story in relation to an action that is displaced, that occurs elsewhere. There is a fascinating moment at the end of Sophocles' *Electra* when the classic bad guy, Aegisthus, is about to be killed by Orestes. He pleads,

> Why take me inside?
> If the deed is honorable, what need of darkness?" (lines
> 1982–83)

For reasons that are not at all clear but that are axiomatic for the entirety of tragedy, there is great need of darkness. The action has to take place offstage. All that happens onstage are words, words, words.

43

The Birth of Tragedy (and Comedy)

For Aristotle, there are two causes that engender poetry, both natural (*physikai*) (1448b4). Firstly, there is the instinct to engage in *mimesis,* which follows from the fact that we are imitative animals. Secondly, everyone *enjoys* mimetic objects: we like seeing the likenesses of things, such as images, pictures, and so on. More particularly, we take pleasure at the sight of the likenesses of things whose actual sight would cause pain, such as the lowest, vilest animals and corpses (1448b3–13). We are mimetic creatures who take pleasure in pain, not a pain that is directly experienced, but in what we might call a dramatically distanced pain. Theater is the imitation of pain, a *mimesis* that we enjoy and that flows directly from our nature. All theater is a theater of cruelty, and it would appear to have little if nothing to do with moral education.

Mimesis is what comes naturally to us, like melody and rhythm. "From the beginning" (*ex arches*), Aristotle writes, those with "special natural talents" for imitation, rhythm, and melody "gradually progressed and brought poetry into being from improvisations" (1448b21–23). The *arche* of poetry, then, lies in forms of musical improvisation that combine words, tunes, and beats and that are performed by those creatures with the requisite natural ability. This is an intriguing thought. From this improvisational basis, poetry developed into the two branches suggested by the major distinction between the elevated and the base. Imitation therefore divides into the *mimesis* of noble and vulgar characters. Nobility leads to encomia, panegyric, and hymns of praise, whereas vulgarity leads to the varieties of invective. Interestingly, both branches are present in Homer, with the imitation of nobility in the *Iliad,* but with laughable invective in the *Margites,* the lost burlesque epic (which it would have been so much fun to read). The iambic lampoons of the *Margites* stand in the same relation to comedy as the *Iliad* and the *Odyssey* stand to tragedy (1448b–49a).

This brings us to Aristotle's famous speculation on the birth and history of drama. Again, both tragedy and comedy have an improvisatory origin, or *arche* (1449a9). Tragedy begins with the dithyramb, the chorus of the followers of Dionysos, to which the mysterious Thespis added the first actor. Comedy derives from the leaders of the phallic songs, which, as Halliwell notes, "were normally obscene and scurrilous."[1] But early, improvised tragedy was clearly also comic, suffused with satyric ethos, and went through many changes until it shook off its slight and laughable elements. Nietzsche makes much of this linking of tragedy to the satyr play in *The Birth of Tragedy,* as he does with the ancestry of tragedy in Dionysian dithyrambs. The wider question is the relation of ontological priority between the birth of tragedy and what Aristotle calls its proper nature *(ten autes physin)* (1449a15). This occurs when Aeschylus adds a second actor and Sophocles a third, along with scenography. But the key factor in tragedy finding its proper nature was the achievement of grandeur (*megethos*) when the poetry changed to iambic trimeter, which, according to Aristotle, most closely echoes the rhythms of natural speech and conversation. Aristotle has a particular interest in the birth of tragedy, but, unlike Nietzsche and many influenced by him, doesn't attribute any ontological significance to its genesis story. As will be clear from what I said in Part 2, I am inclined to agree with Aristotle.

Comedy is the *mimesis* of base but not vicious characters. Its field is the laughable or the ridiculous (*to geloion*). The early history of comedy—unlike tragedy—was forgotten because no serious interest was taken in it, which also explains why comedy was granted only a chorus at the Athenian City Dionysia in 487/6 BCE, whereas one had been granted to tragedy around 532. After a brief description of the similarities and differences between epic and tragic poetry—they are both elevated and in verse, but where epic uses a single hexameter form and observes no limit in time, tragedy uses a variety of meters and tends to keep within one revolution of the sun—Aristotle makes two promises before turning to the essence, being, or *ousia* of tragedy. Firstly, he says that he will speak later about epic, which he does; and secondly he says he will discuss comedy, which he doesn't. This is because the second book of the *Poetics* either wasn't written or no longer exists, a topic to which we will return at length below.

44

Happiness and Unhappiness Consist in Action

What, then, is the being of tragedy? Here we turn to the famous definition already touched on above. Tragedy is *mimesis praxeos,* imitation of action or enactive imitation, *prattein mimeseos.* It is elevated and complete, possessing magnitude and grandeur, in language that is "embellished by distinct forms in its sections" (1449b25–26). Embellishment means that the language of tragedy is marked by rhythm and melody. "Distinct forms" signifies that some of the language works through various meters alone, like single-line dialogue (*stichomythia*) or long speeches, where other language communicates through song, as with the choral odes or *stasima.* On just one occasion, in *Poetics* XIV, Aristotle refers to "horror and pity," where *phrittein* denotes a shuddering as the effect of enactive *mimesis,* and which might lead one to ponder the aesthetics of horror in relation to tragedy. Otherwise, pity is always paired with fear, and the enactment of tragedy accomplishes the catharsis of these twin passions. Read neutrally, literally, and flatly, as I think they should be, Aristotle's words seem to lean closer to the more minimal understanding of catharsis suggested above. The enactment of imitation in tragedy accomplishes, completes, or brings to an end (*perainousa*) the clearing away of the passions of fear and pity. Nothing more dramatic than that.

There are six components to tragedy: plot, character, diction, thought, spectacle, and song (or lyric poetry). To understand Aristotle's argument in the *Poetics,* it is necessary to grasp the absolute centrality of plot (*mythos*). Plot is the "soul of tragedy"(1450a38) and denotes the quality of the structure of events and actions. This is where the definition of the being of tragedy is so important. Tragedy is the imitation of events and not persons, actions and not character (*ethos*). It is not in order to provide *mimesis* of character that agents act, but in order to imitate actions and events. Although it is by virtue of character that a person has certain qualities, like virtues, it is only through their actions that they either find happiness or unhappiness (*eudaimonia kai kako-daimonia*) (1450a17).

This is an interesting moment where we can read across from the *Poetics* to Aristotle's ethical writings. The purpose or goal of life, for Aristotle, is happiness or flourishing, and this is achievable only in action. It is such actions that are imitated in tragedy, and a poet is a maker of plots and not characters or verses (1450a25). A plot is not unified if, as some people think, it is built around an individual character (1450a16). Think of a tragedy like Aeschylus's *The Suppliant Maidens,* where there is action (well, a little) but no individual character, and the protagonists in the drama are the fifty daughters of Danaus. The centrality of plot in Aristotle is revealing, I think, because one of the traditional charges made against the *Poetics,* by Hegel, Nietzsche, and many others, is that he psychologizes tragedy and thereby anticipates and legitimates the subjectification of art and aesthetic experience in the modern world. He doesn't. By making character secondary to action, or *praxis,* Aristotle in many ways *pragmatizes* tragedy. And, by conceiving of *mimesis* in instinctual terms, as he does, we might say that Aristotle *naturalizes* art as well.

Tragic action requires grandeur, but also magnitude. It requires action of a certain size. But what size? The magnitude of an action is that which allows what Aristotle calls *metabole,* change or transformation, to occur. This can be the change from prosperity to adversity or from adversity to prosperity (1451a15). If the scale of a tragedy is determined by *metabole,* then Aristotle is clear that the size should not be too big. The size of a tragedy has to be the right size, which is repeatedly illustrated in organicist metaphors. We can conceive of an animal a thousand miles long, Aristotle says, but that is too large to keep in one's mind, just as the minuscule is too small (1450b35–51a1–5). If we were to object that the tragedy of a thousand-mile-long Leviathan or a tiny amoeba might be either infinitely or infinitesimally sublime, then we have to understand that the sublime was not a category that was available to Aristotle. Although Aristotle later speaks of the pleasure of "awe" (*thaumaston*) (1460a17), the sublime awaits its formalization several centuries later with the shadowy Longinus. Beauty, by contrast, is what we feel when presented with a body of the right magnitude, namely one that allows for what Aristotle calls "coherent perception" (1451a5).

It is on analogy with the perception of coherence in a living body that Aristotle addresses the coherence of a drama and the idea of completeness in the definition of tragedy. To say that a tragedy is complete means that it is of the right magnitude and it constitutes a whole. What is a whole? At which point, Aristotle makes the seemingly blindingly obvious point that "A whole is what has a beginning, a middle, and an end" (1450b26). Whatever one thinks of this idea of wholeness—and here Aristotle begins to resemble a rather prosaic creative writing instructor or screenplay coach—it is interesting to note that many of the extant tragedies appear to ignore his advice. Sophocles' *Electra* begins in the middle and ends there too. Euripides' *Hecuba* begins at the end, with the destruction of Troy, and doesn't move beyond that endpoint, and so on. This organicist idea of wholeness and its refusal of the arbitrary (1450b30–32) makes little sense of some of the dramatic effects of tragedy, especially Euripides' complex marshaling of the deus ex machina, as we will see in Chapter 49. Directly linked to this idea of wholeness is the claim that a good plot must possess unity (1451a16–17). What Aristotle means here is that a good plot should not include everything, but just a unitary action of the right magnitude. Thus, Homer did not tell the whole history of the Trojan War in the *Iliad,* but just enough of the story to exert the right effect, namely the wrath of Achilles and its bloody consequences.

It is with this emphasis on the coherence, unity, and the whole beginning-middle-and-endedness of tragedy that Aristotle will infer what he sees as the right effect of poetry, which is the universal. In *Poetics* IX, he makes the distinction between poetic truth and historical truth: the latter tells of what happened, the former of what might happen; the latter is concerned with particulars, the former with the universal or general (*ta katholou*) (1451b7). Poetry is more philosophical than history and more elevated, Aristotle says, having greater import and scope than history. Aristotle betrays a rather low view of history here, which is at the very least questionable, specifically in the light of the clear historical contents of tragedies like Aeschylus's *Persians* and other historical events that show up refracted in tragedy, such as the Melian massacre in Euripides' *The Trojan Women.* But we might also want to think about apparent self-evidence of Aristotle's argumentation here, where the definitional criteria for tragedy lead directly to a claim for universality. On this view, which is admittedly the dominant view in the history of art, the validity of a particular artwork is granted only by virtue of its symbolic access to the universal. But can we not at the very least question this hierarchy and conceive of tragedy, or indeed the artwork as such, as the presentation of the particular in its particularity? At stake here would not be what might happen, but what actually took place historically, a history that might not be coherent, whole, and unified, and for good reason. This is one way of thinking about the relation between tragedy and what Benjamin calls *Trauerspiel,* the forms of early modern mourning play which, in his analysis, do not merely serve as conduits to universality, but as allegories of their own place and perhaps ours too.[1] History is not only the midwife of the universal, it is a bloody archive of particulars that might be generative of tragedies in ways that refuse the possibility of coherence, unity, and wholeness.

Single or Double?

It is action, the imitation of action, that produces tragedy's most "potent means of emotional effect," what Aristotle calls *psychagogia* (1450a33 and 1450b16). Lear nicely translates *psychagogia* as "soul-capturing."[1] We might recall that this is the same word, close to necromancy, that Socrates used to describe the pernicious effects of rhetoric in the *Gorgias* and that also describes the effects of the mighty lord that is *logos* in Gorgias's texts themselves. The two most important means of *psychogogia* that tragedy employs are key components of the plot: reversal and recognition, *peripeteia* and *anagnorisis* (1450a33–34).

In *Poetics* XI, Aristotle defines *peripeteia* as an unexpected change or *metabole* from one state of affairs to another. This change must conform with probability or necessity, and Aristotle gives his favorite example of Sophocles' *Oedipus the King,* where the messenger's news, which is intended to rid him of his anxiety about killing his father and bedding his mother, has exactly the opposite effect. *Anagnorisis* is the change from ignorance to knowledge. The most beautiful recognition is accompanied by reversal, and once again the example is Oedipus, whose knowledge of his identity leads simultaneously to his sudden fall from prosperity into adversity, self-blinding, and exile. When reversal and recognition are combined as two complementary motions that mesh in the wheel of a well-constructed tragic plot, then the effect will be pity or fear, the passions that find catharsis in tragedy.

After a brief, helpful enumeration of the parts of tragedy (*prologue, parados, episode, stasimon, exodos*), Aristotle turns in *Poetics* XIII to pity and fear, *eleos* and *phobos*. Now, in *Poetics* X, the distinction is made between simple and complex plots. Simple plots are simply episodic, where one damn thing happens after another, driven by no force of necessity. Complex plots contain reversal and recognition, and are therefore superior because they arouse the pity and fear that are appropriate to tragic *mimesis*. Pity is aroused by the sight of undeserved misfortune. Fear is generated by seeing the suffering of someone who is not us, but like ourselves. Pity and fear together are felt in the face of the unmerited adversity into which someone like us can fall. Interestingly, Aristotle also talks here of *philanthropia*, a fellow feeling or sympathy (1453a2). In order for tragedy to have the right effect, namely catharsis, it has to resonate with our philanthropic and not misanthropic sentiments. The latter is appropriate to invective, comedy, or satire, but not to tragedy.

This is where the much-discussed concept of *hamartia*, or error, is introduced, often misunderstood as a fatal, tragic flaw. The thought here, and again Oedipus is exemplary for Aristotle, is that the fall from prosperity into adversity and misery is not because of some evil or sinfulness in one's nature for which one is responsible, as Christianity later maintained in the doctrine of original sin. No, the fall is due solely to an unwilled error of character that is not our fault. Halliwell is illuminating on this point and sees *hamartia* as a basic human vulnerability that involves human beings in actions that lead them to profound suffering.[2] Expanding on this idea of vulnerability or fallibility, *hamartia* can be seen as a basic ontological weakness, lack, and limitedness that defines the human being. As Heidegger will show in *Being and Time*, existence is marked by a basic experience of thrownness and indebtedness that should not be interpreted in moralistic or Christian theological terms.

In addition to thinking that the best plots are complex rather than simple, Aristotle also claims that the well-made plot is single rather than double (1453a12–13). That is, the best tragedies are called *Oedipus* or *Antigone,* and not *Oedipus and His Mum* or *Antigone and Her Power-Crazed Uncle.* But seriously, this raises an important point. Although Aristotle says very clearly that plot is much more important than character, he also insists that the best tragedies turn on the *hamartia* of an individual like Oedipus or Thyestes. By contrast, as I sought to show above, tragedy is all about doubling, which can be the doubleness of an individual character like Oedipus, pulled this way and that and divided over against himself, showing a ravaged interior duplicity. But tragedy also very often turns around double deaths, like Eteocles and Polynices, Agamemnon and Cassandra, Clytemnestra and Aegisthus, and so on.

I have argued that in tragedy everything and everyone is doubled over and the effects of this are most clearly seen in the chorus, which, in plays like *Seven Against Thebes* and elsewhere, itself becomes twinned into a double dirge and divides into two distinct parts chanting strophe and antistrophe. It is very revealing that the chorus gets scant attention in the *Poetics,* with Aristotle writing a few sentences on the topic at the end of *Poetics* XVIII, where he takes a swipe at Euripides. He claims that the chorus should be treated as one of the actors and should participate in the action "not as in Euripides, but as in Sophocles" (1456a27–28). Although he does not express it explicitly, Aristotle is implying that the chorus in Euripides becomes a spectator on the action rather than a participant in it. This is a point that Nietzsche insists upon in *The Birth of Tragedy* with the rise of what he calls "aesthetic Socratism," when the philosophical spectator steps on the stage, which is why Nietzsche fallaciously insists that Socrates helped Euripides write his plays. I would argue that this claim about the chorus as actor and not spectator is of a piece with the constant emphasis upon the need for coherence, unity, and integrity in the construction of tragedy. We might oppose the latter to the tragedies of disintegration, disunity, and incoherence that define many of the plays of Euripides and which I prefer to see as a virtue rather than a vice.

We can link the relative unimportance of the chorus in Aristotle to what Simon Goldhill sees as the silencing of the civic frame of tragedy in the *Poetics*. If tragedy is all about doubling, then the subject who is doubled over in tragedy is the *polis* itself, divided and in some cases destroyed by the opposed forces that constitute what Hegel would see as the substance of ethical life. The political life of the city is divided by claim and counterclaim. It is the very conflict between those claims, say, the competing views of *dike* in the *Oresteia* or *nomos* in the *Antigone,* that both makes up and shakes up the experience of justice in tragedy. The individual character, Oedipus or Antigone, is a vital element in this conflictual experience of justice, but not the only element, and perhaps not the most important one.

46

Most Tragic Euripides

Returning to *Poetics* XIII, we find another fascinating passing reference to Euripides. Aristotle's claim is that the best tragedies, namely single tragedies, are constructed around the reversal from prosperity to misery. This reversal is caused not by depravity, which would not be tragic as it would not allow for any philanthropic sentiment like pity, but by error, *hamartia*. Aristotle tells us, and we have to assume he is right as there is no extant counter-evidence, that "Originally, the poets recounted any and every story." But "nowadays," namely in the second half of the fourth century BCE, Aristotle continues, "the finest tragedies are composed about only a few families" (1453a17–19). So, the finest or most beautiful (*kalliste*) (1453a22–23) tragedies of which Aristotle is aware take a few families as their subjects, such as the Palace of Thebes or the House of Atreus. Therefore, Aristotle adds, those who complain that Euripides has too few family narratives in his plays—many of which are focused on the events closely connected to the Trojan War—and that most of his plays end in adversity, are wrong. "For this, as explained," Aristotle adds, slightly impatiently, "is the right way" (1452a26–27).

As proof of this claim, Aristotle says that in theatrical contests, namely the *agon* at the City Dionysia and elsewhere, the plays that deal with a few families and that end badly are found to be the most tragic. To which he adds, fascinatingly, "And Euripides, even if he does not arrange other details well, is at least found the most tragic [*tragikotatos*] of the poets" (1452a28–30).

What is the meaning and force of the word *tragikotatos*? I think that Aristotle is condemning Euripides with faint praise here. The "other details" that Euripides does not arrange well include the chorus, as we have seen, and the deus ex machina, to which we will turn presently. What Aristotle is saying in claiming that Euripides is the most tragic poet is not that he is the best poet, who would presumably have to be Sophocles for Aristotle, but that he wins in the theatrical contests. Euripides is a *winner,* even if he arranges all sorts of details incorrectly and even when he is criticized by those Aristotle calls the *polloi* (1452a25). The latter are the many who govern in a democracy, a form of government, as Aristotle makes clear in the *Politics,* that has a perverted constitution. This is a fascinating moment because, as we will see when we turn to Aristophanes' *The Frogs*, one of the claims made by the comic character of Euripides is that he made tragedy democratic. This is the major reason as to why he is left in Hades after his death. It is Aeschylus who is resurrected and brought back to the city by the god Dionysos at the end of Aristophanes' comedy in order to rescue the martial valor of Athens.

Aristotle is clear that the fall of the central character in tragedy—he does not use the word "hero"—is not due to any depravity on his part. If Oedipus were depraved, then we would have no fellow feeling for him and the play would not therefore be a tragedy, as it would not evoke pity and fear. Now, part of the extraordinary power of many of Euripides' plays, such as the *Orestes* and *The Trojan Women,* is the way in which the line between what Aristotle sees as the properly tragic and the depraved is continually crossed. Characters like Orestes and Electra, for whom we might feel pity in Aeschylus, are exposed as mere self-interested brigands or bloodthirsty killers in Euripides, which seriously risks upending the balance in the emotional scales of tragedy as Aristotle conceives it. It is in this way that Euripides continually pushes against the constraints of the genre of tragedy and produces another kind of theater, which might be described as tragicomic, darkly ironic, or indeed a theater of depravity. With such a theater, which we linked earlier to Brecht's idea of epic theater, the question of catharsis is suspended.

47

Monstrosity—Or Aristotle and
His Highlighter Pen

In *Poetics* XIV, we find another passing but revealing delimitation in Aristotle's understanding of tragedy. Aristotle is clear that pity and fear should take their rise from the structure of events in the play, namely the plot. The plot should be so conceived that the mere recounting of the story is enough to yield the proper tragic emotions (1453b1–7). Plot is the superior element in tragedy and Aristotle is imagining that if a listener simply hears the story of Oedipus, then they would shudder with horror. However, fear and pity can also be produced by the spectacle (*ex tes opseos*), namely the visual dimension of theater: set, costume, and the like. But Aristotle goes on to claim that those dramatists who use spectacle to generate what he calls *to teratodes,* "have nothing in common with tragedy" (1453b8–9). The adjective *to teratodes* is translated by Halliwell as "sensational," but it might better be rendered as "the monstrous," and linked to what Liddell and Scott's *Greek-English Lexicon* calls "monstrous, of strange births."

This is an admittedly slight, passing moment in the unfolding of the *Poetics,* but significant, I think. We might recall that Hölderlin, in his enigmatic and fascinating "Remarks on Oedipus" from 1803, defines the essence of the tragic as the monstrous (*das Ungeheure*). This monstrosity is the awful coupling of the divine and the human; a strange birth indeed.[1] For Hölderlin, tragedy is entirely marked by a rhythm of momentary union with the divine—and he is thinking specifically of the godlike *hybris* of Oedipus at the beginning of Sophocles' play or Empedocles declaring himself an immortal—and separation from the god, which equals death or annihilation. The very title of Hölderlin's unfinished *Trauerspiel,* or mourning play, *The Death of Empedocles,* suggests this rhythm where the godlike man experiences the agony of separation from the divine and seeks to overcome it in union with god in the form of nature through his suicide in the flames of Mount Etna. But we might also link this thought of the monstrous to the idea we saw in Vernant and Vidal-Naquet that the tragic hero, like Oedipus, is a kind of monster. Oedipus breaches the proper political order of the city through parricide and incest. The tragic hero is the monster who is the source of the pollution in the city that must be expelled. Tragedy is the process by which we see the city attempt to confront and cleanse monstrous pollution. It is an open question as to how successful such attempts might be. Indeed, it is completely unclear how successful they were meant to be. Is political life possible without pollution? Might not tragedy be the presentation of the necessity of pollution?

More broadly still, just as the aesthetics of beauty in Aristotle's understanding of the necessary coherence that shapes the magnitude of tragedy has no place for the sublime, then a fortiori there can be no monstrosity in tragedy. In Kant's *Critique of the Power of Judgment,* he makes a distinction between the sublime, which is what he calls "almost too much," and the monstrous, which is "absolutely too much." That which is monstrous defeats our capacity for conceptual comprehension, and for Kant, there can be no room for it in the realm of aesthetic judgment.

This exclusion of the monstrous from poetics can be interestingly juxtaposed with the presence of the monstrous in the experience of tragedy itself. What I mean here is that there is something absolutely too much or uncontainable in tragedy, which resists and exceeds our capacity to comprehend it. This is one way of understanding what I called at the beginning of Chapter 30 the transcendentally opaque. Nietzsche's name for the uncontainable dimension in tragedy is the Dionysian, which can only be tolerated through the beautiful shining forth of the Apollonian. As we saw with *Prometheus Bound,* beneath the rational back-and-forth of the dialogue, there is the mute, irrational, uncontainable presence of violence. Such violence can also be seen in the background of the *Oresteia,* whether we think of the hallucinatory visions of Cassandra where language breaks apart into one long scream, or the silent bloodlust of the laconic Pylades, the quietly violent accomplice to Orestes. But what is uncontainable in tragedy is not just violence, it can be the mute presence of incestuous desire in *Oedipus the King* or even the fact of a traumatic wound in *Philoctetes.*

In the first words of *Poetics* XVII, Aristotle says—once again in the guise of the writing coach with a highlighter pen—"One should construct plots, and work them out in diction, with the material as much as possible in the mind's eye" (1455a21–22). On the contrary, I think that the experience of tragedy allows us to look, just for a moment, or perhaps for a sustained series of moments, at what is beyond or behind the mind's eye. Beneath the back-and-forth of speech and counterspeech, the play of conflictual reasoning that we hear in drama, some uncontainable and vast dimension of life flickers and flares up, something that we would rather keep out of view but that presses in upon us with an unbearable insistence. Such is the monstrous.

The affective response to monstrosity in tragedy is not pity and fear, but, I think, a feeling of *disgust,* where we are simply appalled by the sufferings of Cassandra, the endless woes heaped on Hecuba, or the coiled incestuous twinning of Oedipus and Jocasta that spins off through their four progeny. Although this uncontainable dimension is present along the edges of Aeschylus and Sophocles, it is brought to a boiling point of exaggeration and almost intolerable depravity in Euripides, where he twists the mechanisms of tragedy toward something altogether more unpleasant and disturbing. I think this is one reason why Euripides feels so much like our contemporary and the precursor to what we might call the art of the monstrous that we can find in Artaud's Theatre of Cruelty, Hermann Nitsch's blood orgies, or the theater of Heiner Mueller and, more recently, Sarah Kane. If we look back at much of what is most radical in the art of the last century or so, we can see that we are no longer dealing with an Aristotelian poetics of beauty or even a Kantian analytic of the sublime, but with an art of desublimation that attempts to adumbrate the monstrous, the uncontainable, the unreconciled, that which is unbearable in our experience of reality.

48

The Anomaly of Slaves and Women

In *Poetics* XV, Aristotle lists four apparently innocuous criteria for the depiction of characters in tragedy: they should be good, appropriate, lifelike, and consistent. But what is revealing here are the caveats on character. As concerns goodness, Aristotle says that every class of person can be good, even women and slaves, "even if the first of these is an inferior class, the other wholly paltry" (1454a19–20). Warming to his admittedly thoughtless misogyny, appropriateness is explained in the following way: "There is courage of character, but it is inappropriate for a woman to be courageous or clever in this way" (1454a23–24). Women characters, who it must be remembered were played by men, probably young men, should not be too bold or smart. Think of the way in which a character like Clytemnestra in the *Agamemnon* is repeatedly described by the patriarchal chorus of the elders as taking the part of the man and not the woman. This is not just because of her seizure of political power and by taking a compliant male consort. It is also due to the intelligence of her planning in setting up the vast beacon relay system of fires from Troy to Argos to warn her of the imminent arrival of her husband's return from the Trojan War. But think also of the clever flattery of her deception in luring Agamemnon and Cassandra along the crimson carpet and into the palace that serves as their slaughterhouse. Or again, when Antigone displays ferocious courage in the defense of her brother and her attacks on Creon, she is described as manly. The curious fact about so many Greek tragedies—and we should also think of Hecuba, Helen, Medea, and many others—is the persistent intelligence and courage of female characters, and so it is hard to make sense of, let alone tolerate, what Aristotle is suggesting here. But he clearly doesn't approve of the depiction of clever, courageous women.

The two further criteria, although seemingly benign, also betray clear moral prejudice and make little sense of the phenomenon of tragedy. That a character should be lifelike or possess likeness or *homoiosis,* really means that they should be "like us," namely like a decent, normal, adult patriarch like Aristotle. In a society, such as classical Athens, based on a very rigid hierarchy of the sexes where women were denied access to education and political participation, the repeated displays of clever, courageous women could hardly be described as lifelike. Which then raises the question—which we discussed in Part 2—about what might be going on in the inversion of gender roles in tragedy. Is tragedy lifelike, namely like life under Athenian patriarchy, or is something more subversive, troubling, and insurrectionary taking place in drama?

Consistency (*to omalon*) is also fascinatingly explained by Aristotle. Even when a character is clearly inconsistent—think of Euripides' Heracles, who is like two different people before and after the appearance of Madness (*Mania*—who is paradoxically the only sane character in the play)—they "should still be consistently inconsistent." The Greek here is the wonderfully oxymoronic *omalos anomalon* (1454a27). What Aristotle is suggesting is that anomaly must be avoided in depictions of character. Characters must not be uneven or irregular, which are other ways of rendering *anomalos.* And if a character is anomalous, they must be evenly uneven or regularly irregular. Again, it is tempting to introduce Euripides as counterevidence as he is the master of theatrical anomaly. Picking up on Aristotle's passing remark about the paltriness of slaves, think of the moment in Euripides' *Orestes* when Helen's Phrygian slave comes onstage toward the end of the play. He can't speak Greek and while this might not have been one of the job qualification criteria for his paltry role, he becomes suddenly hugely important in the drama. The slave is obliged to report to the chorus what happened to Helen inside the palace when Orestes and Pylades were trying to murder her. Then he has to prevent himself being killed when Orestes turns up in a foul temper. "Please remove your blade from my throat," the slave says, "I don't like the glare"(*Orestes* 1153). The effect of the slave's inability to speak Greek, combined with the intelligence he deploys to outwit Orestes and save his own skin, is wonderfully comic and a sheer anomaly in the flow of the drama. Tragedy, particularly Euripidean drama, is replete with stunning displays of inconsistency.

49

Mechanical Prebuttal

What is driving so much of Aristotle's argument in the *Poetics* is the insistence that there should be nothing irrational (*alogon*) (1454b6) in tragedy. If there is an irrationality in the plot, then it should lie outside the drama as part of the backstory. Aristotle gives the example of the irrationality of Oedipus's ignorance of the death of his father, Laius. Yet, this is permissible because it is extraneous to the action of Sophocles' *Oedipus the King.* The plot should unravel entirely on the basis of its own momentum and not by appealing to anything implausible or unintelligible. It is in this connection that Aristotle mentions the deus ex machina: "Clearly, the denouement of plots should issue from the plot as such, and not from a deus ex machina as in *Medea*" (1554a36– 54b1). The Greek here is *mechane,* which means both the crane or theatrical machine by means of which the gods appeared to be in the air, but also any artificial means of contrivance that is extraneous to the rationality of the plot. The specific allusion that Aristotle makes is to the end of the *Medea,* when she appears in the chariot of the sun, possibly drawn by dragons, with the corpses of her murdered children before she makes her escape to Athens after negotiating refuge with King Aegeus in exchange for her sorcery services. Here is another clever, courageous woman, but this time she isn't killed, but gets away with murder, multiple murders, while lording it over Jason, the hapless opportunist.

What interests me in this moment in the *Poetics* is the way in which Aristotle wants to draw a clear line not just between the rational and the irrational, but also the organic and the mechanical. A good tragedy has a tight, internal rationality that allows the drama to have the right magnitude and to be complete, like a living being of the appropriate proportions—not too big and not too small. It is in the presence of such a tragedy that we experience pity, fear, and catharsis. For Aristotle, the *mechane* is a machinic device, a moment of pure artifice, that is extraneous to the organic unity, coherence, and integrity of the properly tragic plot.

But what if we were to look at the *mechane* in another way, not as some sort of dramatic failure, but as a deliberately deployed artifice that is designed to frustrate and forestall any organicist conception of tragedy. What if the machinic is the truth of the organic that the latter has to exclude and repress. What I mean is that Euripides employs the mechanism of the *mechane* not in order to bring about a fake denouement of the drama, but precisely in order to show the fakery of any denouement as such. Euripides knows exactly what he is doing when he uses the *mechane*. He is showing how our desire for reconciliation and for a rational tidying up of all the loose ends of a drama is what has to be exposed as fraudulent. Fake reconciliation here functions as a deconstructive dismantling of the very idea of reconciliation. Euripides uses the deus ex machina to frustrate our wish for a neat conclusion, tragic catharsis, and a good night's sleep. As B. M. W. Knox says of Euripides, "He was born never to live in peace with himself and to prevent the rest of mankind from doing so."[1]

Let me give some examples. At the end of the killing field that is Euripides' *Orestes,* we find the unholy trinity of Orestes, Pylades, and Electra—looking like The Clash in 1977—on the roof of the palace engaged in a vicious argument with Menelaus and his troops with orders to kill them all. Orestes has a sword at the throat of Helen's daughter, Hermione. The three of them have torches in their hands and they are about to burn down the palace. It's an ugly scene. Euripides, as so often in his dramas, takes us to a boiling point of absolute deadlock. At which point, on the *mechane,* the god Apollo suddenly appears and gives a bizarre set of prophetic instructions. He tells Orestes that he will marry Hermione, the maiden whom he is about to slaughter. The quiet killer Pylades is told that he will marry Electra and that "great happiness awaits him" (line 1659)—it is completely unclear what that might mean. After a year or so in exile, in order to atone for killing his mother, Orestes will be allowed to reign as king in Argos. And in the meantime, Helen, the source of everyone's woe, whom Orestes and Pylades were just trying to murder, has been magically transfigured into a deity and will shine in the night sky like a star as a guiding light to sailors (to which one feels like replying, "Yeah, right").

Matters get even stranger in Euripides' *Electra.* After a bloodbath of revenge killing that exposes Orestes and Electra as amoral killers just going at it—Electra says to Orestes, "I urged you on, I touched the sword beside your hand" (lines 1224–25)—the Dioscuri, Castor and Pollux, suddenly appear. Castor disputes the justice of Orestes' murder of Clytemnestra: "You have not worked in justice" (line 1244). Of course, the matricide was legitimated by a prophecy from Phoebus Apollo and this forms the central claim to justice in Aeschylus's *The Libation Bearers.* When Castor asks Apollo for his counsel on Orestes' action, he receives "silence." Castor adds that "he knows the truth, but his oracles were lies" (line 1245). In addition to showing that the truth of the claim to justice was a lie, Castor tells Pylades that he will go on to found a city, possibly called Oresteion. Interestingly, Castor adds that Menelaus will bury Clytemnestra with due ceremony, accompanied by his apparently cheating wife, Helen.

The cheating is apparent because it is then revealed by the Dioscuri that the real Helen didn't go to Troy, but a Helen image was sent instead in order to deceive everyone. The idea that it was not Helen herself who was sent to Troy, but a simulacrum—which incidentally implies that the entire Trojan War was fought

for nothing, just a fake image—also provides the central conceit of Euripides' *Helen.* It would appear that Helen spent the
whole period of the Trojan War in Egypt. Poseidon's anger at
the Argives made their journey home from the war a very stormy
affair, as Odysseus knew to his cost. By sheer chance, Helen's
husband, Menelaus, washes up ashore in Egypt after losing his
way. A whole series of rather comic romantic intrigues ensue;
Helen and Menelaus eventually escape from the grip of the lech-
erous Egyptian bad guy, Theoclymenus, with the help of his sister, the priestess Theonoe, whose sole aim in life is to remain a
maiden. Theoclymenus is at the point of murdering Theonoe for
her betrayal, when there is a sudden *mechane.* Castor and Pollux
make a return appearance, stop the murder, and promise to serve
as guides to Helen and Menelaus so that they can return to Sparta
and live happily ever after.

Other examples of the deus ex machina could be given, like
the end of the *Bacchae* or *Andromache* or indeed the beginning
of the *Hippolytus* or *The Trojan Women,* but hopefully the point
is made. The *mechane* is deployed by Euripides in order to show
the inherent irrationality of the desire for organic integrity, clear
denouement, and neat endings that Aristotle requires from tragedy. Euripides is a kind of "prebuttal" of Aristotle in this and many
other ways. The apparent resolution of the deus ex machina in fact
resolves nothing and everything spirals into what Arrowsmith
rightly calls with reference to the *Orestes,* "a negative tragedy of
total turbulence."[2] Everything in Euripides seems to hurtle toward
deadlock, blockage, or standstill that can only be broken through
the fake reconciliation of the *mechane.* By exposing the fakery of
our desire for clean narrative arcs and happy endings, Euripides
exposes the sheer artifice of tragedy, allowing the mechanical to
erupt into the organic and twisting tragedy away from the rationality of catharsis toward something irrational, uncontainable,
disturbing, and morally devastating.

50

The God Finds a Way to Bring About What We Do Not Imagine

A widespread view has been held since antiquity that Euripides is a skeptic about the gods, or some kind of pagan atheist. Aristophanes famously suggested that Euripides was irreligious because he was seeking to promote a belief in newfangled gods. One can find modern echoes of this view in Schelling, where Euripides is seen as a decadent poet who committed sacrilege with the myths and the use of the deus ex machina is evidence of his impiety.[1] But I am not so sure. In *Euripides and the Gods,* Mary Lefkowitz powerfully argues that far from undermining traditional Greek religion, Euripides can be seen to be buttressing the existence of the ancient gods and reverence toward them. Closing out her compelling argument, Lefkowitz adapts the final lines from the *Medea* to make a general point about the role of the gods across the entirety of Euripides' dramas:

> Many are the forms of divinity; the gods bring many things to pass unexpectedly. And what people think will happen does not come to pass, but the god finds a means to bring about what we do not imagine. That is the outcome of action.[2]

The use of the *mechane* does not therefore entail disbelief in the gods, as much as show the absolute distance between the human and divine orders. As the chorus of Greek captive women say in *Helen,* "What is god, what is not god, what is between man and god who shall say?" (lines 1137–38).

What we think will come to pass in the rational unfolding of a good Aristotelian plot does not come to pass. The unexpected happens. And the gods in Euripides find a means to bring about what we do not imagine. The outcome of tragic action, on this view, is that we do not know the nature of divinity; it is closed from mortal eyes by a kind of epistemic mist. But this view is not some precursor of a mystical Christian belief in a cloud of unknowing. Within Christianity and the other monotheisms, we cannot know the true nature of the divine, but we can have faith that God loves us and cares for us. The radicality of ancient Greek polytheism is that the gods do not love and care for us and indeed they did not even create us. They can take the side of a certain person at a certain time, but that can and does change. Through the artifice of the *mechane,* divine action appears arbitrary, but this is due to the limitation of human reason. What tragedy gives its audience, seated like gods in the theater, is a momentary awareness of the proper relation between gods and mortals, which is one of distance and separation. The gods do not exist in order to console or comfort human beings, but in order to bring to pass what we might not at all expect. If there is an absurdity in Euripides' plays, then it is not that of an atheistic universe without a God, but rather the absurdity of the belief—the belief that arguably animates philosophy from Plato and Aristotle onward—that human rationality can intuit and render intelligible the nature of God and find a correspondence or likeness between the human and the divine. Tragedy is not committed to such a belief.

51

Misrecognition in Euripides

This Euripidean logic can be extended in relation to the next topic in the *Poetics:* recognition. The latter is the transition from ignorance to knowledge and Aristotle is clear in *Poetics* XVI that the best kind of recognition is accompanied by reversal. This was the case with *Oedipus the King,* where the two mechanisms mesh and unfold together from the events described in the plot itself and require nothing external. Aristotle then categorizes four other, inferior kinds of recognition. (1) That which is prompted by external signs like a sword, a necklace, or a scar, as was the case with Odysseus. (2) Recognition through poetic contrivance, such as a letter exchange. (3) Memory can trigger recognition where the sight of something familiar but overlooked can bring about awareness. (4) Reasoning of a syllogistic kind can also bring about recognition. Aristotle gives the example of Electra's recognition of her brother Orestes in *The Libation Bearers,* "That someone like her has come, no one is like her except Orestes, therefore *he* has come" (1455a4–6). If recognition combined with reversal is the highest kind, then "second-best are those by reasoning" (*syllogismou*) (1455a20).

"How do you overturn a cliché?" Anne Carson asks. "From inside."[1] Returning to Euripides and the way in which he continually overturns and twists tragic conventions inside out, it is fascinating to see how the recognition scene from Aeschylus's *The Libation Bearers* is replayed in his *Electra,* probably performed around forty-five years after the *Oresteia*. As Simon Goldhill shows, Euripides directly parodies Aeschylus.[2] The stately ritual libations become a water pot, and Electra serially dismisses the Old Man's Aeschylean suggestions to find clues for the proof of Orestes' return. When the Old Man says, "Look at the lock of hair and match it to your own head" (lines 520–23), Electra replies,

> How could a lock of hair match with mine?
> One from a man with rugged training in the ring
> And games, one combed and girlish? (lines 527–29)

When he replies,

> At least go set your foot in the print of his hunting boot
> and see if it is not the same as yours, my child." (lines
>   532–33)

Electra becomes enraged, as Greece has notoriously rocky ground:

> You make me angry. How could rocky ground receive
> the imprint of a foot? And if it could be traced,
> it would not be the same for brother and for sister,
> a man's foot and a girl's—of course his would be bigger.
>   (lines 534–37)

When the Old Man suggests that Electra might recognize Orestes by a piece of clothing that she wove, she quips,

> You know quite well Orestes went away in exile
> when I was very small. If a little girl's hand
> could weave, how could a growing boy still wear that cloth
> unless his shirt and tunic lengthened with his legs? (lines
>   541–44)

Boys' feet are bigger than girls'. Boys' hair is rougher than girls'. And why would Orestes be wearing the same clothing as he wore when he was a kid? As Goldhill says of Electra, "Her sarcastic rationalism offers a sophistic critique of the Aeschylean token."[3] Euripides offers a critical parody of the idea and ideal of recognition by syllogistic reasoning. Euripides' *Electra* is a metatheatrical takedown of Aeschylus. And the irony in the play deepens because Electra is wrong: Orestes is already there onstage. Which rebounds into the question of the point and goal of rational argumentation in tragedy. The deus ex machina in *Electra,* discussed above, provides the final contradiction in the play. Apollo knows the truth but his oracle was a lie. Aristotelian syllogisms stall in a swirl of paradox. Everything is turned inside out.

Euripides willfully extends recognition scenes to the point where tragedy flips over into farce. In *Iphigenia in Tauris,* there is a painfully long scene between Iphigenia and Orestes whose sheer banality becomes ridiculous. Back and forth they go, reasoning relentlessly to little effect. When Iphigenia says, "Orestes is not here. He is in Argos," Orestes replies, "Poor sister, not in Argos! I am here!" (lines 746–48). But Iphigenia still doesn't get it, adding many lines later, "Are you Orestes? Is it really you?" The extended recognition scene is also used to great comic effect in Euripides' *Helen.* Here is a small portion of what runs for several pages of rapid *stichomythia,* or single-line interchange:

Menelaus: You are more like Helen, my lady, than any I know.
Helen: You are like Menelaus, too, what does it mean?
Menelaus: The truth. You have recognized that most unhappy man.
Helen: Oh, you are come at long last here to your wife's arms.
Menelaus: Wife? What wife do you mean? Take your hands off my clothes. (lines 563–67)

Indeed, Euripides has a fondness for these kinds of one-line takedown punch lines, as we saw above in Menelaus's quip to Hecuba that it would be dangerous to let Helen set foot on his ship: "What can you mean? That she is heavier than she was?" (*The Trojan Women,* 1050). When Electra explains that the kind farmer to whom she has been married has never had sex with her, Orestes replies, "He finds you unattractive?" (*Electra*, 256). When the newly happily married couple of Helen and Menelaus are coolly planning a murder, she says that it would be impossible to kill the Egyptian king, to which he replies, "You mean he has a body that no steel can pierce?" (*Helen*, 810). Or again, when the broken body of the boy Astyanax—freshly hurled from the burning battlements of Troy—is brought to Hecuba, she turns on the Greeks: "This baby terrified you?" (*The Trojan Women,* 1165).

52

Smeared Makeup

In Euripides, everything that we think we know about tragedy begins to fall apart. Goldhill adds, "Here are Greeks who do not believe their myths, even as they tell them."[1] Consider the scene of matricide in *Electra*. In Aeschylus, Orestes doubts the legitimacy of his action in killing his mother, and turns to Pylades, who, in his only line in the play, reassures Orestes that Apollo has ordained the act. In Euripides, Electra has her hand on the sword, urging Orestes on with ruthless violence. The guidance of action by the gods in Aeschylus becomes sheer bloodlust in Euripides. As Anne Carson says,

Aeschylus looked at the story of Agamemnon and saw a parable of human grandiosity and tragic *katharsis,* leading through bloodshed and strife to an eventual restoration of civilized order. Euripides looked at the same story and saw smeared makeup.[2]

Euripides' Electra is a particularly nasty piece of work. When the Old Man counsels the murder of Clytemnestra and the plan is set, Electra defies him and says, "I will be the one to plan my mother's death" (line 647); adding, with murderous simplicity, "She will come; she will be killed. All that is clear" (line 660). Should the plan fail and Orestes not kill his mother, then Electra

makes plain, in what might be a line from a Nick Cave song, "I
will stab my belly with a two-edged sword" (line 688).

The authority of oracles and ritual, which is so important to the
action of the *Oresteia,* is hollowed out in Euripides and twisted.
Aegisthus is presented as a rather two-dimensional opportunist by
Aeschylus. But in Euripides he is described as solemnly slaughter-
ing a bull in honor of the Nymphs and being exceptionally pleasant and hospitable to his stranger guests, Orestes and Pylades.
Aegisthus is then brutally stabbed in the back by Orestes as he
is ritually disjointing the beast, and "The vertebrae of his back
broke" (line 841). It is hard to see any courageousness or nobility
in this murder. When Aegisthus's corpse is dragged and dumped
onstage, Orestes says to Electra, "He is all yours" (line 895). She
then proceeds to give a wildly vindictive and rather pointless
speech over the corpse. At which point, it is reported that Clytemnestra is on her way to visit Electra and make the accustomed
sacrifices to a fake baby to which she believes her daughter has
just given birth. Orestes once again has doubts as in *The Libation
Bearers,* but this time it is not the oracle of a god that is invoked
but vengeance pure and simple. Electra insists, "Kill her just the
way she killed my father. And yours" (line 970).

When Clytemnestra turns up, she is presented as a remarkably
sympathetic and even contrite figure. In a remarkable moment of
confession, she admits, "Perhaps I drove my hate too hard against
my husband" (line 1110). What drives Electra's rage at her mother
is certainly not justice, nor even pride and honor, but the most
powerful motivator in the realm of human affairs: *real estate.* She
says, and this is amazing,

If, as you say, our father killed your daughter,
Did I do any harm to you, or did my brother?
When you killed your husband, why did you not bestow
The ancestral home on us, but took to bed the gold

Which never belonged to you to buy yourself a lover? (lines
1086–90)

Electra is saying, "Okay, you killed Dad because he killed my
sister in order to go to war, and maybe that's understandable, but
why didn't you give us the palace after you did it?" After the deed
is done and the gory corpses are displayed, both Orestes and Electra collapse into pathetic self-pity, with Electra whining,

Oh weep for me. Where am I now? What dance—
what wedding may I come to? What man will take me bride
to his bed? (lines 1198–1200)

When Castor and Pollux appear, it soon becomes clear that
Electra will be married to Pylades and do just fine.

What, then, is the moral of this tale? In her translator's introduction to the play, Emily Townsend Vermeule offers a rather
pious critique of Euripides' *Electra* that inadvertently says much
that is true. She says that it is a play in deliberately bad taste where
Euripides deploys a technique of double vision: seducing the audience into sympathy with Electra and Orestes and then destroying
it with wanton brutality. Oracles are disbelieved, ritual is ridiculed, and "Aeschylean morality is somehow missing."[3] She won-
ders whether Euripides had a moral purpose in writing this play,
which raises the metaquestions: What exactly is a moral purpose?
And why should theater exhibit it? Euripides offers his spectators no comfort or reassurance and I would argue that this is a
strength rather than a failing. If our moral expectations of tragedy
are warped by Euripides, then this might lead us to question those
expectations rather than judge his drama to be the falling away
from an earlier tragedy ideal.

Of course, Aristotle was no dunce. He was aware of the kinds
of twisting of Aeschylus that Euripides produced. There is a brief

moment in *Poetics* XXII when Aristotle notes that Euripides composed exactly the same iambic line as Aeschylus, but replaced just one word, using a loan term rather than the standard expression. Where Aeschylus in his lost *Philoctetes* writes, "the cancer which eats the flesh of my foot," Euripides replaces "eats" (*esthiei*) with "feasts on" (*thoinatai*) (1458b23–24). The effect of this substitution changes what is beautiful (*kalon*) into something tawdry (*euteles*). By overturning Aeschylus from the inside, Euripides completely transforms tragic grandeur into something low, paltry, and unseemly.

53

Sophocles' Theater of Discomfort

But the truth is that this warping and subversion of tragic conventions is not restricted to Euripides. It is already present in Sophocles (and, who knows, it might also be abundant in Aeschylus himself, but sadly we do not possess any of the earlier tragedies that he might have subverted as models). In Sophocles' *Electra,* which was very possibly written in the same period as Euripides' play of the same name—the dating is uncertain, and it is possible that Sophocles' play is later than Euripides', which was probably staged in 413 BCE—there is also a direct allusion to the lock of hair recognition scene in *The Libation Bearers* (lines 1198–99). Like Euripides, Sophocles seems to be quite deliberately both subverting the dramatic conventions of the *Oresteia* and unraveling *avant la lettre* Aristotle's understanding of tragedy. Sophocles' *Electra* is a play entirely without comfort. It is also a play where the imitated action is constantly shifted into the background and actionless words fill the stage. From the moment she enters, around 100 lines in, until the play ends some 1,400 lines later, Electra simply stands in the doorway of the palace and laments excessively, interrupted by an extraordinary series of screams. Indeed, she outscreams all the other screamers in tragedy, even Cassandra. And once Electra has begun talking it is impossible to make her stop.

As Virginia Woolf says, Electra is a figure so tightly bound that she can move only an inch this way or that.[1] She is a creature of pure negation, whose identity is secured by the continuous out-pouring of her grief alone. "Actionless," as Anne Carson says, "she feeds on her own negativity."[2] And the negations double throughout the play: "I cannot not grieve" (line 181); "I must not violate Electra" (line 495). And in a manner more excessive even than Euripides' *Helen*, she is surrounded by fakery, the fraudulence of the palace in which she lives with her murderous mother, Clytemnestra, and her opportunist lover, Aegisthus. Electra says to her mother,

> I don't think of you as mother at all.
> You are some sort of punishment cage
> Locked around my life. (lines 801–4)

Her most extreme lamentation occurs when she holds the urn that she believes contains the ashes of her brother. But the urn is empty, the news that she hears is fake, and the only way in which she can respond is through negation. Holding the dummy urn, she cries,

> I send you out, I get you back:
> tell me
> how could the difference be simply
> nothing?
> Look!
> You are nothing at all.
> Just a crack where the light slipped
> through. (lines 1505–11)

Like a character in Beckett (one thinks of Winnie in *Happy Days*), Electra is a talking ball, a speaking wound in a world of fake trash locked in an urn of language and lament.

The effect of the fakery and negation pushes the tragic once again toward the farcical. Addressing the urn, she screams,

Look how you got smaller, coming back.
OIMOI TALAINA
All my love
Gone for nothing. (lines 1528–31)

During the extended final recognition scene with Orestes, the effect is painful. Electra is so shocked that she receives any sympathy for her plight that she simply cannot believe it. But it is also painfully funny. When it finally becomes clear to Electra that the person standing in front of her really *is* Orestes, and he wants to carry out his plan of double murder, she simply won't stop talking. Orestes says, "Yes, I am here. No, keep silent for a while" (line 1654). To which Electra replies "Why?" When she erupts again in lamentation, "OTOTOTOTOTOI TOTOI. You drive me back down my desperation" (line 1663), Orestes insists, "No long speeches" (line 1678). But it is to no avail and she cannot stop; Electra cannot not be herself. When Orestes' accomplice, the Old Man, tells her directly, "Now cut short the speechmaking" (line 1777), Electra screams on, incessant in her lament.

The tragicomedy reaches a weird crescendo at the end of the play, when Aegisthus realizes that he is doomed and tries to speak. To which Electra replies, "Don't let him speak—by the gods! Brother—no speechmaking now!" (line 1970). Her only action, such as it is, is to leave the doorway where she has been standing sentinel for what seems like an eternity, and walk into the palace behind her brother. Whatever else Sophocles' *Electra* might be, it is certainly not an imitation of action designed to achieve the catharsis of the affects of pity and fear. There is no reversal here and no *metabole* in the plot. Electra is the same at the end of the play as she was at the beginning. Nothing has changed. *Electra* is a play where action is sidelined by language, redemption is subtracted, and justice seems a massive irrelevance. We might be terrified by the negative intensity of Electra and pity her condition, but there is no question of catharsis. The audience is never let off the hook. The emotions in this play are simply opened and left gaping like the vast wound of grief that defines Electra's being.

In a passing clause of *Poetics* XXV, Aristotle appears to quote Sophocles when he said that the latter "created characters as they ought to be, Euripides as they really are" (1460b32–33). Based on our reading of Sophocles' and Euripides' versions of Electra, the truth would appear to be somewhat more complex.

54

Vulgar Acting and Epic Inferiority

After a series of chapters (XIX–XX) that might well be a partial
interpolation from another text, like *De Interpretatione* or possibly one of his lost works on poetry, Aristotle ends the analysis
of tragedy or enactive imitation (*to prattein mimeseos*) (1450a15–
16) and turns, as promised in the first words of *Poetics* VI, to epic
poetry. Epic is explained by analogy with tragedy. Although epic
is *mimesis* that works through narration rather than imitation, like
tragedy it should be centered on a single action. The dominant
example in these pages is, unsurprisingly, Homer, who possesses
"inspired superiority over the rest" of the epic poets (1459a30–
31). Epic also requires reversals and recognitions, and, like tragedy,
it must be of an appropriate size to be seen in a single, coherent
view. Epic needs a beginning, a middle, and an end, although its
scale can obviously be larger than tragedy. Namely, there is much
more action in the *Iliad* than, say, in Euripides' *Rhesus*, which is
the only play we have that is lifted entirely from Homer (although
its authorship is strongly disputed), where the action concerns
a moment in Book X. The grandeur and elevation of epic are
achieved, in part, by the use of the heroic hexameter, "the most
stately and dignified of metres" (1459b34).

In a fascinating and direct reversal of Socrates' argument
in the *Republic* that narration is better than imitation because
it constrains the vicious excesses of mimicry, Aristotle insists

that "the poet should say as little as possible in his own voice" (1460a7). Namely, that although epic is narrative verse, it should be as mimetic as possible and the poet should seek to speak in the voices of others. This leads to the last question that Aristotle deals with in the *Poetics:* which is superior, epic or tragic imitation? Otherwise said, is tragedy inferior to epic because it is vulgar (*phortike*) (1461b28–29), namely it appeals to the vast audiences assembled in theaters like that on the south slope of the Athenian Acropolis?

Aristotle makes two very interesting claims here. Firstly, to call tragedy vulgar is not a critique of the tragic poets, but of the performances of tragedy. Hence, vulgarity is the fault of acting and not writing. The historical context for this remark is important. Aristotle is writing in the second half of the fourth century after a long period when much more prominence had been given to actors than the kind of citizen-soldiers who took part in the original productions of Aeschylus. A celebrity Attic star culture had clearly emerged, when famous actors would freely adapt and elaborate parts from classic plays in order that they might be seen in a better light. *Plus ça change,* one might respond. Indeed, according to David Kovacs, there is evidence from medieval scholia of the suspicion that actors had tampered with the original texts of the plays.[1] Aristotle singles out actors who clearly "overdo visual signals" (1462a6) like the otherwise entirely unknown rhapsode Sosistratus. Or again, Aristotle has no patience for "crude performers" (1461a8) such as Callipides and other actors who portray "low women" (1461a10). Aristotle clearly did not like attention-seeking, flashy actors who overdo it.

The second claim directly follows from the first. Aristotle says that "Tragedy achieves its effect even without actors' movements, just like epic; reading makes its qualities clear" (1461a10–11). The effect of tragedy is the catharsis of the emotions of pity and fear. But this effect does not require performance. It can be felt by simply reading the text. Aristotle is probably thinking of reading texts out loud rather than the modern habit of reading silently in solitude. But this is a precious indication that by the time of the composition of the *Poetics*, the texts of the tragedies were available. Namely, that the performance papyri had been collated and archived in a way that could be studied. What we see here in this moment in the *Poetics* is something self-evident to us, but not to the fifth-century productions of the extant plays. Namely that there could be a gap between text and performance, and the effects of tragedy could be gleaned by the former and didn't necessarily require the latter. Indeed, scholars have suggested that Lycurgus, the Athenian statesman from 338 to 326 BCE (close to the possible dates of the composition of the *Poetics*), arranged for the collection of official state copies of the plays of Aeschylus, Sophocles, and Euripides, and established by law that actors could not deviate from established texts in their performances.

The combination of these two claims allows Aristotle to answer the question raised by *Poetics* XXVI. Aside from vulgar performances by crude actors, where tragic drama would presumably veer into melodrama, tragedy is a higher form of imitation than epic. Tragedy possesses all of epic's poetic resources, namely its metrical quality of speech in verse, but it also has music and spectacle, "which engender the most vivid pleasures" (1462a16). And this vividness, which can be seen in performance, but also felt through reading, is superior because it is more concentrated and compact. For Aristotle, it is self-evident that what is compact is more pleasurable than what is diluted. Although Homeric epics like the *Iliad* are structured "as well as could be" (1462a10), they still consist of multiple, related actions and therefore constitute diluted delights. By focusing on a single action, like Sophocles' *Oedipus the King*, we are granted a unified, concentrated, and higher pleasure. Therefore, Aristotle concludes, tragedy is superior to epic in achieving the goal of catharsis.

At which point, in a typical moment of bathos, Aristotle concludes his discussion of tragic and epic poetry with the words "Let this count as sufficient discussion"(1462a19). The text of the *Poetics* ends with a lacuna, which is where the lost analysis of comedy would have begun.

55

Is Aristotle Really *More Generous to Tragedy Than Plato?*

Before turning to the question of the existence of the second book of the *Poetics,* I'd like to make some general remarks about Aristotle, particularly thinking back to the discussion of Plato's *Republic.* The first thing to note is the apparent difference between the treatment of tragedy in Plato and that given by Aristotle. As we saw in the opening pages of this part, it is very much a moot point whether the *Poetics* must be read as the defense or apology for poetry called for in Book X of the *Republic.* But the contrast between the two approaches is startling, particularly as they both begin from the understanding of poetry as *mimesis.* But in Aristotle *mimesis* is not part of a metaphysical and moral critique of imitation that seeks to denigrate poetry with respect to the world of phenomena and the realm of transcendent forms that allegedly guide that world. *Mimesis* is more of a supple principle than an Occam's razor dividing truth from lies. There is also nothing in Aristotle to suggest that the tragic poets should be excluded from the philosophically well-ordered city. Rather, imitation is understood to be an instinct that human beings possess and that distinguishes them from other animals. Human beings are mimetic animals and it is out of this natural drive that poetry emerges, especially as it is first expressed in musical and linguistic improvisation. We are imitative beings, and poetry is enactment and, crucially, reenactment. As I said above, Aristotle is a proto-

Darwinian and sees *mimesis* in naturalistic terms as a process of behavioral development through adaptation.

Aristotle shows himself to be sensitive to the considerable effects of tragedy on the emotions, as did Socrates in the *Republic*. But Aristotle is not suspicious or distrustful of the moral consequences of the passions in the sphere of poetry. Tragedy evokes pity and fear (and, in one instance, horror), but these emotions are not to be restrained, controlled, held in, and massively inhibited in the manner suggested by Socrates because they threaten our self-mastery. Rather, we are led by tragic poetry toward a catharsis of those emotions, although it is rather unclear, as we showed above, whether the key concept in the *Poetics* is to be understood in moralistic, ritualistic, or purely physiological terms.

What is striking in the *Poetics* is the extensive use of empirical sources and quasi-botanical samples and examples, together with the serious interest in the historical origins of poetry in general and tragedy in particular. Also, crucially, the rules of tragedy are not deduced *a priori* as they are in the *Republic* or desiccated into a series of aesthetic principles as in French neoclassicism's obsession with the three unities of time, place, and action. Aristotle works through *a posteriori* inference from a number of specific cases, like *Oedipus the King,* and then generalizes his views into a series of flexible guidelines, while acknowledging that there will always be exceptions to his rules. Aristotle plays the pragmatist to Plato's metaphysician. As we said above, the *Poetics* is a theory of tragedies rather than a metaphysical critique of tragedy (nor is it a speculative philosophy of the tragic of the Schellingian or early Nietzschean varieties). Aristotle is someone who obviously both saw a lot of plays and had access to the texts independently of performance.

The relative or perhaps *apparent* absence of judgment in the *Poetics* is striking. Aristotle's style is direct and monological, rather than indirect and dialogical. Unlike Plato in the *Republic, Phaedrus,* and elsewhere, Aristotle does not write a competing counterdrama to the drama of tragedy, a mimetic metacritique of *mimesis,* but simply gives us a lecture, or quite possibly a series of lectures. Aristotle's pedagogical style is flawless. It is defined by abundant examples, an apparent generosity of spirit toward the matter discussed, and most of all by a clear, analytic rigor that works formalistically through particulars toward the elucidation of general concepts. Most of all, Aristotle's style is defined by a sympathetic but utterly self-confident *rationality.*

In the subsequent history of aesthetics, despite their obvious philosophical differences, Aristotle might be seen as the progenitor of Hegel in the sheer empirical diversity and scope of the artistic examples and genres discussed. Hegel, and I am thinking here of his late lectures on aesthetics rather than earlier works like the *Phenomenology of Spirit,* is like a benevolent philosophical steamroller, flattening out examples and arranging, categorizing, and, crucially, hierarchizing artistic genres. But one has the sense that neither Aristotle nor Hegel is *troubled* by the art that they analyze. They are neither perturbed nor disturbed by art. No, they analyze, they sift and sort, and offer cool, rational analyses. In this similarity, both Aristotle and Hegel are dissimilar to Plato and Nietzsche, who are profoundly pained by that which they are pushing against, whether *theatrokratia* in the former or the vicious moralistic effects of Platonism in the latter. It is this sense of being deeply disturbed by the pernicious effects of tragedy on the city or aesthetic Socratism on the world that perhaps unites the otherwise opposed forces of Platonism and anti-Platonism. It is also what leads both Plato and Nietzsche to be violently unfair to the objects of their antipathy: to declaim, to distort, and to exaggerate. What is so distinctively different about Aristotle is his evenly disposed (and sometimes maddening) fairness toward the poetry he discusses.

But is Aristotle *really* more generous to tragedy than Plato? To which I'd like to answer: yes and no. *Yes,* insofar as tragedy is taken very seriously in its own terms, both empirically and historically, and then elevated above epic and very possibly above comedy too. Aristotle very clearly inverts the Socratic privileging of narration over imitation, and therefore of epic over tragic poetry. Tragic *mimesis* is not seen as some falling away from rational self-mastery that descends through democracy into tyranny. The tragic poets are not the lackeys of tyrants. On the contrary, as we saw in *Poetics* XXVI, tragedy is not condemned or judged to be inferior for appealing to the many, the *hoi polloi*. Thus, although Aristotle gives us a philosophical account of tragedy in a discourse that is very clearly theoretical, its spirit is remote from the kind of philosophical autocracy and political authoritarianism described in the *Republic*. To be clear, I am not saying that Aristotle's analysis of tragedy is democratic, as Aristotle was critical of democracy. Let's just say that, for Aristotle, tragedy has a place in the existing political order and the tragic poets do not therefore need to be summarily expelled.

No, insofar as one might claim that the *Poetics* gives ample proof of the self-assuredness and hegemony of philosophical discourse after Plato, especially the primacy of monological philosophical rationality. Platonic dialogue is a discursive invention that is in clear competition with tragic poetry and sees tragedy as the real rival, the genuine opponent and worthy enemy, in the way that Nietzsche will much later view Socrates. Aristotle's discourse, on this view, is written after the battle between philosophy and poetry has been won and Attic tragedy has lost out to theory, whether naturalistic, moral, or metaphysical. What we see in Aristotle is the beginning of a scientific approach to poetry, and of course to all the other matters in the vast scope of his writings. Might one not suggest that Aristotle describes tragedy from the unquestionably superior rational vantage point of scientific or theoretical discourse? If this is plausible, then it is this assurance of superiority that is the source of Aristotle's undoubted generosity to tragedy. In this sense, Aristotle is once again closer to Hegel, who is also extraordinarily generous to the whole world of the aesthetic, but where that world is comprehended from a necessarily higher and systematic philosophical standpoint. Aristotle is so fair, so confident, so reasonable, so measured, so virtuous, so gently but insistently opinionated, that it sometimes makes you want to scream. We might recall Aristotle's passing remark on women and slaves discussed above. Aristotle is just a normal Greek patriarch. As Jonathan Lear argued, Attic tragedy is not intended for the ignorant who require some kind of moral education in the simpler form of a visual spectacle with a gripping, slightly scary, story. The audience for Aristotle's view of tragedy is composed of well-educated, well-adjusted, virtuous male citizens. And that is the problem.

Continuing this line of thought, there is something about the eminent reasonableness of Aristotle that leads one's critical faculties to shut down. In his cool, calm, measured, impersonal manner, Aristotle draws the reader along and somehow leads one to submit to him, to give up any protest and accept his basic premises. For example, and this is one premise we have discussed, Aristotle defines tragedy as *mimesis praxeos,* and he gives us an etymological and historical narrative—with a moral twist—in order to back this claim up. But why should one assume that Aristotle is right about tragedy being the imitation of action? And if tragedy is understood in this way—and this was Nietzsche's point above—then why is so much of tragedy concerned with inaction, with the often vapid back-and-forth and speech and counterspeech, where action slips into the background or takes place offstage? My sense is that reading Aristotle can have a lulling, almost soporific effect that can draw one into a too-ready acceptance of his understanding of tragedy. The point of my readings of certain tragedies, particularly those of Euripides, is to question that understanding by showing how it is complicated—indeed negated—by the more turbulent logic of the plays themselves.

Is there not finally something simply fateful about Aristotle's *Poetics*? Does it not describe the way in which we have come to see and judge artworks, as requiring coherence, unity, a beginning-middle-and-end integrity, an organic quality like a living being, all based on the tight internal rationality of plot? As we have seen, Aristotle can be read as being full of advice for budding dramatists: benign, measured, and full of a quiet, but haughty, self-assurance. The point is, whether we like it or not (and I don't), Aristotle is fatefully right about our responses to art. What I mean here is that Aristotle has informed, shaped, or somehow finds an echo in our very ordinary aesthetic judgments. We make these not when we're trying to be clever in relation to experimental, edgy, or avant-garde work that defies our expectations, but in our more humdrum, everyday aesthetic pleasures. Think, for example, of the ways in which we respond to mainstream Hollywood cinema or popular television series. We bring a whole host of aesthetic presumptions to bear in our modest little judgments to friends, say. We might complain that a story didn't quite hold together, that a character was ill formed, the ending was gratuitous or added on and we didn't feel that the whole story hung together in a way that allowed us to emote in the way we like to emote, namely with pity and fear and a little bit of catharsis. In our ordinary, slightly thoughtless but well-intended aesthetic judgments, we are all Aristotelians.

56

Poetics II—*Aristotle on Comedy*

Let's move into the realm of speculation. Might the *Poetics* be read in terms of what is missing from it? Namely, in terms of an absence? As we have seen, the text ends with an ellipsis. Aristotle promised that the transition from tragedy to epic was going to be followed by a discussion of the comic. But what is known as the second book of the *Poetics* has disappeared. The question is: Did it disappear? Was Aristotle's book on comedy lost?

These questions provide the central conceit of Umberto Eco's well-known and widely read *The Name of the Rose* from 1980.[1] In this gripping murder mystery, whose central protagonist is the Sherlock Holmes–like Franciscan friar William of Baskerville, the plot turns on a copy of the second book of the *Poetics.* The sole extant copy of the book is hidden away in a secret room at the center of a labyrinth-shaped library in a monastery in the hills of Piedmont. The library is administered by the blind Jorge of Burgos, a thinly veiled caricature of Jorge Luis Borges, who was himself director of the National Public Library in Buenos Aires. The pages of the second book of the *Poetics* are infused with deadly poison, so that whosoever might find their way to the forbidden book will die by licking their fingers when turning the pages. This explains the many monkish murders that punctuate Eco's story. Jorge of Burgos hated laughter, which he considered ungodly and unbecoming for monks, in an analogous way to Socrates' prohibition of ribald laughter for the philosopher-guardians. In the climax to Eco's tale, when asked by William why the book on comedy had to be locked away, Jorge answered that it would not be proper for "the Philosopher," as the medievals called Aristotle, who provided the core to Thomistic Christian dogma, to be seen to endorse laughter by dignifying it with his words. Jorge then takes his own life by eating the forbidden book and sets fire to the library, ensuring that it would be lost forever to the world.

It's a wonderful story. But was the second book of the *Poetics* really lost to the world? Did the text even exist? Here, we need to tell the equally wonderful story of the *Tractatus Coislinianus,* a text brought to light in 1839 by J. A. Cramer. Cramer's remarks on the *Tractatus* proved to be highly influential through the work of the philologist Jacob Bernays, whose *Zwei Abhandlungen über die Aristotelische Theorie des Dramas* was first published in 1880. Bernays's theory of catharsis, to which we will briefly turn below, is better known through the significant effect it had on Sigmund Freud's *Jokes and Their Relation to the Unconscious.* Indeed, the kinship between Bernays and Freud is closer than one might imagine, as the former was the uncle of the latter's wife, Martha Bernays. The *Tractatus Coislinianus* is a Byzantine text, probably from the tenth century or arguably even from the sixth century, which was sent on a ship from Cyprus to Paris in 1643. It then sat in the de Coislin collection of the Bibliothèque Nationale de Paris. The tractate purports to be nothing less than a summary of the second book of the *Poetics.* The case for its authenticity—which is a highly controversial claim among classicists—has been made with impressive detail and no little courageous aplomb by Richard Janko in his *Aristotle on Comedy.*[2]

The text of the *Tractatus Coislinianus* appears quite odd to the contemporary reader as it is not a prose summary, but a schematic representation with concepts arranged in family trees, although this was apparently a common Byzantine style of presentation. It is very short, just a few pages in Greek. It is an example of the classical genre of the "epitome," a summary or abstract of a longer piece of writing. We begin with a definition of tragedy, which is said to "remove" the mind's emotions of fear by means of pity and terror and which is described, strangely to our ears, as having "painful feelings as its mother."[3] The reference to the maternity of pain in relation to tragedy is interesting, as is the understanding of catharsis as a process of removal. We then get the definition of comedy, which is a clear variant, perhaps even a parody, of *Poetics* VI:

> Comedy is an imitation of an action [*mimesis praxeos*] that is absurd and lacking in magnitude [or grandeur, *megethous*], complete (with embellished language), the several kinds (of embellishment being found) separately in the (several) parts (of the play); (directly represented) by person(s) acting, and (not) by means of narration; through pleasure and laughter achieving the purgation [*katharsin*] of the like emotions. It has laughter [*gelota*] for its mother.[4]

It is a splendidly baroque definition, but we should note that if pain is the mother of tragedy then laughter is the matrix of comedy, which is absurd and lacking in tragic grandeur. Comic catharsis is achieved through pleasure and laughter rather than pity and fear.

What follows the definition is a highly elliptical description of the various mechanisms of comedy. The laughable can function through homonyms, or what we would call puns, and through synonyms, which work through pleonasm, where the example given is "I'm here and am arrived,"[5] which is obviously the same thing twice, a technique used by the character of Euripides in his mocking of Aeschylus in Aristophanes' *The Frogs*. When Aeschylus writes, "I have come back. I have returned," Euripides says, "Ha! The great Aeschylus has said the same thing twice" (lines 1152–54). Synonyms function similarly to the next mechanism, which is repetition, an ageless comic technique of using the same

word continually for comic effect. Next are paronyms, where a
redundant and extraneous element is added to a standard term;
the example is "I'm Midas the scrounger," or through subtrac-
tion, "I'm Midas the scrounge." Laughter can also arise from
diminutives, where Socrates becomes "Socratiddles" and Euripides becomes "Euripidipides," or through the slight alteration of
sound, "O Clod Almighty" instead of "O God Almighty" (admittedly, some of these examples don't work so well in translation).[6]
The final mechanisms are interrelated, namely parody, transfer-
ence, and manner of speaking. What is meant here is simply the
way in which laughter can be provoked by an alteration in the
patterns of speaking through comic delivery, where meaning can
be transferred through mimicry. The stately Sophoclean words "I,
Oedipus, whom all men call the Great" become funny when imitated in a slightly higher or lower tone of voice or simply through
being repeated.

Matters turn to the ways in which laughter can arise from
actions. This can occur in various forms: through knowing deception, from logical impossibility, from the possible but entirely
inconsequential, from things happening incongruously contrary
to expectation, and from elevated characters becoming base.
Laughter also arises from innuendo, when a process of reasoning
is shown to be disjoined and flawed, and "from using vulgar dancing."[7] The latter might be a reference to the cordax, a licentious
and obscene dance in ancient comedy, which involved the use of
finger cymbals and provocative bodily movement: think of the
classical equivalent of twerking. The *Tractatus Coislinianus* continues, "The joker aims to expose faults of mind and body."[8] All
that it takes for a tragic character to become comic is through some
minor bodily malfunction, like a sneeze or a fart. If the grandeur of
tragedy requires the unity of mind and body, then comedy works
through their disunity, where the body takes its noisy revenge on
the mind. There follows a very brief and Aristotelian-sounding
summary of the parts of comedy (plot, character, thought, dic-

tion, song, and spectacle) and the division of comic drama into prologue, choral song, *episode,* and *exodos.* The author of the tractate states that a comic plot is structured around laughable events, the characters are buffoonish, ironists, or boasters, and the diction is local, common, and low. With that, and a very brief statement of the differences in the degree of absurdity in Old, Middle, and New Comedy, the brief *Tractatus Coislinianus* comes to an end.

57

Tormented Incomprehensibly—Against Homeopathic Catharsis

Janko engages in a fascinating and extended piece of scholarly detective work, amassing philological detail, and even offers a hypothetical reconstruction of the entire text of the *Tractatus Coislinianus*.[1] It is highly probable that the second book of the *Poetics* would have been shorter than the extant text, possibly around five thousand or six thousand words. And Janko claims that the deficiencies in the tractate are in part due to Aristotle's undoubted propensity for stating the obvious rather than offering a deeper and more satisfying explanation of the nature and causes of comedy. Pulling together all the evidence, the following conclusions are reached: (1) the *Tractatus Coislinianus* is a unified text and not a farrago from different sources. (2) It has a coherent structure. (3) It is Aristotelian in both diction and content. And (4) it corresponds well to what we know of the second book of the *Poetics,* where the skeletal structure of the *Tractatus Coislinianus* strongly suggests that it represents the living body of the lost book.[2]

Is Janko right? As a nonclassicist, I do not feel qualified to pass judgment, but I am rather inclined to agree. As we have seen, Aristotle promises the reader that he is going to give an account of comedy, he provides the rough outlines of that account in the opening chapters of the *Poetics*, and the text ends with a lacuna, which Umberto Eco, among others, has tried to fill. Indeed, whether the text is authentic or not, the *Tractatus Coislinianus* still provides a compelling outline of what Aristotle *might* well have said about comedy and therefore merits a significant place in the history of literary criticism.

But there is one more fascinating detail that I would like to pull out of Janko's book, which allows us to circle back to where this chapter began. There is a long discussion of the concept of catharsis and the relation between tragic and comic catharsis.[3] Janko engages in a vigorous critique of Bernays's physiological theory of catharsis as purgation, which was so influential on the work of Herbert Spencer and Freud. On this view, both tragedy and comedy function as a kind of draining of the swamp of our inhibited, pent-up emotions, where pleasure is experienced because we are relieved or purged of affect. Aesthetic pleasure is the experience of the lowering of the excessive energy in the organism and this has a therapeutic effect. Tragedy is where neurotics go to find some curative solace and comedy is understood as comic relief, where laughter is the best medicine. Appealing as it might be, the problem with this view of catharsis is that there is not a word to support it in Aristotle's *Poetics*. There is no hint that the goal of drama is therapy for tortured souls. On the contrary, as we saw in Chapter 55, Aristotle's audience was composed of educated, adult male citizens who went to the theater for neither moral education nor psychotherapy.

Against this purgative view, Janko argues that catharsis is not a draining of the emotions, but a kind of moral moderation: "Instead, it is to predispose us to feel the right emotion in the right way, at the right time, toward the right object, with the right motive, and to the proper degree."[4] What is clearly being alluded to is Aristotle's idea of prudence or *phronesis* and the prudential person or *phronimos* from the *Nicomachean Ethics*. The *phronimos* is the person who does the right thing, at the right time, in the right way. Catharsis is not purgation, then, but a kind of moral recalibration of the emotions that brings the audience closer to the behavior of the decent, prudential person. Against the medical or therapeutic conception of catharsis, Janko is proffering a *homeo-pathic* view, where "Pity and fear drive out pity and fear. . . . It is no more problematic than curing fever by piling on blankets."[5] By representing the pitiful and the fearful, tragedy arouses pity and fear in the audience and acts so "as to *relieve* them by giving them moderate and harmless exercise; and with relief comes pleasure."[6] On this view, tragic catharsis is both a simulation and a stimulation of the emotions that allows the audience to feel them in a more measured way and where moderation leads to pleasure. For Janko, matters are similar when we turn to comic catharsis and indeed this linkage could be justified negatively with reference to Book X of the *Republic,* where both tragedy and comedy are judged to be equally bad because they arouse an excess of either lamentation or laughter (606a). Janko's view is different: that there is indeed an analogy between tragic and comic catharsis, where they both have similar ethical effects, namely "the achievement of proportion or balance in the emotions."[7]

I think Janko's view suffers from the same deficiency as the moralistic interpretation of catharsis that we saw Jonathan Lear very gracefully dismember. It is highly dubious that Aristotle wishes to attribute any ethical significance to tragedy. A more minimalist view of catharsis would simply see it as the outcome of the emotions of pity and fear aroused by drama. We see the suffer-ing of Oedipus, we feel pity for him because of his plight and fear or *philanthropia* because he is somewhat like us, and then we no longer feel those emotions. There is a pleasure in the experience of tragedy, as Aristotle repeatedly insists, but there is no moral instruction that occurs through that pleasure. We simply like feel-ing pleasure in pain for a while and this is what we are accustomed to expect when we go to see a tragedy. Although he is against Ber-nays's purgative theory of catharsis, Janko is still committed to the idea of catharsis as a kind of relief. This relief is not administered through heavy, theatrical drugs, but with a softer, homeopathic cure that gently leads the audience toward the proper prudential disposition. Sometimes one might be able to cure a fever by piling on blankets, but sometimes one might not and it is possible that the fever becomes fatal. What is questionable in my view is that tragedy is in the fever curing business at all.

What is driving Janko's homeopathic view of catharsis is a strongly normative idea of aesthetic comprehensibility. In order to experience catharsis in the appropriate prudential way, the drama must make sense to us and be a kind of simulation or echo chamber of our moral view of the world. Janko writes, "If the tragic events are badly motivated, and the characters tormented incomprehensibly, we are simply shocked; our feelings are not worked through and made comprehensible."[8]

What I have tried to show in this chapter is that this experience of shock where nothing is worked through is precisely what happens in Euripides. In his *Hecuba*, we see the eponymous Trojan queen "tormented incomprehensibly," layering one indignity upon another until she is finally told that she will be cursed in the afterlife by returning in the form of a dog. In Euripides' *Electra, Medea,* and *Orestes,* we witness catastrophe upon catastrophe, events that are so "badly motivated" that they require the external, mechanical intercession of the deus ex machina that Aristotle criticizes. In such dramas, we are opened up and left exposed to a series of incomprehensible experiences that defy homeopathic moral moderation. Euripides, but equally Sophocles too as we saw in his *Electra,* leads us step by step toward something much more devastating where catharsis is suspended. Tragedy does not comfort our fever like a warm blanket; it inflames that fever and the fire begins to burn.

58

Aristophanes Falls Asleep

Are matters significantly different with comedy? If Aristotle's entire discussion of tragedy is formed around the conceptual lacuna of tragic catharsis, then can we speak with any more confidence about comic catharsis, which has laughter and not painful feelings "as its mother"? I'd like to approach these questions, in conclusion, by turning to Aristophanes' *The Frogs*.[1]

We might recall the extraordinary passage, at the very end of Plato's *Symposium,* the drinking party or booze-up. Around the crack of dawn, after a night of drinking and long speeches about love, only Socrates, Aristophanes, and the beautiful Agathon, who had just won the prize for his first tragedy, are still awake, "drinking out of a large cup which they were passing around from left to right" (223c–d).[2] Although drowsiness and drink make the narrator's memory blurry, "The main point was that Socrates was trying to prove to them that authors should be able to write both comedy and tragedy: the skilful tragic dramatist should also be a comic poet" (223d). Agathon, the tragedian, should be able to write comedy and Aristophanes, the comedian, should be able to write tragedy. Interestingly and perhaps ironically, this is something that Socrates explicitly denies in the *Republic* (395a). Just at the point when Socrates was about to clinch his argument, "Aristophanes fell asleep" (223d). It's a wonderful image. Socrates' philosophical argument for the interchangeability of tragedy and comedy leads, first Aristophanes and then Agathon, to drop off into slumber. Socrates is the last one awake and he heads off to the Lyceum to wash up and then spends the day "just as he always did" (223d), before going home in the evening to rest.

As if to prove Socrates' point, *The Frogs* is a comedy about tragedy. Together with Gorgias's fragment, discussed in Part 1, it gives us our earliest "theoretical" response to tragedy in the sense of the *theoros,* the spectator in the theater. If theory is born in theater, where tragedy is a deception that leaves the deceived wiser than the nondeceived, then *The Frogs* is a comedy that gives us some precious theoretical indications about the nature of tragic deception. The play suffers from all the difficulty in understanding ancient comedy, or indeed any historical comedy. Comedy feeds on the present and it always dates very fast. But what is fascinating in *The Frogs* is the extended, closing debate, or *agon,* between Aeschylus and Euripides as to who is the best tragedian. Aristophanes is hardly in the business of being fair to people, and the play gives us flat, two-dimensional caricatures used for comic effect. But Aristophanes provides a clear sense of how the tragedians were seen in the late fifth century that has been hugely influential. Indeed, the dating of *The Frogs,* from 405 BCE, is significant. Although Aeschylus had been dead for a half century, Euripides had died just the previous year, in 406 BCE, and Sophocles died shortly afterward. So, the comic character of Euripides in Hades that Aristophanes presents had only very recently descended to the Underworld.

The political stakes of the drama are revealed in the *parabasis,* which is the moment in comedy when the actors leave the stage and the chorus addresses the audience directly. Although, as Nan Dunbar reminds us, it is impossible to form any clear view of Aristophanes' personal opinions on the issues of the day based on his dramas, the words of the leader of the chorus are strikingly reactionary.[3] Having been at war with Sparta more or less continuously since 431 BCE, and in the aftermath of the disastrous Sicilian expedition, Athens was crawling toward the endgame of the Peloponnesian Wars. The city is in crisis because native Athenian virtue has been lost, and the city has been taken over by vicious foreigners. The Leader directly addresses the citizens of Athens in the following words:

> We have some stately gentlemen,
> modest, anciently descended, proud and educated well on
>   the wrestling ground, men of distinction who have been
>   to school.
> These we outrage and reject, preferring any foreign fool,
>   redhead slave, or brassy clown or shyster. This is what we
>   choose to direct our city—immigrants. (lines 728–33)

Decent native Athenians are sidelined and vilified; flashy immigrants and metics are preferred and promoted. The question is which tragedian should be brought back from Hades to Athens in order to restore its martial valor and save the city?

Aeschylus holds the Chair of Tragedy in Hades. Sophocles (who is presented as a nondescript lackey of Aeschylus throughout) kissed Aeschylus after he died, shook hands with him, and "gave up his claim on the chair" (lines 788–90). But Aeschylus's place has been questioned and threatened by Euripides. At this point, the *agon* between Aeschylus and Euripides begins, arbitrated by the god Dionysos. Aeschylus is presented, however unjustly, as a patrician patriot who describes *The Persians* as the "Best play I ever have written" (line 1032) and *Seven Against Thebes* as inducing "heroic endeavour" (lines 1027–28) in its audience. Aeschylus's verse is seen by him as a model of decorum and moral purity, as opposed to the corruption of Euripides, especially the character of Phaedra, "the floozie" (lines 1043–44). In his defense, Euripides claims, "*I* made the drama *democratic*" (line 955). The everyday, down-to-earth intelligibility of his verse is compared by Euripides to the obscurity and turgid repetitiveness of Aeschylus, with his penchant for pregnant, but empty, silences. Euripides says to Aeschylus,

> But you, with your massive construction,
> huge words and mountainous phrases, is that what you call
> useful instruction?
> You ought to make people talk like people. (lines 1061–62)

In his defense, and in the funniest moment in the play, Aeschylus says that he will ruin Euripides' prologues with a little bottle of oil. At which point, in a manner reminiscent of the hard-boiled-egg scene from the Marx Brothers' *A Night at the Opera,* every time that Euripides begins to quote from one of his plays, Aeschylus adds the phrase "lost his little bottle of oil" (line 1209). The effect is deflationary bathos, which nails what Aeschylus sees as the folksy and sentimental way in which Euripides plays on the emotions of his audience (lines 1052–88).

And so it goes, back and forth, with abundant and telling quotations and even close metrical prosodic analysis. Eventually, scales are brought onstage and the lines of Aeschylus and Euripides are weighed for their literary and moral heft. Who will save the city? Dionysos, after some deliberation, decides in favor of Aeschylus and dumps Euripides back into Hades. Against what is seen as the democratic decay of tragedy in Euripides, Aeschylus's drama will restore the heroic virtue of the Athenians and give them back some proper patriotism. There is even a fascinating parting critique of Socrates, which could be linked to the depiction of Socrates as a Sophist in Aristophanes' *The Clouds,*

> Better not to sit at the feet
> Of Socrates and chatter
> Nor cast out of the heart
> The high serious matter
> Of tragic art [*tragodikes technes*]. (lines 1491–95)

The Frogs is a contradictory thing: it is a comedy that defends tragedy. More specifically, it is a defense of the "high serious matter" of Aeschylean tragedy against the sophistical and sentimental corruption of Euripides and Socrates—a linking of the two that would please Nietzsche and those who claim that the latter helped the former write his plays.

Aeschylus says that his Chair of Tragedy can be given to the compliant Sophocles while he is upside trying to save the city from itself. Euripides is condemned as a pseudopoet and a vile, lying clown. And in the final lines of the choral *exodos*, Kleophon, leader of the popular party, the war party, is attacked for being an alien (line 1532). The chorus voice the hope that Aeschylus's drama will allow Athens to prosper and the sorrows that accompany war will come to an end. Sadly, nothing of the kind happened and Athens was humiliated in a surrender to Sparta in 404 BCE, the year after *The Frogs* was produced.

59

Make Athens Great Again

Regardless of the unknown personal opinions of Aristophanes, it appears hard to avoid the conclusion that the message of *The Frogs* is conservative. The comedy here is a plea for the restoration of political order through the stately ritualism of Aeschylean tragedy. The comic pokes fun at the newfangled, empty novelty of the Euripidean present, with its sentimentality, its warmongering populism, its subjectivism, its litigiousness, and its sophistry. There is a yearning to return to a lost social order when patriotic virtue ruled the city and foreigners and immigrants were treated with rightful suspicion. At the heart of Aristophanes' comedy about tragedy is an apparent longing for the vanished substance of communal life, a city governed by peace where the citizens would feel comfortable and at home.

But is the message of Aristophanes' comedy simply that we can make Athens great again? Is a play like *The Frogs* telling the Athenians they can recover the lost substance of political life by going back to the old version of tragedy? I am not so sure. The delight that we feel in watching a play like *The Frogs,* or indeed *The Clouds* or *The Birds,* derives from watching the faddish, silly trends that govern the present openly mocked and roundly ridiculed. Everything evaporates into the air and we feel the liberating lightness of absurdity. This is how I would choose to read a play like *The Birds*.[1] In the latter, we see two lost souls, an Athenian Laurel and Hardy, mired in debt, running away from the city.

All that they want is a "nice cushy city, soft as a woollen blanket, where we could curl up" (lines 121–22). This is what eventually leads, through an elaborate series of intrigues, to the establishment of a vast bird republic, without walls and as big as the sky. In the *parabasis,* the leader of the chorus outlines a legitimating cosmogenic myth about the birds having the right to govern because "We're far older than all the blessed gods" (line 702). Eventually, Cloudcuckooland brings all other cities in Greece, and even the Olympian gods themselves, to kneel in servitude.

Now, what is at stake in *The Birds* is clearly not the practical feasibility of constructing Cloudcuckooland—which is why it is called Cloudcuckooland. Nor is *The Birds* some proto-Orwellian animal parable about the dangers of totalitarianism. Not at all. The ethereal city of *The Birds* is simply a fanciful way of imagining an escape from the human condition: "Oh suffering mankind . . . creatures of clay, hear us now, the ever-living birds" (lines 685–89). This is also how I would read the plea for the restoration of Aeschylean tragedy in *The Frogs.* There is no question of such a thing ever happening. It is far too late for the city to be saved. The game is up, Aeschylus is long dead, Euripides has won, and sophistry, sentimentality, and subjectivism govern the city as it drifts toward defeat and destruction.

To that extent, Aristophanic comedy and Euripidean tragedy are mirror images of each other. Or, perhaps better, Euripides provides a set of piercing night vision goggles rather than the Ray-Bans that Aristophanes gives us to dim the glare of a ridiculous world. But tragedy and comedy are complementary aspects of the same substance, or rather the same lack of substance. In Hegelian terms, we know that substance and subject have fallen apart and the communitarian core of political life has dissolved into a vast cloud of tiny individual atoms. Hegel sees Euripides' plays as "lamentable," as the betrayal of the stately substance of the ethical life that is played out in Aeschylus and Sophocles.[2] By contrast, he judges Aristophanes as a "true patriot," yearning for the old religion and true morality.[3] I disagree. I think that both Euripidean tragedy and Aristophanic comedy are dramatic echoes of the same reality: absurd, crazy, lighthearted escape on the one hand and a cold, dispassionate staring into the fiery core of existence on the other. But they are ultimately united by a shared somber realism. The world is a tragicomedy defined by war, corruption, vanity, and greed, and entirely without the capacity for redemption. Perhaps this is why it is so hard for us to parse the difference between tragedy and comedy. Who knows, perhaps Socrates was right in the *Symposium* after all: the tragedian should be a comedian and vice versa. At which point, like Aristophanes, we feel the irresistible urge to fall asleep.

PART VI

Conclusion

60

Transgenerational Curse

It is easy enough to talk glibly of reconciliation and harmony over the dead bodies on the tragic stage. It may be true that the cry of the blood of Agamemnon is satisfied at last with revenge, that Oedipus comes to rest in a glorious grave in quiet Colonus, that Heracles ascends to sit on the right hand of Zeus; but can we suppose that to Cassandra, to Jocasta, to Dejanira all seemed to end so pleasantly in a pink sunset of satisfaction? Does the world of tragedy or the tragedy of the world really bear any relation to this Universe squirted with philosophic rose-water? It is an astonishing conception. Many another Dr. Pangloss has endeavoured to make mankind swallow the world like a pill by coating it with sugar.[1]

—Frank L. Lucas

Characters in tragedy are acted on by histories conveyed by a story, a riddle, a prophecy, or a command. They are acted upon, yet acting. That is, tragic characters occupy the space between autonomy and heteronomy, in an experience of ever-partial agency. They are neither free nor are they causally determined. They exist in some space between freedom and necessity, where both are present, deeply interdependent, yet quite distinct, like the white and the yolk of a hard-boiled egg.[2] The name of this space is fate, which is not simply out of our hands, but requires our hands in order to accomplish it. One reason to study tragedy is to see precisely about how in acting, we are acted upon, and how that being acted upon can and does convert to a certain action that takes place in our own name. Action is motivated by something—a prophecy, say—that leads to the destruction of the one who acts. Action is not causally determined by necessity, nor is it free. It is somehow that in our free, volitional action there is an experience of being acted upon by a curse, a transgenerational curse. This is how we might interpret the nasty incident at the crossroads between Oedipus and Laius, where the former killed the latter, son killed father.

The structure of this incident might indicate a general feature of action. In acting thoughtlessly or in rage and hurt, we are acted upon, not quite causally, and not quite volitionally. And then Oedipus's arm raises to strike. I think about this in relation to our lives, in our moments of rage. It is not so much a question of rage against the machine, but against those we call kin, those to whom we are bound, those whom we love. What happens when we act like assholes and lose it with them? What happens when we act hatefully to those we love? In rage, in anger, we act freely, but something acts through us, some kind of curse, the largely unconscious effect of the past on the present. We need to reflect in order to meet the curse, forestall the curse. Can we do this? Is this what tragedy is showing its spectators in the theater? It is one thing it shows.

Oedipus doesn't reflect. He knew the prophecy. This is why he fled Corinth. Why didn't he ponder this when he met the man in the chariot who wouldn't give way? Did anger blind him? Rage blinds us. Oedipus is blind with rage and sees only when he is blind. Something is also revealed here about the nature of prophecy. It does not make the future happen as it foretells. It is not inevitable. Rather, it relies on the power of words to foretell what will happen, as if the one who speaks these words is already witnessing the events from a future perspective. Prophecy is a kind of speaking that is out of time, out of joint, producing a kind of disjunction in the flow of time, in the usual order of succession. The past happens right now in an action that shapes the future. Words act on us unknowingly, as Oedipus was walking down that road to meet and kill his father. There is something that he knows without knowing it. Or some sort of knowledge that works upon him and drives him to the boiling point but which he cannot quite claim as his own. Is this just true of tragedy, or is this tragedy's version of the truth? I think it is the latter. At the end of the tragedy, of *Oedipus the King,* once the curse is fulfilled, Oedipus becomes monstrous, becomes an exile from the city. He can neither be identified publicly by his identity as king nor privately by the bonds of kinship. He is an abomination. As Oedipus exits the city, is he still human? He has no identity: he is neither human nor animal, and certainly not divine. We might ponder the double function of monstrosity here, at the beginning and end of Sophocles' play. For Hölderlin, who identifies—as we saw above—the tragic with the experience of the monstrous, Oedipus moves from the monstrosity of the union with the god, to that of the abject ejection from the city where all that counts for identity is stripped away from him. Tragedy is defined by the quasi-dialectical rhythm of unification and division, where the unity with the divine gives way to the disunity of the self from itself.

Oedipus's blindness is so odd. When he sees and is seen, he sees nothing. Oedipus comes onstage and delivers his first lines: you see me and know me, I am Oedipus, I solved the riddle, "whom all men call the Great [*kaloumenos*]" (*Oedipus the King,* line 8). It is only when he is blind that he finally sees. This is perhaps what Hölderlin means when he says, *"Der König Oedipus hat ein Auge zuviel vielleicht"* ("King Oedipus has an eye too many perhaps").[3] And when he cannot see, we see him finally in his truth. At this point, he does not want to be seen, for shame. And yet we see, we look. So where are *we* in the theater? Who are *we* in the theater? Is this our shame? To watch shamelessly? If shame lies on the eyelids of the tragic protagonist at the end of the drama, then where is our shame?

As I said in the opening paragraphs of this book, there is a link between this structure of seeing and *theoria,* the theory that spectates on the unraveling theatrical praxis. This is one function of irony in *Oedipus the King,* opening the gap between theory and praxis. If tragedy is *mimesis praxeos,* then it is praxis viewed theoretically, an imitation of action where we become ironic spectators on praxis, our praxis. And praxis falls apart, internally divides against itself, becoming *mimesis apraxeos.* We no longer know how to act or what to do. Like Sophocles' *Electra,* action collapses into inaction and we stand rigid against the door of the palace speaking a torrent of words, words, words. Words take the place of action. And words *do* nothing.

Oedipus persists with a crazed drivenness, a drive for knowledge that leads to self-destruction. And this is the deep contradiction of his tragedy: he knows the curse and yet does not know it. He continually misrecognizes the curse, but keeps scratching away at it until he is undone. He claims not to know, but still seems at another level to know and is unrelenting in his drive to find out, despite his rage. And Oedipus's rage is boundless. His self-justifying blaming of others, of anyone but himself. And remember that Tiresias tells him the truth straight to his face early in the play. He doesn't hear it. And behind his back, we watch. Not with an ironic superiority, but with a sullen-faced horror. This couldn't happen to us, could it? After all, we *know,* right? Tragedy raises questions about the conditions for seeing. But it also raises questions about hearing. When do we actually hear anything? Rarely, I think. This is especially the case when children listen to parents and parents to children, and here the twisted coupling of Oedipus and Jocasta (mother/son, wife/husband) has a doubling, troubling power. When do parents really listen to children and children to parents? At times, it seems that everyone is deaf, with ears blocked with wax, wearing Theban headphones playing mellow mood music.

Oedipus is living out and living through a transgenerational curse that disrupts the proper order of generations attached to kinship and kingship, where son becomes mother's husband and father becomes brother and sister. Once again, the curse does not act on its own volition, but requires our action, our partly unknowing complicity with it. Tragic action happens in this hard-boiled-egg-like space between freedom and necessity. It is a kind of voluntary servitude. The curse interpellates us as subjects behind our backs, as it were. It makes subjects subject, it makes subjects exist in terms of subjection. Yet that subjection requires our free complicity. This is the enigma of ideology. It operates behind our backs and without our consent yet still requires our free action, our complicity with it. We know all right, but we still act as if we didn't. Ideology is also not deterministic. It requires my desire, my more or less free desire. We are never just victims, as comforting as that seems, as it gives us someone to blame. But we are also perpetrators. We know that ideology is not true, yet we still believe.

Following Anne Carson, tragedy has been understood in this book as the experience of rage that flows from grief, usually in a situation of war. As we saw in the discussion of the *Republic,* Plato's suspicion of tragedy is largely a deep concern about the political effects of grief, that the audiences of tragedies would become fattened on grief, in a kind of voluptuous melancholic lamentation, the kind of exquisitely pleasurable pain described by Gorgias. Grief is appetitive for Plato, and that's the problem. Philosophy is the metaphysical critique of *mimesis* from the standpoint of the *idea* and it is a moral economy of lamentation. One suggestion is that there is something in grief that is politically unstable, unruly, and ungovernable, that contests the hierarchical rule of the city or state. If one thinks of the politicization of funerals all over the world in the past decades—in Ireland, in Argentina, in Ukraine, in North Africa, all across this wide world—then this point would appear to be massively confirmed. Security forces massacre protesters attending a funeral procession for protesters murdered by security forces. We seem locked within repetitive loops of violence.

Antigone, that grieving machine, is kind of a political monster, like her dad. Butler writes that Antigone's rage-filled grief is something that has always "haunted the polis and its philosophical defenders, not because of some enduring truth about women, but because of the ways they figure in the building and unbuilding of power."[4] Grief is something that women in tragedy do, whether one thinks of Antigone, Hecuba, Tecmessa in *Ajax,* Atossa in *The Persians,* or Electra, the most extreme of all. Women are raging and grieving in tragedy in the context of war. But this is not because of some essentialist truth about women that can be explained through some romanticization of the "feminine." Tragedy returns again and again to those monstrous figures, like Oedipus or indeed Prometheus, who form a kind of defining outside, or perhaps what Ernesto Laclau called a "constitutive outside," out of which the *polis* is built and who threaten at every moment to unbuild the *polis.*[5] What seems to be figured in tragedy is the genealogy of sovereign political power, in its doing and undoing. Tragedy is about a moment where the sovereign is a person, a person who has this role because of kinship, and the crimes against kinship perpetrated by the tragic hero culminate in the dissolution of political power. Oedipus is a disfiguration of the sovereign at the end of the play and might stand for the possible dissolution of sovereignty.

Tragedy is neither simply affirmative nor negative, neither optimistic nor pessimistic. It cannot be defined by affixing either a plus or a minus sign. And such oppositions are pretty fatuous. Rather, tragedy provides something like a theatrical archive, a memory theater perhaps, that is shared, for who we are in public and private, in the inseparability of public and private, in their layerings and intrigues and intrications. It gives us a genealogy of who we are, an account of our origins and how the curse of the past can unknowingly take shape in the present, and we don't see it and we rage when we are told what it is. Can it provide a way of escaping the curse? No, I don't think so. But we can perhaps see it for what it is, and this would be the moment of the spectacular blinding of Oedipus. At this moment, at least we experience shame . . . on the eyelids. Not his, ours.

Aliveness

Throughout this book, especially, in the commentaries on Plato and Aristotle, I have expressed caution about finding a tidy metaphysical essence of tragedy with clear moral consequences. I have sought to see tragedy as a kind of prebuttal of philosophy that refuses to sprinkle idealistic rosewater on reality. But if I am justified in that caution, then what is it that tragedy does? What experience does it offer?

Let me finish by telling you a story. A couple of years ago, I was lucky enough to have a long public conversation at the Brooklyn Academy of Music with the French actor Isabelle Huppert. We were meant to talk about the production of *Phaedra(s)*[1] in which she was starring as the ill-starred Cretan queen consumed with illicit incestuous desire for her stepson, where both are destroyed in the process. What was interesting about this production was the way in which it counterpointed the many different and seemingly contradictory treatments of the story of Phaedra that one can find in Euripides, Seneca, Racine, and, most recently, Sarah Kane's *Phaedra's Love*. It didn't try to unify these different Attic, Roman, neoclassical, and contemporary versions of Phaedra or blend them together into some syncretic whole. Rather, Krzysztof Warlikowski's production of the play placed those versions alongside each other—hence the plural "Phaedra(s)"—in an uneasy tension and conjunction that drew in the spectator. New theatrical elements were added with dialogue adapted from Wajdi

Mouawad and J. M. Coetzee. Isabelle Huppert appeared as at least three different Phaedras, as the Australian writer Elizabeth Costello, and even as the goddess Aphrodite, who seemed to have been fused with the god of ancient theater: Dionysos. She was onstage pretty much constantly for more than three hours.

Anyhow, Isabelle Huppert and I talked and I tried, with some trepidation and limited success, to get her to address the ideas in the play: desire, love, incest, violence, and the relation between gods and mortals. She was very obliging, polite, and intelligent and the conversation went back and forth for a good while. And then at a certain point, perhaps slightly exasperated by my philosophical probing, she said, "Of course, what theater is about is aliveness, a certain experience of aliveness. That's all that matters. The rest is just ideas. Good ideas, maybe. But just ideas."

I was internally stopped in my tracks and had to take several quiet, deep breaths. She was right. Theater is not just about ideas. Nor is it about a message of any kind. If you want to send a message, get a smartphone or use your laptop. It is rather about being permitted, allowing oneself to be permitted, to enter what Peter Brook called "the empty space." If one allows oneself to be completely involved in what is happening onstage, one enters a unique space that provides an unparalleled experience of sensory and cognitive intensity that is impossible to express purely in concepts or to abstract stratospherically to the status of an *idea,* however sugarcoated. This intensity happens in theater. And it doesn't always happen, as there can obviously be really bad theater. But when it does happen, then no other experience comes close. It is this experience that one hopes for as the houselights dim and the play begins. Sometimes, it happens.

By watching tragic personages in the most extreme situations, such as the horrors that befall Phaedra and Hippolytus, we look into the *core,* the core of life, of aliveness, in all its burning intensity, moral ambiguity, emotional devastation, erotic doubling, and political complexity. Suspicious of the concept of catharsis as something that somehow explains the effect of theater, Anne Carson talks of tragedy as a process whereby something concealed shows up onstage and we look at "this hidden thing." She goes on, "I think of walking around Detroit. Sometimes at night you might pass the Foundry—a place with molten metal inside. You can glance at it and see—you glance into the core. It's burning away in there. Then you go down the street. What remains in the mind is the core."[2] If we are lucky, and we allow ourselves, then we can be afforded a glance at the burning core. If the hidden thing shows itself, just for a moment, then we can be taken to a place where our usual, everyday vision of the world, our common-place predictable reactions to events and our habitual moral judgments, are suspended, temporarily switched off, alleviated if you will. At that point, we are both deepened and raised up. It is not that we become someone else at that moment, but that theater at its best somehow allows us to become ecstatically stretched out into another time and another space, another way of experiencing things and the world. At that moment, it is not so much the scales that fall from our eyes, but our eyes that fall like scales. We stumble about seemingly blinded, like Oedipus at the end of his tragedy, or sagacious, blind Tiresias. But suddenly, at the same moment, we see farther.

What can happen in tragedy is that we can give ourselves over to that intensity of life, to the happening of aliveness, and open ourselves to the core. One looks at the core of aliveness and it looks back. Just for a moment. And then one walks down the street, and the world resumes its relentless hum. But the memory of the core remains with us.

ACKNOWLEDGMENTS

Why This Book Was Hard to Write—and Thanks

My obsession with tragedy and its relation to philosophy goes back for decades, and I have taught seminars on the topic over the years, first at the University of Essex and then at the New School for Social Research. Matters became deeper and more developed when I gave a semester-long lecture course at the New School with Judith Butler, in 2011. I extended the argument in two further lecture courses in 2014 and 2017. The oral and pedagogical origin of long stretches of this book is not something that I have sought to disguise in preparing it for publication. I would like to thank students at the New School, the School of Criticism and Theory at Cornell University, and the European Graduate School for their patience, interest, and countless contributions to this project.

This is a book that I found fiendishly difficult to finish. This is, in part, because of my hesitancy in writing about classical themes as a nonclassicist. My tribulations with trying and failing to master ancient Greek (especially the verb forms) are not something I am proud of or I wish to recount here. But the difficulty is also linked to the feeling that this book is my attempt to come to terms with the discipline that I have spent my career teaching: philosophy. As will become clear from the opening pages of the book, I am engaging with tragedy in order to take aim at a certain style of philosophy whose origins I trace to Plato and Aristotle. I have come to find the metaphysical and moral assumptions to which that style is linked questionable. It is not that this book is antiphilosophical. Far from it. It is rather that tragedy offers another way of thinking and experiencing, a dialectical modality of reflection that is at once more realistic, more negative, more modest, and more devastating than much that takes the name of philosophy, conventionally understood, which tends to confuse art with moral tutorial.

But the difficulty in writing this book is also linked to a long-standing fascination with theater and finding it hard to say exactly why it is that drama compels me so much. Having come from a working-class English family that most decidedly did *not* go to the theater, I recall the fascination of first watching theater as a university student in Colchester in the early 1980s. These plays often took place in small studios in provincial theaters, and I remember very clearly being absolutely gripped by probably fairly humdrum productions of *Oedipus the King, Othello,* and some short pieces by Beckett. From that time, I was completely hooked and a faith in the experience that theater can offer (obviously, sometimes it doesn't—in fact, very often it doesn't) is something that has never left me. What I find in theater is a particularly intense and vibrant sense of sheer *aliveness.* This experience, at once sensory and intellectual, is spectacularly tricky to render into concepts, however supple they might be. This book represents an attempt at such a rendering.

This is my book about the Greeks, at least as I imagine them. To be clear, my interest in ancient Greek tragedy is far from any form of cultural conservatism. I see it rather as a subversive traditionalism that is in no way traditional. Simply as a way of avoiding ever more egregious forms of cultural stupefaction that arise from being blinded by the myopia of the present, each generation has an obligation to reinvent the classics. The ancients need our blood in order to revive and live among us. By definition, such an act of donation constructs the ancients in our image. In seeing them, we see ourselves turned around, in a new light, under a new aspect. As I try and make clear in the opening pages, the character of this book is invitational and at its center is an invitational "we" that asks the reader to join with me in pondering the ancient Greek past as a way of questioning and destabilizing the present. As such, tragedy constitutes a powerful critique of ideology. My amateur passion for antiquity goes back to my history teacher when I was eleven years old, Mr. Parker. You might say he made me nosy. At a certain point in the early 1970s, after noticing my interest in ancient history, he took me aside after class and recommended that I read *The Greeks* by H. D. F. Kitto, which I did. It had the force of a revelation. After failing pretty dramatically at school, I eventually went to university when I was twenty-two years old. A large part of the reason why philosophy appealed to me was that it revived my love for the ancient Greeks. I remember reading fragments of the pre-Socratics as if they were surrealist poetry and from there I began to read Sophocles and the Socratic dialogues. In recent years, I have had the immense good fortune to visit Greece regularly, and this book would not have taken the shape that it did without the support of the Onassis Foundation and especially conversations over many years with its president, Anthony Papadimitriou. I would like to dedicate this book to the Foundation and their support for both my work and for those of doctoral students in philosophy at the New School for Social Research.

In addition, I would like to thank Nemonie Craven, Dan Frank, Mark Ellingham, Andrew Franklin, Afroditi Panagiotakou, and thanks to Yi Wu for her invaluable help with references and footnotes. Something more than thanks are owed to Ida Lødemel Tvedt, who accompanied every step of the way in the completion of this book with grace, kindness, mirth, and love.

—Simon Critchley

NOTES

I. FEEDING THE ANCIENTS WITH OUR OWN BLOOD

1. Simon Goldhill, "The Audience of Athenian Tragedy," in *The Cambridge Companion to Greek Tragedy*, ed. P. E. Easterling (Cambridge: Cambridge University Press, 1997), 62–66.
2. Ulrich von Wilamowitz-Moellendorff, *Greek Historical Writing and Apollo*, trans. Gilbert Murray (Oxford: Clarendon Press, 1908), 25.
3. Raymond Geuss, *A World Without Why* (Princeton, NJ: Princeton University Press, 2014), 234.

2. PHILOSOPHY'S TRAGEDY AND THE DANGEROUS PERHAPS

1. Anne Carson, *The Beauty of the Husband* (New York: Vintage Books, 2001), 134.
2. Judith Butler, *Frames of War: When Is Life Grievable?* (London: Verso, 2009).
3. Friedrich Nietzsche, *Beyond Good and Evil: Prelude to a Philosophy of the Future*, trans. Walter Kaufmann (New York: Vintage Books, 1966), 11.

3. KNOWING AND NOT KNOWING: HOW OEDIPUS BRINGS DOWN FATE

1. Rita Felski, introduction to *Rethinking Tragedy*, ed. Rita Felski (Baltimore: Johns Hopkins University Press, 2008), 2.
2. Euripides, *Grief Lessons—Four Plays by Euripides*, trans. Anne Carson (New York: New York Review of Books, 2006), 311.

4. RAGE, GRIEF, AND WAR

1. Anne Carson, preface, "Tragedy: A Curious Art Form," in *Grief Lessons—Four Plays by Euripides,* trans. Anne Carson (New York: New York Review of Books, 2006), 7.
2. For a contemporary defense of the ancient Greeks that begins from the theme of rage, see Emily Katz Anhalt, *Enraged: Why Violent Times Need Ancient Greek Myths* (New Haven, CT: Yale University Press, 2017). Katz's final chapter is a discussion of Euripides' *Hecuba,* pp. 149–83.
3. Raymond Williams, *Modern Tragedy* (London: Vintage Books, 1966), 105.
4. Ibid.

5. GORGIAS: TRAGEDY IS A DECEPTION THAT LEAVES THE DECEIVED WISER THAN THE NONDECEIVED

1. Kathleen Freeman, *Ancilla to the Pre-Socratic Philosophers* (Cambridge, MA: Harvard University Press, 1983), 138.
2. Henry G. Liddell and Robert Scott, *A Greek-English Lexicon* (Cambridge: Clarendon Press, 1996), 181.
3. Stephen Halliwell, "Learning from Suffering—Ancient Responses to Tragedy," in *A Companion to Greek Tragedy,* ed. Justina Gregory (Malden, MA: Blackwell Publishing, 2005), 394–95.
4. And see Plato, *Republic* 595b, "For you will not betray me to the tragic poets and all other imitators [*mimetikous*]—that kind of art seems to be a corruption of the mind of all listeners who do not possess, as an antidote [*pharmakon*], a knowledge of its real nature [τὸ εἰδέναι αὐτὰ οἷα τυγχάνει ὄντα]."

6. JUSTICE AS CONFLICT (FOR POLYTHEISM)

1. Stuart Hampshire, *Justice Is Conflict* (London: Duckworth, 1999), 21–23.

7. TRAGEDY AS A DIALECTICAL MODE OF EXPERIENCE

1. George Steiner, *The Death of Tragedy* (New Haven, CT: Yale University Press, 1996); Raymond Williams, *Modern Tragedy* (London: Vintage Books, 1966).

9. A CRITIQUE OF THE EXOTIC GREEKS

1. Louis MacNeice, *Selected Poems,* ed. Michael Longley (London: Faber & Faber, 2007), 59–60.
2. Erika Simon, *Das antike Theater* (Heidelberg: F. H. Kerle, 1972); Bruno Snell, *Die Entdeckung des Geistes: Studien zur Entstehung des europäischen Denkens bei den Griechen* (Hamburg: Claaszen & Goverts Verlag, 1946). And see Bernard Williams's convincing critique of Snell in Bernard Williams, *Shame and Necessity* (Berkeley: University of California Press, 1993), 21–33.
3. Friedrich Nietzsche, *Basic Writings of Nietzsche,* ed. and trans. Walter Kaufmann (New York: The Modern Library, 2000), 99–100.
4. Ian Christopher Storey and Arlene Allan, *A Guide to Ancient Greek Drama* (Malden, MA: Blackwell Publishing, 2005), 31.
5. Simon Goldhill, "Modern Critical Approaches to Greek Tragedy," in *The Cambridge Companion to Greek Tragedy,* ed. P. E. Easterling (Cambridge: Cambridge University Press, 1997), 331.
6. René Girard, *Violence and the Sacred,* trans. Patrick Gregory (Baltimore: Johns Hopkins University Press, 1979), 65; cited in Goldhill (1997), 332.
7. Scott Scullion, "Tragedy and Religion: The Problem of Origins," in *A Companion to Greek Tragedy,* ed. Justina Gregory (Malden, MA: Blackwell Publishing, 2005), 34.
8. P. E. Easterling, "A Show for Dionysus," in *The Cambridge Companion to Greek Tragedy,* ed. P. E. Easterling (Cambridge: Cambridge University Press, 1997), 46.
9. Friedrich Nietzsche, *Basic Writings of Nietzsche,* ed. and trans. Walter Kaufmann (New York: The Modern Library, 2000), 37.

10. DISCUSSION OF VERNANT AND VIDAL-NAQUET'S
MYTH AND TRAGEDY IN ANCIENT GREECE

1. Jean-Pierre Vernant and Pierre Vidal-Naquet, *Myth and Tragedy in Ancient Greece* (New York: Zone Books, 1990).
2. Ibid., 14–15.
3. Ibid., 25.
4. Ibid., 186.
5. Ibid., 181.
6. Ibid., 187–88.
7. Ibid., 35.
8. Ibid., 26.
9. Ibid.

11. MORAL AMBIGUITY IN AESCHYLUS'S *SEVEN AGAINST THEBES* AND *THE SUPPLIANT MAIDENS*

1. Martin Heidegger, *Introduction to Metaphysics,* trans. Gregory Fried and Richard Polt (New Haven, CT: Yale University Press, 2000), 156–76.
2. Paul Cartledge, "'Deep Plays': Theatre as Process in Athenian Civic Life," in *The Cambridge Companion to Greek Tragedy,* ed. P. E. Easterling (Cambridge: Cambridge University Press, 1997), 20.

12. TRAGEDY, TRAVESTY, AND QUEERNESS

1. Terry Eagleton, "Commentary," in *Rethinking Tragedy,* ed. Rita Felski (Baltimore: Johns Hopkins University Press, 2008), 344; W. B. Yeats, "Crazy Jane Talks with the Bishop," in *The Poems of W. B. Yeats: A New Edition,* ed. Richard J. Finneran (London: Macmillan, 1933).
2. Vernant and Vidal-Naquet, *Myth and Tragedy,* 43.
3. Nicole Loraux, *The Experiences of Tiresias: The Feminine and the Greek Man,* trans. Paula Wissing (Princeton, NJ: Princeton University Press, 2014); Nicole Loraux, *The Invention of Athens: The Funeral Oration in the Classical City,* trans. Alan Sheridan (New York: Zone Books, 2006); Nicole Loraux, *Mothers in Mourning,* trans. Corinne Pache (Ithaca, NY: Cornell University Press, 1998).
4. Nicole Loraux, *Tragic Ways of Killing a Woman,* trans. Anthony Forster (Cambridge, MA: Harvard University Press, 1987), 17.
5. Ibid.
6. Ibid., 28.
7. Ibid., 30.
8. Ibid., 64.
9. Ibid., 65.
10. Judith Butler, *Antigone's Claim: Kinship Between Life and Death* (New York: Columbia University Press, 2000).

13. POLYPHONY

1. Simon Goldhill, "The Audience of Athenian Tragedy," in *The Cambridge Companion to Greek Tragedy,* ed. P. E. Easterling (Cambridge: Cambridge University Press, 1997), 57.
2. Cartledge, "'Deep Plays,'" 5.
3. Ibid., 6.
4. Simon Goldhill, "Generalizing About Tragedy," in *Rethinking Tragedy,* ed. Rita Felski (Baltimore: Johns Hopkins University Press, 2008), 2.
5. Cartledge, "'Deep Plays,'" 9.

6. Goldhill, "Audience of Athenian Tragedy," 62.
7. Ibid., 64.
8. Thomas S. Eliot. *The Waste Land*, ed. Michael North. (New York: W. W. Norton & Company, 2001), lines 218–19.
9. Edith Hall, "The Sociology of Athenian Tragedy," in *The Cambridge Companion to Greek Tragedy*, ed. P. E. Easterling (Cambridge: Cambridge University Press, 1997), 93–126.
10. Ibid., 105.
11. Ibid., 121.
12. Ibid., 109.
13. Ibid., 99.
14. Ibid., 125.
15. Ibid., 118.

14. THE GODS! TRAGEDY AND THE LIMITATION OF THE CLAIMS TO AUTONOMY AND SELF-SUFFICIENCY

1. Vernant and Vidal-Naquet, *Myth and Tragedy*, 44.
2. Ibid., 48.
3. Ibid., 46.
4. Ibid.
5. Ibid., 46–47, emphasis mine. A very similar claim is made by Vernant and Vidal-Naquet in "Oedipus Without the Complex," in *Myth and Tragedy*, 92.
6. Karl Marx, *Grundrisse: Foundations of the Critique of Political Economy*, ed. and trans. David McLellan (New York: Harper & Row, 1971), 44–46.
7. Bernard Williams, *Shame and Necessity* (Berkeley: University of California Press, 1993), 16.
8. Ibid.
9. Ibid., 16–17.
10. Ibid., 163.
11. Ibid., 164.
12. Simon Critchley and Jamieson Webster, *Stay, Illusion!: The Hamlet Doctrine* (New York: Pantheon Books, 2013).
13. Both quoted in Williams, *Shame and Necessity*, 164.
14. Rubin Museum, "Happy Talk: Simon Critchley + Philip Seymour Hoffman," filmed December 2012; https://www.youtube.com/watch?v=TiQkdprJs00.
15. Williams, *Shame and Necessity*, 166. Emphasis mine.
16. Ibid., 163.
17. Vernant and Vidal-Naquet, *Myth and Tragedy*, 247.
18. Ibid., 242.

16. THE PROBLEM WITH GENERALIZING ABOUT THE TRAGIC

1. Goldhill, "Generalizing About Tragedy," 46–47.
2. Ibid., 47.
3. Halliwell, "Learning from Suffering," 401–5.
4. Goldhill, "Generalizing About Tragedy," 49.
5. Friedrich Hölderlin, *Essays and Letters on Theory,* trans. Thomas Pfau (Albany: State University of New York Press, 1988), 83.
6. F. W. J. Schelling, *The Unconditional in Human Knowledge: Four Early Essays, 1794–1796,* trans. Fritz Marti (Lewisburg, PA: Bucknell University Press, 1980), 192–93.
7. Ibid., 193.
8. F. W. J. Schelling, *The Philosophy of Art,* ed. and trans. Douglas W. Stott (Minneapolis: University of Minnesota Press, 1989).
9. Ibid., 255.
10. Ibid., 257.
11. Goldhill, "Generalizing About Tragedy," 55.
12. Walter Benjamin, *The Origin of German Tragic Drama,* trans. John Osborne (London: Verso, 1998), 101.
13. Martin Heidegger, *Introduction to Metaphysics,* trans. Gregory Fried and Richard Polt (New Haven, CT: Yale University Press, 2000).

17. GOOD HEGEL, BAD HEGEL

1. Peter Szondi, *An Essay on the Tragic,* trans. Paul Fleming (Stanford, CA: Stanford University Press, 2002).
2. Emmanuel Levinas, *Totality and Infinity,* trans. Alphonso Lingis (Pittsburgh, PA: Duquesne University Press, 1969).
3. G. W. F. Hegel, *Natural Law: The Scientific Ways of Treating Natural Law, Its Place in Moral Philosophy, and Its Relation to the Positive Sciences of Law,* trans. T. M. Knox, H. B. Acton, and John R. Silber (Philadelphia: University of Pennsylvania Press, 1975).
4. Szondi, *Essay on the Tragic,* 17.
5. Hegel, *Natural Law,* 105.
6. Ibid., 108.
7. Szondi, *Essay on the Tragic,* 19.
8. Ibid., 21.
9. Ibid.
10. Ibid., 54.
11. Ibid., 55–56.
12. William Shakespeare, *Troilus and Cressida: The Cambridge Dover*

Wilson Shakespeare, ed. John Dover Wilson (Cambridge: Cambridge University Press, 1957), 121.

18. FROM PHILOSOPHY BACK TO THEATER

1. Philippe Lacoue-Labarthe, *Métaphrasis: Suivi de Le théâtre de Hölderlin* (Paris: Presses Universitaires de France, 1998).
2. Ibid., 57–58.
3. Jacques Taminiaux, *Le Théâtre des philosophes: La tragédie, l'être, l'action* (Grenoble: Jérôme Millon, 1995).
4. See especially Brecht's essays from 1918 to 1932 in Bertolt Brecht, *Brecht on Theatre: The Development of an Aesthetic,* ed. and trans. John Willett (New York: Hill and Wang, 1964), 3–62.
5. Walter Benjamin, *Understanding Brecht,* trans. Anna Bostock (New York: Verso, 1998), 4. See especially the first and second versions of the essay, "What Is Epic Theatre?," 1–22.

19. AGAINST A CERTAIN STYLE OF PHILOSOPHY

1. Friedrich Nietzsche, *Beyond Good and Evil: Prelude to a Philosophy of the Future,* trans. Walter Kaufmann (New York: Vintage Books, 1966), 11.
2. Simon Critchley and Jamieson Webster, *Stay, Illusion!: The Hamlet Doctrine* (New York: Pantheon Books, 2013).

20. AN INTRODUCTION TO THE SOPHISTS

1. Alain Badiou, *Plato's Republic: A Dialogue in Sixteen Chapters,* trans. Susan Spitzer (New York: Columbia University Press, 2012).
2. Barbara Cassin, *Sophistical Practice: Toward a Consistent Relativism* (New York: Fordham University Press, 2014), 3–4.
3. Quoted in Hermann Diels, *The Older Sophists,* ed. Rosamond Kent Sprague (Indianapolis, IN: Hackett Publishing Company, 1972), 1.
4. Kathleen Freeman, *Ancilla to the Pre-Socratic Philosophers* (Cambridge, MA: Harvard University Press, 1983), 125.
5. Ibid., 126.
6. Ibid., 162.
7. Ibid., 126.

21. GORGIASM

1. Philostratus and Eunapius, *The Lives of the Sophists,* trans. Wilmer Cave Wright (New York: G. P. Putnam's Sons, 1922).

2. Ibid., 29–31. I will follow closely the excellent and helpful presentation of Gorgias in John Dillon and Tania Gergel, *The Greek Sophists* (London: Penguin Books, 2003), 43–97.

3. These anecdotes are assembled from evidence in the books of Dillon and Gergel, and Sprague.

22. THE NOT-BEING

1. Dillon and Gergel, *The Greek Sophists,* 42–45.
2. Ibid., 67–76.
3. Jean-François Lyotard, *The Différend: Phrases in Dispute,* trans. Georges Van Den Abbeele (Minneapolis: University of Minnesota Press, 1988), 14–16.
4. See Eric Kaplan, "Can We Live with Contradiction?" *The New York Times,* January 29, 2017.

23. I HAVE NOTHING TO SAY AND I AM SAYING IT

1. Barbara Cassin, *Sophistical Practice: Toward a Consistent Relativism* (New York: Fordham University Press, 2014), 4.
2. Ibid., 5.
3. John Cage, *Silence: Lectures and Writings* (Middletown, CT: Wesleyan University Press, 1973), 109.
4. Samuel Beckett, *The Beckett Trilogy: Molloy, Malone Dies, The Unnameable,* trans. Patrick Bowles (London: Pan Books, 1979), 295. I'd like to thank Charles Snyder for drawing my attention to the parallels between Gorgias and Beckett.
5. Ibid., 353.
6. Ibid., 367.

24. HELEN IS INNOCENT

1. Dillon and Gergel, *The Greek Sophists,* 78.
2. Ibid., 83.
3. Ibid.
4. Ibid., 79.
5. Ibid., 80.
6. Ibid.
7. Ibid., 81.
8. Ibid., 82.
9. Ibid., 84.
10. Ibid., 84–93.

11. Ibid., 95.

12. Thucydides, *On Justice, Power, and Human Nature: Selections from The History of the Peloponnesian War,* trans. Paul Woodruff (Indianapolis, IN: Hackett Publishing, 1993), 42.

25. TRAGEDY AND SOPHISTRY—THE CASE OF EURIPIDES' *THE TROJAN WOMEN*

1. Euripides, *Grief Lessons,* 126.

2. Simon Goldhill, "The Language of Tragedy: Rhetoric and Communication," in *The Cambridge Companion to Greek Tragedy,* ed. P. E. Easterling (Cambridge: Cambridge University Press, 1997), 134.

3. Ibid., 135.

4. Ibid.

5. Ibid., 143.

6. Ibid., 149.

28. *PHAEDRUS,* A PHILOSOPHICAL SUCCESS

1. Plato, *Phaedrus,* trans. Alexander Nehamas and Paul Woodruff (Indianapolis, IN: Hackett Publishing, 1995). All references are to the Greek pagination.

2. Ibid., ix–xlvii.

3. G. W. F. Hegel, *Phenomenology of Spirit,* trans. A. V. Miller (New York: Oxford University Press, 1977), 409.

29. *GORGIAS,* A PHILOSOPHICAL FAILURE

1. Plato, *Gorgias,* trans. W. C. Helmbold (Upper Saddle River, NJ: Prentice Hall, 1997).

30. INDIRECTION

1. G. W. F. Hegel, *Lectures on the History of Philosophy,* Vol. 1, trans. Elizabeth S. Haldane and Frances H. Simson (London: Kegan Paul, Trench, Trübner & Company, 1892), 384–448.

31. A CITY IN SPEECH

1. Plato, *The Republic of Plato,* trans. Allan Bloom (New York: Basic Books, 1991).

33. THE MORAL ECONOMY OF *MIMESIS*

1. Hannah Arendt, *The Human Condition* (Chicago: University Chicago Press, 1998).

35. WHAT IS *MIMESIS*?

1. Plato, *Republic*, trans. Bloom, 426–27.
2. Martin Heidegger, *Nietzsche*, Vols. 1 and 2, trans. David Farrell Krell (New York: HarperCollins, 1991), 142.
3. Plato, *Republic*, trans. Bloom, 430.

37. THE INOCULATION AGAINST OUR INBORN LOVE OF POETRY

1. Jean-Jacques Rousseau, *Politics and the Arts: Letter to M. D'Alembert on the Theatre*, trans. Allan Bloom (Ithaca, NY: Cornell University Press, 1960).

38. THE REWARDS OF VIRTUE, OR WHAT HAPPENS WHEN WE DIE

1. I'd like to thank Melanie Swan for pointing this out to me.

39. WHAT IS CATHARSIS IN ARISTOTLE?

1. Aristotle, *Poetics*, trans. Stephen Halliwell (Cambridge, MA: Harvard University Press, 1995), 19. All subsequent references to this edition are given in the text with reference to the Greek pagination.
2. Ibid., 19.
3. Alexander Nehamas, "Pity and Fear in the Rhetoric and the Poetics," in *Essays on Aristotle's Poetics*, ed. Amélie Rorty (Princeton, NJ: Princeton University Press, 1992), 303.
4. Ibid., 307.
5. Jonathan Lear, "Katharsis," in *Essays on Aristotle's Poetics*, ed. Amélie Rorty (Princeton, NJ: Princeton University Press, 1992), 315–35.
6. Ibid., 335.
7. Ibid.

40. MORE DEVASTATING

1. Lear, "Katharsis," 315.
2. Lauren O'Neill-Butler, "Freaks and Greeks," Artforum.com, September 2015; https://www.artforum.com/slant/id=55046.

41. REENACTMENT

1. Aristotle, *Poetics*, trans. Halliwell, 8.

42. *MIMESIS APRAXEOS*

1. Friedrich Nietzsche, *The Birth of Tragedy and the Case of Wagner,* ed. and trans. Walter Kaufmann (New York: Vintage Books, 1997), 174.

43. THE BIRTH OF TRAGEDY (AND COMEDY)

1. Aristotle, *Poetics*, trans. Halliwell, 42.

44. HAPPINESS AND UNHAPPINESS CONSIST IN ACTION

1. Walter Benjamin, *The Origin of German Tragic Drama,* trans. John Osborne (London: Verso, 1998), see esp. 159–67.

45. SINGLE OR DOUBLE?

1. Lear, "Katharsis," 334.
2. Aristotle, *Poetics*, trans. Halliwell, 17.

47. MONSTROSITY—OR ARISTOTLE AND HIS HIGHLIGHTER PEN

1. Hölderlin, *Essays and Letters,* 107.

49. MECHANICAL PREBUTTAL

1. Euripides, *Grief Lessons,* trans. Carson, 8.
2. William Arrowsmith, "Introduction to Orestes," in *Euripides IV*, ed. David Grene and Richmond Lattimore (Chicago: University of Chicago Press, 1958), 106.

50. THE GOD FINDS A WAY TO BRING ABOUT WHAT WE DO NOT IMAGINE

1. F. W. J. Schelling, *The Philosophy of Art,* ed. and trans. Douglas W. Stott (Minneapolis: University of Minnesota Press, 1989), 262.
2. Mary Lefkowitz, *Euripides and the Gods* (New York: Oxford University Press, 2015), 194.

51. MISRECOGNITION IN EURIPIDES

1. Euripides, *Grief Lessons,* trans. Carson, 14.
2. Goldhill, "Generalizing About Tragedy," 56.
3. Ibid., 57.

52. SMEARED MAKEUP

1. Goldhill, "Generalizing About Tragedy," 58.
2. Euripides, *Grief Lessons,* trans. Carson, 93.
3. Emily Townsend Vermeule, "Electra: Introduction," in *Euripides V,* ed. David Grene and Richmond Lattimore (Chicago: University of Chicago Press, 1959), 3.

53. SOPHOCLES' THEATER OF DISCOMFORT

1. Virginia Woolf, *The Common Reader* (London: Pelican Books, 1938), 36.
2. Sophocles, *Electra,* trans. Anne Carson (New York: Oxford University Press, 2001), 41–49. All subsequent references to this edition are given in the text with reference to Anne Carson's own pagination.

54. VULGAR ACTING AND EPIC INFERIORITY

1. David Kovacs, "Text and Transmission," in *A Companion to Greek Tragedy,* ed. Justina Gregory (Malden, MA: Blackwell Publishing, 2005), 381.

56. *POETICS II*—ARISTOTLE ON COMEDY

1. Umberto Eco, *The Name of the Rose,* trans. William Weaver (New York: Mariner Books, 2014).
2. Richard Janko, *Aristotle on Comedy: Towards a Reconstruction of Poetics II* (Berkeley: University of California Press, 1984).
3. Ibid., 23.
4. Ibid., 25.
5. Ibid., 29.
6. Ibid., 31.
7. Ibid., 37.
8. Ibid.

57. TORMENTED INCOMPREHENSIBLY—AGAINST HOMEOPATHIC CATHARSIS

1. Janko, *Aristotle on Comedy*, 42–90.
2. Ibid., 87.
3. Ibid., 139–51.
4. Ibid., 141.
5. Ibid., 150.
6. Ibid., 142. Emphasis mine.
7. Ibid., 149.
8. Ibid., 142.

58. ARISTOPHANES FALLS ASLEEP

1. Aristophanes, *Aristophanes: Four Comedies*, ed. William Arrowsmith, trans. Richmond Lattimore (Ann Arbor: University of Michigan Press, 1969).
2. Plato, *Symposium*, trans. Paul Woodruff and Alexander Nehamas (Indianapolis, IN: Hackett Publishing, 1990).
3. Aristophanes, *Birds*, trans. Nan Dunbar (Oxford: Oxford University Press, 2002), 2.

59. MAKE ATHENS GREAT AGAIN

1. Aristophanes, *Birds. Lysistrata. Women at the Thesmophoria*, trans. Jeffrey Henderson (Cambridge, MA: Harvard University Press, 2000).
2. G. W. F. Hegel, *Aesthetics: Lectures on Fine Art*, trans. T. M. Knox (New York: Oxford University Press, 1975), 1202.
3. Ibid., 1222.

60. TRANSGENERATIONAL CURSE

1. Frank L. Lucas, *Tragedy: Serious Drama in Relation to Aristotle's Poetics* (London: Hogarth Press, 1927), 66. I'd like to thank Manya Lempert for drawing this passage to my attention.
2. Image borrowed from Anne Carson, *Grief Lessons,* 168. Also, the remarks that follow are deeply indebted to notes taken during lectures and conversations with Judith Butler.
3. Friedrich Hölderlin, "In lieblicher Bläue," in *Sämtliche Werke: Frankfurter Ausgabe. Gesänge, 7–8*, ed. D. E. Sattler (Frankfurt: Stroemfeld Verlag, 2000), 1012.
4. Judith Butler, "The Tragic and Its Limits," unpublished lecture transcript, 2011.

5. Ernesto Laclau, *New Reflections on the Revolution of Our Time* (London: Verso, 1990).

61. ALIVENESS

1. *Phaedra(s)*, by Odéon-Théâtre de l'Europe, script by Sarah Kane, Wajdi Mouawad, and J. M. Coetzee, directed by Krzysztof Warlikowski, Brooklyn Academy of Music, New York, September 13, 2016.
2. O'Neill-Butler, "Freaks and Greeks," Artforum.com.

BIBLIOGRAPHY

Anhalt, Emily Katz. *Enraged: Why Violent Times Need Ancient Greek Myths.* New Haven, CT: Yale University Press, 2017.

Arendt, Hannah. *The Human Condition.* Chicago: University of Chicago Press, 1998.

Aristophanes. *Aristophanes: Four Comedies.* Edited by William Arrowsmith. Translated by Richmond Lattimore. Ann Arbor: University of Michigan Press, 1969.

———. *Birds. Lysistrata. Women at the Thesmophoria.* Translated by Jeffrey Henderson. Cambridge, MA: Harvard University Press, 2000.

———. *Birds.* Translated by Nan Dunbar. Oxford: Oxford University Press, 2002.

Aristotle. *Poetics.* Translated by Stephen Halliwell. Cambridge, MA: Harvard University Press, 1995.

Badiou, Alain. *Plato's Republic: A Dialogue in Sixteen Chapters.* Translated by Susan Spitzer. New York: Columbia University Press, 2012.

Beckett, Samuel. *The Beckett Trilogy: Molloy, Malone Dies, The Unnameable.* Translated by Patrick Bowles. London: Pan Books, 1979.

Benjamin, Walter. *The Origin of German Tragic Drama.* Translated by John Osborne. London: Verso, 1998.

———. *Understanding Brecht.* Translated by Anna Bostock. New York: Verso, 1998.

Brecht, Bertolt. *Brecht on Theatre: The Development of an Aesthetic.* Edited and translated by John Willett. New York: Hill and Wang, 1964.

Butler, Judith. *Antigone's Claim: Kinship Between Life and Death.* New York: Columbia University Press, 2000.

———. *Frames of War: When Is Life Grievable?* London: Verso, 2009.

———. "The Tragic and Its Limits." Unpublished lecture transcript, 2011.

Cage, John. *Silence: Lectures and Writings.* Middletown, CT: Wesleyan University Press, 1973.

Carson, Anne. *The Beauty of the Husband.* New York: Vintage Books, 2001.

Cassin, Barbara. *Sophistical Practice: Toward a Consistent Relativism.* New York: Fordham University Press, 2014.

Critchley, Simon. *Infinitely Demanding: Ethics of Commitment, Politics of Resistance.* New York: Verso, 2007.

Critchley, Simon, and Jamieson Webster. *Stay, Illusion!: The Hamlet Doctrine.* New York: Pantheon Books, 2013.

Critchley, Simon, and Philip Seymour Hoffman. "Happy Talk: Simon Critchley + Philip Seymour Hoffman." YouTube video. Posted by "Rubin-Museum," 2012; https://www.youtube.com/watch?v=TiQkdprJsoo.

Dillon, John, and Tania Gergel. *The Greek Sophists.* London: Penguin Books, 2003.

Easterling, P. E., ed. *The Cambridge Companion to Greek Tragedy.* Cambridge: Cambridge University Press, 1997.

Eco, Umberto. *The Name of the Rose.* Translated by William Weaver. New York: Mariner Books, 2014.

Eliot, Thomas S. *The Waste Land.* Edited by Michael North. New York: W. W. Norton & Company, 2001.

Euripides. *Grief Lessons—Four Plays by Euripides.* Translated by Anne Carson. New York: New York Review of Books, 2006.

Felski, Rita, ed. *Rethinking Tragedy.* Baltimore: Johns Hopkins University Press, 2008.

Freeman, Kathleen. *Ancilla to the Pre-Socratic Philosophers.* Cambridge, MA: Harvard University Press, 1983.

Geuss, Raymond. *A World without Why.* Princeton, NJ: Princeton University Press, 2014.

Girard, René. *Violence and the Sacred.* Translated by Patrick Gregory. Baltimore: Johns Hopkins University Press, 1979.

Gregory, Justina, ed. *A Companion to Greek Tragedy.* Malden, MA: Blackwell Publishing, 2005.

Grene, David, and Richmond Lattimore, eds. *The Complete Greek Tragedies.* Chicago: University of Chicago Press, 1959.

Hampshire, Stuart. *Justice Is Conflict.* London: Duckworth, 1999.

Hegel, G. W. F. *Lectures on the History of Philosophy,* vol. 1. Translated by Elizabeth S. Haldane and Frances H. Simson. London: Kegan Paul, Trench, Trübner & Company, 1892.

———. *Aesthetics: Lectures on Fine Art.* Translated by T. M. Knox. New York: Oxford University Press, 1975.

———. *Natural Law: The Scientific Ways of Treating Natural Law, Its Place in Moral Philosophy, and Its Relation to the Positive Sciences of Law.* Translated by T. M. Knox, H. B. Acton, and John R. Silber. Philadelphia: University of Pennsylvania Press, 1975.

———. *Phenomenology of Spirit.* Translated by A. V. Miller. New York: Oxford University Press, 1977.

Heidegger, Martin. *Nietzsche,* vols. 1 and 2. Translated by David Farrell Krell. New York: HarperCollins, 1991.

——. *Introduction to Metaphysics.* Translated by Gregory Fried and Richard Polt. New Haven, CT: Yale University Press, 2000.

Hölderlin, Friedrich. *Essays and Letters on Theory.* Translated by Thomas Pfau. Albany: State University of New York Press, 1988.

——. "In lieblicher Bläue." In *Sämtliche Werke: Frankfurter Ausgabe. Gesänge 7–8.* Edited by D. E. Sattler. Frankfurt: Stroemfeld Verlag, 2000.

Janko, Richard. *Aristotle on Comedy: Towards a Reconstruction of Poetics II.* Berkeley: University of California Press, 1984.

Kaplan, Eric. "Can We Live with Contradiction?" *The New York Times,* January 29, 2017.

Laclau, Ernesto. *New Reflections on the Revolution of Our Time.* London: Verso, 1990.

Lacoue-Labarthe, Philippe. *Métaphrasis: Suivi de Le théâtre de Hölderlin.* Paris: Presses Universitaires de France, 1998.

Lefkowitz, Mary. *Euripides and the Gods.* New York: Oxford University Press, 2015.

Levinas, Emmanuel. *Totality and Infinity.* Translated by Alphonso Lingis. Pittsburgh, PA: Duquesne University Press, 1969.

Liddell, Henry G., and Robert Scott. *A Greek-English Lexicon.* Cambridge: Clarendon Press, 1996.

Loraux, Nicole. *Tragic Ways of Killing a Woman.* Translated by Anthony Forster. Cambridge, MA: Harvard University Press, 1987.

——. *Mothers in Mourning.* Translated by Corinne Pache. Ithaca, NY: Cornell University Press, 1998.

——. *The Invention of Athens: The Funeral Oration in the Classical City.* Translated by Alan Sheridan. New York: Zone Books, 2006.

——. *The Experiences of Tiresias: The Feminine and the Greek Man.* Translated by Paula Wissing. Princeton, NJ: Princeton University Press, 2014.

Lucas, Frank L. *Tragedy: Serious Drama in Relation to Aristotle's Poetics.* London: Hogarth Press, 1927.

Lyotard, Jean-François. *The Différend: Phrases in Dispute.* Translated by Georges Van Den Abbeele. Minneapolis: University of Minnesota Press, 1988.

MacNeice, Louis. *Selected Poems.* Edited by Michael Longley. London: Faber & Faber, 2007.

Marx, Karl. *Grundrisse: Foundations of the Critique of Political Economy.* Edited and translated by David McLellan. New York: Harper & Row, 1971.

Nietzsche, Friedrich. *Beyond Good and Evil: Prelude to a Philosophy of the Future.* Translated by Walter Kaufmann. New York: Vintage Books, 1966.

———. *The Birth of Tragedy and the Case of Wagner.* Edited and translated by Walter Kaufmann. New York: Vintage Books, 1967.

———. *Basic Writings of Nietzsche.* Edited and translated by Walter Kaufmann. New York: The Modern Library, 2000.

O'Neill-Butler, Lauren. "Freaks and Greeks." Artforum.com, last modified September 22, 2015; https://www.artforum.com/slant/id=55046.

Philostratus, and Eunapius. *The Lives of the Sophists.* Translated by Wilmer Cave Wright. New York: G. P. Putnam's Sons, 1922.

Plato. *Symposium.* Translated by Paul Woodruff and Alexander Nehamas. Indianapolis, IN: Hackett Publishing, 1990.

———. *The Republic of Plato.* Translated by Allan Bloom. New York: Basic Books, 1991.

———. *Phaedrus.* Translated by Alexander Nehamas and Paul Woodruff. Indianapolis, IN: Hackett Publishing, 1995.

———. *Gorgias.* Translated by W. C. Helmbold. Upper Saddle River, NJ: Prentice Hall, 1997.

Rorty, Amélie, ed. *Essays on Aristotle's Poetics.* Princeton, NJ: Princeton University Press, 1992.

Rousseau, Jean-Jacques. *Politics and the Arts: Letter to M. D'Alembert on the Theatre.* Translated by Allan Bloom. Ithaca, NY: Cornell University Press, 1960.

Schelling, F. W. J. *The Unconditional in Human Knowledge: Four Early Essays, 1794–1796.* Translated by Fritz Marti. Lewisburg, PA: Bucknell University Press, 1980.

———. *The Philosophy of Art.* Edited and translated by Douglas W. Stott. Minneapolis: University of Minnesota Press, 1989.

Shakespeare, William. *Troilus and Cressida: The Cambridge Dover Wilson Shakespeare.* Edited by John Dover Wilson. Cambridge: Cambridge University Press, 1957.

Simon, Erika. *Das antike Theater.* Heidelberg: F. H. Kerle, 1972.

Snell, Bruno. *Die Entdeckung des Geistes: Studien zur Entstehung des europäischen Denkens bei den Griechen.* Hamburg: Claaszen & Goverts Verlag, 1946.

Sophocles. *Electra.* Translated by Anne Carson. New York: Oxford University Press, 2001.

Sprague, Rosamond Kent, ed. *The Older Sophists.* Indianapolis, IN: Hackett Publishing Company, 1972.

Steiner, George. *The Death of Tragedy.* New Haven, CT: Yale University Press, 1996.

Storey, Ian Christopher, and Arlene Allan. *A Guide to Ancient Greek Drama.* Malden, MA: Blackwell Publishing, 2005.

Szondi, Peter. *An Essay on the Tragic.* Translated by Paul Fleming. Stanford, CA: Stanford University Press, 2002.

Taminiaux, Jacques. *Le Théâtre des philosophes: La tragédie, l'être, l'action*. Grenoble: Jérôme Millon, 1995.

Thucydides. *On Justice, Power, and Human Nature: Selections from the History of the Peloponnesian War*. Translated by Paul Woodruff. Indianapolis, IN: Hackett Publishing, 1993.

Vernant, Jean-Pierre, and Pierre Vidal-Naquet. *Myth and Tragedy in Ancient Greece*. New York: Zone Books, 1990.

Warlikowski, Krzysztof, dir. *Phaedra(s)*, by Sarah Kane, Wajdi Mouawad, and J. M. Coetzee. Theater performance, September 13, 2016, by Odéon-Théâtre de l'Europe, Brooklyn Academy of Music, New York.

Wilamowitz-Moellendorff, Ulrich von. *Greek Historical Writing and Apollo*. Translated by Gilbert Murray. Oxford: Clarendon Press, 1908.

Williams, Bernard. *Shame and Necessity*. Berkeley: University of California Press, 1993.

Williams, Raymond. *Modern Tragedy*. London: Vintage Books, 1966.

Woolf, Virginia. *The Common Reader*. London: Pelican Books, 1938.

Yeats, W. B. *The Poems of W. B. Yeats: A New Edition*, ed. Richard J. Finneran. London: Macmillan, 1933.

INDEX

A Note about the Author

Simon Critchley is Hans Jonas Professor of Philosophy at the New School for Social Research. His many books include *Very Little . . . Almost Nothing, The Book of Dead Philosophers, The Faith of the Faithless,* and *Memory Theater.* He is the series moderator of "The Stone," a philosophy column in *The New York Times,* to which he is a frequent contributor.

A Note on the Type

This book was set in Adobe Garamond. Designed or the Adobe Corporation by Robert Slimbach, the fonts are based on types first cut by Claude Garamond (c. 1480–1561). Garamond was a pupil of Geoffroy Tory and is believed to have followed the Venetian models, although he introduced a number of important differences, and it is to him that we owe the letter we now know as "old style."

Composed by North Market Street Graphics,
Lancaster, Pennsylvania

Printed and bound by Berryville Graphics,
Berryville, Virginia

Designed by M. Kristen Bearse